VILLAINS
AND
VIGILANTES

OTHER BOOKS BY STANTON A. COBLENTZ

Prose

MARCHING MEN

THE DECLINE OF MAN

THE SUNKEN WORLD

AFTER 12,000 YEARS

THE WONDER STICK

INTO PLUTONIAN DEPTHS

THE ANSWER OF THE AGES

WHEN THE BIRDS FLY SOUTH

THE LITERARY REVOLUTION

THE TRIUMPH OF THE TEAPOT POET

AN EDITOR LOOKS AT POETRY

NEW POETIC LAMPS AND OLD

FROM ARROW TO ATOM BOMB

Poetry

TIME'S TRAVELERS

GARNERED SHEAVES

THE PAGEANT OF MAN

GREEN VISTAS

SONGS BY THE WAYSIDE

WINDS OF CHAOS

ARMAGEDDON

THE LONE ADVENTURER

SHADOWS ON A WALL

THE ENDURING FLAME

SONGS OF THE REDWOODS

THE MOUNTAIN OF THE SLEEPING MAIDEN

THE MERRY HUNT AND OTHER POEMS

SENATOR GOOSE AND OTHER RHYMES

THE THINKER AND OTHER POEMS

Anthologies

UNSEEN WINGS

THE MUSIC MAKERS

MODERN AMERICAN LYRICS

MODERN BRITISH LYRICS

EXECUTION OF JENKINS BY THE VIGILANCE COMMITTEE

Villages igilantes

The Story of William
and Pioneer Justice in California

BY

STANTON A. COBLENTZ

A Perpetua Book

A. S. Barnes & Company, Inc.

New York

CONTENTS

ILLUSTRATIONS

VILLAINS
AND
VIGILANTES

INTRODUCTION

Amid the engrossing political events and turbulent international affairs that characterize the twentieth century, we moderns are not unnaturally inclined to lose sight of many turbulent, engrossing, and colorful episodes of the past. We are apt, subconsciously, to assign many of the deeds and struggles of yesterday to the realm of dusty documents and not less dusty text-books; we are prone to forget that they represent living occurrences, in which live, feeling, palpitating human beings indulged with all that man is capable of hope, agony and despair. We are inclined not to recognize that the trials which they endured were as real as any of our own, that their aspirations were as keen, their longings as gusty, their temptations as tantalizing, their courage as high and their defeats and triumphs as poignantly experienced as anything the present-day world has to offer, even though they enacted their rôles in a different drama from ours and to the accompaniment of other stage scenery and accouterments.

These remarks, to be sure, do not apply so much to the outstanding figures—to the Napoleons, the Washingtons, the Lincolns—as to those humbler men whose fights were waged on a narrower arena, and whose deeds, however daring or valorous, did not cause nations to reel or rise. It is the latter group—particularly when they performed their parts on the outskirts of civilization—whose lives frequently possess a human interest and even a social significance all too little realized, and who have been overlooked while biographers of the great have been legion. Yet the careers of these obscure protagonists have often been vivid with a storm and fury, a picturesqueness and glamour denied to men looming far larger in the pageant of history.

It is these considerations that have led me to the treatment of that bizarre, heterogeneous, keenly energetic company who distinguished themselves in San Francisco of the Fifties; it is these considerations which, in particular, have brought me to the story of James King of William, and of the tumultuous events which preceded and followed the short-lived day of his power. Surely, there is no more forceful, attractive, or extraordinary neglected character in American history than James King; surely, no leader of men ever labored in a more fantastic or contradictory environment; surely, in all the records of journalistic achievement there is no exploit which for sheer recklessness, gallantry, and driving effectiveness surpassed that of this journalistic novice in a pioneering community. There is daring and romance in his story, there is conflict and stanch resolution, there is inflexible honesty of purpose against a background of crime that would seem melodramatic did we not know it to have been actual; and, dominating and overtowering all, there is an atmosphere of extravagance; corruption and social anarchy such as the world, we may hope, will not see soon again.

Nevertheless, James King of William remains an obscure character. Although necessarily mentioned in every history of early California, he has become, for the most part, little more than a name; he has not been brought to life for us as the man he was, the reformer fighting perilously for an ideal in a world that recognized no final argument except a pistol-shot. Nor has the present age sufficiently kept in mind the story of that Second Vigilance Committee to which the actions of King directly gave rise,—a Vigilance Committee which has been fittingly described as "the most formidable public tribunal in the history of modern civilization."

There is not, indeed—so far as I have been able to determine

—any single volume extant which adequately covers that whole series of remarkable episodes of which King was the focus and pivot. We are, it is true, indebted to Bancroft for his monumental work on "Popular Tribunals"; but this treatise, aside from being out of print and difficult to procure, reaches the rather forbidding length of some fifteen hundred pages; moreover, it is concerned with many subjects only indirectly related to the Vigilance Committees of San Francisco; nor does it devote a great deal of attention to James King of William. There is, again, Mary Floyd Williams' standard "History of the San Francisco Committee of Vigilance of 1851"; but this work, as the title implies, does not deal except incidentally with James King, nor with the second and more imposing of the two Vigilance Committees. There are, furthermore, Frank Meriweather Smith's pamphlet on the "San Francisco Vigilance Committee of '56", and James O'Meara's "Vigilance Committee of 1856" (issued in 1883 and 1887 respectively, and now very rare); there are a number of valuable but comparatively brief accounts of eye-witnesses and participants, such as William T. Coleman and others; there are the general histories of California or phases of California life, by T. H. Hittell, Royce, and others, which treat of the period of the Vigilantes; yet much of the material still reposes unused in the files of old newspapers, and, aside from the recent cursory presentation by Alan Valentine, a unified one-volume account of the whole tempestuous sequence of occurrences has remained to be written.

It has accordingly been my conviction that here is a chapter of history which cryingly calls for fresh attention; cryingly demands treatment based, so far as is possible, upon a re-examination of first-hand sources. And while, in attempting the task, I have not underestimated the difficulty of resurrecting vanished characters and a vanished era and have not been unaware that much significant material may have been swallowed forever by time, I have been upheld by the belief that there is a large public which will follow the recital sympathetically, and which will be captivated, as I have been, by the flame and tragedy of that hectic, boisterous, blood-spotted universe which was San Francisco in the good old days following the arrival of the Forty-Niners.

CHAPTER I

T HE traveler to modern San Francisco, as he sits upon the deck of a sumptuous liner and gazes out at the roof-covered hills unfolding just within the Golden Gate, can form little idea of the changes accomplished in less than a century. He views a city of imposing proportions, marked by sharp-filed streets and skyscrapers that jut in strange irregularity from the high, house-littered slopes; he views two gigantic bridges flung across the waters of a seemingly unbridgeable bay; his glance wanders far off to the east, where for many miles, in an unbroken sheet, extend the dwellings of Oakland, Berkeley, and Richmond; and he knows that, in this immediate vicinity, at least two million souls live amid all the complexities, strife and refinements of modern civilization. Only to the north, where the bare pointed peak of Tamalpais reposes in silent majesty against the blue skies, have the passing years wrought little if any apparent transformation.

But unless he be of a reflective turn of mind—and, moreover, be well versed in a certain little known phase of history—the visitor to San Francisco will not pause to consider the freaks and alterations of time. It will not occur to him that he is about to step upon a soil where the streams of passion have run unusually high, a shore where blood has flowed, where riot has shouted, where flame and cinders have poured in withering torrents; he will not recall that this small spot of ground has been a meeting-place for all the tempests of emotion of which man is capable, the stage for a thousand dramas of desperation, hatred and fury, of daring, high resolve, and glamorous adventure. Where in the modern city, with its rumbling trolley cars, its dashing automobiles, its blazing electric signs, is there any evidence of the ruder, more turbulent past? Yet the ghost of that past still remains, and whispers in the breath of today. And if the stranger in San Francisco will but pause to peer upon that phantom of yesterday, and will let it return to life in the contours of eighty or ninety years ago, he will witness a series of scenes not less fantastic and in some ways hardly less incredible than anything in the "Arabian Nights."

Therefore we shall let the marvel come to pass; time shall flow backward on its course; and the voyager to San Francisco shall see, instead of the many-towered modern city, its kaleidoscopic predecessor of the Forties and Fifties. And, having scrutinized that strangely fluctuant product of a vanished age, and acquainted himself with some of the whims and foibles, the whirlwinds and the thunderclouds that characterized it, he will be better able to understand those events which gave rise to the Committees of Vigilance, and which constitute the especial object of our present inquiry.

Let us first, accordingly, go back to an era before San Francisco was at all.

It was on the thirty-first of July, 1846, that one of the most notable citizens of early California first sailed through the Golden Gate. His name was Samuel Brannan; his age was twenty-seven; his rank was that of a Mormon elder; and his self-appointed task was to command the destinies of more than two hundred men, women and children, who had set out from New York six months before on the good ship *Brooklyn,* toward the unknown meadows of the Promised Land. Yet it was nothing very promising that Sam Brannan beheld as the *Brooklyn* passed around the eminence of what was later to be Telegraph Hill and he and his young hopefuls stared across the mud-flats of the cove that abutted upon the village of Yerba Buena. A sorry sight the town made!—a few adobe hovels! a few wretched wooden sheds, among which a handful of ragged Indians and indolent whites were to be seen. Westward and to the south, as far as the eye could view, reached the untenanted hills, one rising upon the other, their gullied slopes featured only by the few hardy shrubs and dwarfed trees that could endure the blast of the continual ocean winds; while, on the lower levels, stretched long barren dunes and hummocks of sand.

Nevertheless, there was one sight which proved that the day of change was near. On the flagstaff of "Old Adobe," the Mexican custom-house—a low-lying edifice with something of the appearance of a big barn—the Mexican emblem no longer flew, but the Stars and Stripes waved in the breeze. And this might have been regarded by the incoming voyagers as the symbol of the approaching metamorphosis: the metamorphosis from the lethargic, dreamy, pleasant existence of the old Spanish days, to the alert, hurricane-tossed careers of the new arrivals in the land.

It is hard for us today to realize how serene and even was the tenor of life in that early California into which Brannan and his crew of pilgrims had thrust themselves. The term Arcadia has been well applied to the country of the days before the Gold Rush; for, certainly, there was an Arcadian simplicity, an Arcadian warmth, an Arcadian spirit of hospitality and human kindness. You could then have taken your horse at the remote southern settlement of San Diego, and traveled the five hundred miles or more to Sonoma without once opening your purse; moreover, you could have spent as long as you liked upon the journey, and yet have been everywhere received with cordiality. The missions would have opened their doors, and permitted you to stay for weeks or months; they would have cared for your steed, and, upon your departure, the *padres* would have seen that you were provided with a guide, and with meat, bread, and drink. Similarly, at the great cattle ranches, you would have been greeted with wide-open arms, and no whisper would ever have come to your ears that you were overstaying your welcome; indeed, the attitude of your host and hostess would have been that your presence was conferring a favor upon them. And had you, by any chance, taken out a piece of gold and offered payment, you would have been tendering an insult—for the man of honor, in early California, did not accept payment in return for friendly services.

In spite of the vast extent of the country and its sparsely settled nature, and the consequent opportunity for deeds of violence, pastoral California was a land virtually without crime. There was no public hangman or executioner; there were no jails, juries, or courts, no sheriffs to serve writs, no lawyers to prosecute or defend. It is recorded that, in the twenty-seven years from 1819 to 1846, there were but six murders among the white inhabitants of California (a number that contrasts favorably with the fifty murders reported among the whites alone in the single county of Los Angeles in the seven years beginning with 1850). Nor were the people more given to lesser offenses than to outrages against human life; so high was the standard of honesty that houses were without locks, while sea captains, selling their goods along the coast, were content to return in a year or a year and a half to accept payment in produce—and this system apparently worked without complaint on any one's part.

But now let us look at the upheavals that were to follow—upheavals all the more ironic, all the more tragic because of their contrast with the tranquil, non-acquisitive society which they uprooted. And, first of all, let us return to the city by the Golden Gate; let us view it in the good year 1848, when, having already abandoned the name Yerba Buena in favor of its present appellation, it was a thriving village of rapidly increasing population. In fact, there is reason to suppose that it was already within hailing distance of having a thousand inhabitants! Then lo and behold! the bombshell descended! It was in 1848 that gold was discovered in the Sierras; and from the shock of that revelation the city never quite recovered, nor was it ever again to be quite the same.

At first the effect upon San Francisco seemed to be disastrous —as, indeed, it was in many ways. No earthquake, no tidal wave, no volcanic eruption could have had a much more cataclysmic result. "To the gold-fields! To the gold-fields! To the gold-fields!" rang the cry; and few able-bodied men there were who did not hear that clarion call, and who did not forsake all other interests, duties and obligations in order to join in the intoxicated dash for the mountains. Laborers threw down their tools, merchants abandoned their desks, soldiers forsook their garrisons, whole crews and even captains left their ships to rot at anchor in the bay—and all alike joined in the frantic migration. "To the gold-fields! To the gold-fields! To the gold-fields!" the shout echoed and re-echoed, reaching ever further and further abroad. For a while, San Francisco was almost depopulated; it is said that at one time there were only seven men left in the town! No longer was it possible to hire servants—he who would not do his own work must let it remain undone! The single small school closed for lack of attendance; the newspapers suspended publication, not only for want of readers, but because the sub-editors and the very printer's "devils" had all gone off to the diggings. Curiously revealing is an editorial in the *Californian* on the day when its presses shut down (May 29th, 1848):

"The whole country, from San Francisco to Los Angeles, and from the sea shore to the base of the Sierra Nevada, resounds with the sordid cry of *gold!* GOLD!! *GOLD!!!*— while the field is left half planted, the house half built, and everything neglected but the manufacture of shovels and pickaxes. . . ."

When such a frenzy suddenly descends upon an entire population, driving it from all accustomed roads, one may expect strange and mighty social abnormalities to follow. And strange and mighty were to be the results of that first assault upon the gold-fields.

In order to glance more fully at the developing picture, and to see how the seeds were planted for terror, crime and vigilance committees, let us allow the scenes to shift a little, until the calendar marks the year 1849. For only now has the Gold Rush expanded to its full dimensions; only now have the streams of immigrants begun to pour in from the East; only now has the native of the one-time village of Yerba Buena been provided with any fair clue to the staggering, the appalling proportions of the change that has stormed upon him thanks to the existence of a certain yellow metal amid the gorges and river channels of the Sierra Nevadas.

Let us imagine ourselves to be among the thousands that have dared the perilous migration from the Eastern states. Perhaps we have just completed a voyage of five or six months around Cape Horn, during which we have all but succumbed to seasickness, scurvy, lack of good food, scarcity of fresh water, or crowded and unsanitary sleeping quarters; perhaps we have chosen the shorter route via Panama, and, after threading our way across the fever-smitten Isthmus, have waited for weeks or months for a vessel to bear us up the Coast; perhaps we have traveled via the Mexican Border Route, and have seen companions sag and perish amid the dreadful thirsting waste of the desert; or perhaps we have been members of one of the great covered wagon parties trekking overland from Independence, Missouri, and have arrived at California along a trail littered with the bleaching skulls of oxen and marked with innumerable rude improvised crosses. At all ever. *s*, it is now midsummer or later in the year 1849; and, no matter how we have come, we number ourselves among the citizens of San Francisco. And what do we see as we traverse the streets of the new-risen metropolis?

It is a mushroom town that surrounds us—but a town of marvels. Staring at us from the bay, we see the masts of hundreds of vessels; while, stretching inland from the crescent cove at the city's eastern extremity and high over the slopes of the tumbled, bushgrown hills, we observe a multitude of new-made structures: tents with their canvas flapping fiercely in the wind, tents half covered with blankets and the boughs of trees, crude one-story shanties of wood, and slightly more imposing structures which, taken in pieces from ships in the harbor, are almost instantly set up for occupation. In our ears rings the din of hammers as the housebreakers pursue their tasks; we hear the shouts and cries of vendors, and perhaps the yells of some brawling, tipsy group; our footsteps are impeded by the piles of merchandise which, for lack of other storage space, are heaped up in the sprawling, uneven streets; our eyes are attracted by the vari-colored signs—in Chinese, in Russian, in French, in Italian, no less than in our own mother-tongue—which greet us from the fronts of the shops; while possibly now and then, as we push our way into the city's central thoroughfare, we are forced to step aside for a troop of mounted men, or even for a bull that comes bellowing toward us, with a sombrero-wearing *vaquero* swinging the lariat in hot pursuit.

And the people that we pass—what types, what varieties! Seldom, since the tower of Babel, has such a crowd gathered in any one place! First of all, the population is mostly male, except for some gay-clad lady, of doubtful virtue, who passes on the arm of an insolent-looking gallant; and, moreover, the citizens are almost all young, the vast majority not being out of their twenties, and a man of forty seeming of almost patriarchal age. Not the most difficult to recognize out of this motley crowd is the miner, with his bearded face, his red or blue shirt, his soft slouch hat, his trousers tucked into great rawhide boots, his belt containing bowie-knife or revolver—or possibly both. Close at the heels of this visitor from the diggings one may see a Mexican grandee, with a velvet jacket, and long gaudily colored *serape* hanging down to his silver-spurred heels; next one may note the Chinaman, with his pale blue coat, his slouching gait, his pigtail, and squint eyes; one may observe the Peruvian or Chilean in a brown *poncho,* the white-shirted Negro strutting along in a dandified manner, the swarthy Kanaka with well-formed, handsome features, fur-clad Russians, grotesquely tattooed New Zealanders, Malays, Hindoos, Japanese, Turks, Frenchmen, Italians, Hollanders—in short, representatives of half the lands of the earth; to which must be added, of course, a goodly percentage of our own Yankees.

Now suppose that we continue strolling through the city, and observe a little more of its manner of life and its occupations. Should we go off in search of lodgings, we may find ourselves conducted into a cramped, dark room, with slanting ceiling and partitions in the manner of a vessel, so that a score of men are quartered on the floor or on shelves along the wall. Or should we breathe the brisk out-of-door air at Portsmouth Square (the bare open acre or two which is the center of town) we may be treated to the sight of the auctioneers bawling out their wares, which they sell not for coin, but for gold dust at $16 an ounce; and, if we pause to listen to the prices asked and received, we must be ready for many a shock. With flour selling at times for as much as $27 a barrel (though there are vast fluctuations in price), and with a dollar often given for a single egg or pound of potatoes, we can form some estimate of the scale of charges—though what, after all, are such rates compared with the rents? When the Parker House rents for $110,000 a year, and a canvas tent occupied by gamblers brings $40,000; when real estate, purchased the year before for $20,000, may now command as much as $300,000; when $250 a month is asked for a hole in the ground, no larger than a small hall-bedroom, and when salaries have risen to such an extent that a mere carman may receive $6000 annually—under such circumstances, need we quibble if the prices of commodities are several times as great as in the East? Need we be surprised if any amount under fifty cents seems too small to bother about, and if the population, despite its fierce ardor in gold-getting, displays the most reckless prodigality in the expenditure of its perilously earned "dust"?

As we proceed on our perambulations throughout the city, we may observe what seems to be a miniature commotion. A newspaper vendor stands at a street corner, beside great piles of his wares—the New York *Tribune* and other Eastern dailies—which he has just taken off a newly arrived ship. What matter that they are six months old? What matter that the price of each is a dollar? A greedy crowd, famished for information from the outer world, surrounds him impatiently, and as fast as the seller can dispose of the sheets, they are taken up by the eager outstretched hands. In the course of two hours, he has rid himself of fifteen hundred! Nor is this particularly surprising, in view of certain other occurrences; for example, one of the newly arrived travelers (no less than the aspiring writer, Bayard Taylor) chances to recall some old papers which he has used for wadding in packing his valise, and with these he hastens to a paper merchant at the City Hotel, who looks them over and decides that, wishing to make a good profit, he will not be able to give more than ten dollars for the lot!

If, however, you desire to see money expended with a really bountiful hand, you must visit one of the many gambling houses that cluster about the Plaza. Here you will witness an outstanding activity, not to say industry, of early San Francisco! Let us enter a typical establishment—though it would be well to wait until evening, for it is only after dark that business in this field really begins. We find the house crowded as we make our way into its heavy atmosphere; the air is hot, and foul with alcohol and tobacco fumes; there is a blaze of lights from many lamps and mirrors; gaudy pictures, mostly of nude female forms, are hung upon the walls; at the right is a long counter, at which three or four men are busy handing out drinks in exchange for gold dust; somewhat beyond them is a stand filled with refreshments and a large pot of coffee, which are attended by an enticing Spanish senorita; while at the rear, upon a high platform, the musicians add their notes to vary the monotony of clinking glasses and profane and babbling tongues.

All these, however, are merely the minor appurtenances of the resort. Its most important, its outstanding feature is to be seen in the tables—perhaps ten or twelve of them, if we have entered one of the larger and better equipped places—which greet us in the center of the room, and which are laden in a manner to bring reminders of Croesus and his fabulous wealth. No! do not rub your eyes, and ask yourself when you will awaken! this is not a dream, it is all too real! Those heaps of gold and silver coin piled upon the tables! those bags of gold dust! those lumps, bars and nuggets of the pure metal, sparkling and glittering with a strange yellow brilliance!—do not imagine them to be counterfeit! they represent incalculable fortunes, which no one in the room doubts to be genuine!

Do you not feel something of the excitement of the place invading your very blood as you stare at the tables? as you listen to the rattling of dice? as you see the agitated crowds and the gleaming-eyed players, and watch great heaps of the bright dust and metal changing hands? Even though you are not a gambler by nature, is there not a magnetism, an intoxication in the spectacle of the shuffling cards, the piled-up stakes? Do you not feel something of the lure of victory, the clutch of power, the fascination of wealth that depends upon each turn and stroke of fickle chance? Men of all types stand about you, chewing and smoking, or merely absorbed in the competition—here a rough-clad, bearded laborer, there a wearer of the clerical collar, yonder a respectable-looking merchant, and at his side a reckless-eyed youth of fifteen or sixteen, a swaggering sailor, a silk-hatted dandy, and a rancher just in from the country. Small sums and large are staked upon the games; now you see a player risking but a dollar or two; now a fiery-faced individual, perhaps already reeling a little from the alcohol he has consumed, hazards thousands upon a single toss of the dice, and, losing, shrugs his shoulders with an air of nonchalance, and plunges again into the contest as though nothing has happened. As the hour grows later and the fumes clouding the air become denser, the excitement waxes more intense, the sums ventured are larger, and fortunes change hands with increasing rapidity, until many a man walks away with a swiftly won "pile," and many a toiler, who by arduous labor has accumulated a substantial reward at the mines, slouches off poorer than on the day when he first sought fortune on these Siren shores.

But in spite of all the drains upon the city's energies; in spite of the tremendous human costs of the "gambling hells"; in spite of the vast toll taken by whisky, and by the vicious women imported from Mexico, from Chile, and from far-off France; in spite of that outcropping of crime of which we are shortly to speak; in spite of unhygienic living conditions, and a scarcity of physicians and lack of medical facilities which mean almost certain death to multitudes of the sick, the city prospers and grows at a rate that is bewildering and wellnigh unbelievable. Should we absent ourselves from town for a few weeks or months and then return, we will be astonished at the transformation.

But let us not be content with our own observations; let us summon the testimony of other eye-witnesses. Here, for example, is what Bayard Taylor says in his *Eldorado* regarding his experiences on returning to San Francisco late in 1849 after a four months' absence:

"Of all the marvellous phases of the history of the Present, the growth of San Francisco is the one which will most tax the belief of the Future. Its parallel was never known, and shall never be beheld again. I speak only of what I saw with my own eyes. When I landed there, a little more than four months before, I found a scattering town of tents and canvas houses. . . . Now, on my last visit, I saw around me an actual metropolis, displaying street after street of well-built edifices, filled with an active and enterprising people and exhibiting every mark of permanent commercial prosperity."

So much for the year 1849—but in 1850 we will find the growth equally surprising. Such, at least, is the impression we get from the words of Daniel B. Woods, who, returning to the city in November, 1850, after an absence of five months, is led to declare, in his *Sixteen Months in the Gold Diggings*:

"A new edition, revised and improved, has just been issued. I should not have known the city. Indeed: there was little here—excepting the land—and that cut down and changed—

which had been here when I left. . . . One could not pass through the city without being impressed by the sentiment which seems to describe the whole thing: 'Enterprise run mad.' "

Despite the town's rapid growth, however, there was something less than metropolitan in its looks during the winter of 1849-50. The season had been an extraordinarily rainy one; and even the central thoroughfares, which during the summer had been disagreeable with the blowing dust and sand, had been converted into quagmires. So bad were conditions that one new arrival, Enos Christman by name, could write home in February, 1850, that "The town appeared to be nothing but a mud hole"; while the actual state of the streets would be unbelievable did we not have the testimony of numerous witnesses. "I have seen mules stumble in the street, and drown in the liquid mud," we read in the *Memoirs* of General William T. Sherman. "Montgomery Street had been filled up with brush and clay, and I always dreaded to ride on horseback along it, because the mud was so deep that a horse's legs would become entangled in the bushes below, and the rider was likely to be thrown and drowned in the mud. The only sidewalks were made of stepping-stones of empty boxes, and here and there a few planks with barrel-staves nailed on."

Yet a different type of pavement was to be designed by the enterprising inhabitants. Certainly, it has been well said that necessity is the soul of invention; nevertheless, it is hard to believe that the people of more conservative communities would have taken useful commodities, as did those of San Francisco, and flung them into the mud to provide a passageway. There was a time when, for about seventy-five yards on Kearny Street, one might have stepped gingerly over pavements made not of wood nor of stone, but of bags of coffee beans, boxes of tobacco, and sacks of flour, with an occasional more substantial object such as a cook-stove or piano! And what matter if, to the mind educated under a stricter regime, this did seem a trifle wasteful? Was not the market glutted with such commodities? And, besides, who would not throw away a little coffee or flour in order to protect himself from the possibility of a miserable death in the mud?

And so, mire or no mire, the city continued to progress. A way was found around all difficulties, although the difficulties multiplied. The wind might blow away the flimsy canvas roof of a tent, leaving its occupants exposed to the chilly blast of the night rains—but a substantial wooden structure would rise in its place. The wooden structure might burn (and, indeed, the city was devastated by six great fires, which followed one another in swift succession), but, on each occasion, the indomitable optimism of the people would prevail, and San Francisco would arise again, like the Phoenix, out of its own ruins. The atmosphere was as if trembling with electrical vibrations, which filled all alike with irrepressible energy; men would set off, on hair-trigger impulses, with fabulous schemes for removing precious metal from Gold Bluffs near the Klamath River, or for engaging in filibustering expeditions in Mexico; men would build, plan, create with a dynamic if sometimes erratic force; or, if evilly inclined, would tear down, loot, destroy with equally dynamic power. But whatever they entered into, they seemed not to perform half-heartedly, for life, if sometimes terminated abruptly, was at least lived to the full while it lasted.

It would be possible to continue indefinitely, noting other phases of the life of that remote, vanished San Francisco. We might view the scenes upon the arrival of a vessel, when impetuous men, sometimes unable to keep the tears from their weatherbeaten cheeks, crowd into small boats to greet the loved ones whom they have not seen for many months or even for years; we might observe the line at the post-office, which reaches out for a block or more upon the arrival of the mails, while men wait four or five hours in sun or rain in the hope of news from home; we might glance at the street preaching performed by the Reverend William Taylor on the Plaza, in the midst of saloons and gambling houses; we might gaze at the squatters who calmly take their choice of lots in the sand-hills and amid the chaparral, and, with shotguns and un-bared knives, defy the legal owners to dispossess them; we might cast eyes on the sailors who, hoodwinked and drugged, are shanghaied and sent away like galley-slaves on interminable voyages; we might take note of the palsied beggar on the streets, the insane person chained to a tree or fastened to a post in a stable, the charcoal burners with their ringing bells and donkeys laden with fuel; or we might follow the growth of restaurants, boarding houses, hotels, churches, schools, theatres, and a thousand and one refinements of civilization, which gradually mitigate and overcome the original wild and rough-and-ready atmosphere of the city.

But it is unnecessary to dwell upon all these phases of life, which, indeed, might occupy us to the length of a volume; enough has already been said to provide some idea of the nature of existence in early San Francisco, and to indicate the anarchic character of the environment. It is precisely in such an environment that crime thrives best,—an environment where a thousand currents and counter-currents are flowing, where men are torn away from all familiar sights and objectives, where recklessness predominates and there is little of tempering feminine influence. In the following chapter, accordingly, we shall see how crime did arise, and how it assumed proportions that were monstrous and appalling even for a frontier community.

CHAPTER II

IT is one of the tragedies of history that the reign of Arcadian simplicity and honesty, which we touched upon in the last chapter, should have been dissipated for all time by the incursion of the gold-seekers.

Nevertheless, the old-time conditions, while soon to be as extinct as the dinosaur, showed a certain tenacity of life even after the Gold Rush had begun. The regime of anarchy and lawlessness did not commence *instantly,* as might be imagined; instead, there ensued a period during which men still trusted their neighbors, and still left their doors unlocked. In the mines—those theatres of subsequent turbulence, robbery and murder—the prospectors would leave their bags or bottles of gold-dust unwatched in frail tents or cabins; they would let merchandise stay unprotected by the road, or under flimsy walls of cloth; they would be content to mark their claims with sticks, or with a pick and shovel left upon the ground, in the conviction that all would respect their rights; they would leave piles of gold-bearing earth unheeded for months after the winter rains were over, never doubting that they would still be there when the autumn showers commenced. Similarly, on the ranches, the owner of horses or cattle need not guard them with rifles; while even in San Francisco—so soon to be crimsoned with arrogant crime!— the primitive trustfulness prevailed during the early part of 1849, and much valuable merchandise was piled up along the entire length of Yerba Buena Cove without tempting any one to brigandage.

An illuminating story, indicative of the state of mind in

those almost primeval days, is told by William Tell Coleman —later to win fame as leader of the Vigilantes. In August, 1849, he and his brother entered the Sacramento Valley from the Sierra foothills; when, overtaken by a mounted man, they inquired if it were true that gold had been discovered in California. For reply, the stranger opened his waistcoat, and revealed a long leather bag which, he declared, contained three thousand dollars in gold dust. By way of further proof, he exposed the glittering metal to view, and even gave Coleman several handsome specimens "as a souvenir." Asked if it were not dangerous to display his wealth, the miner answered "that it was perfectly safe; that people were honest, or made to be honest; that there was no room in the country for thieves, and that there was no such thing as highway robbery; that there had been troubles in the country, but the worst men had been summarily punished, the others had learned better, and there was plenty for all who would work."

This report of Coleman does, it is true, make reference to disturbances even before midsummer in 1849; yet it is evident that those disturbances had not pierced the fabric of society, at a time when the miner could still go away and leave his bag of gold dust under his pillow without fear of the consequences, and still need post no guard upon absenting himself from his valuable diggings.

Why, then, did crime arise—and arise so suddenly? Why did an avalanche of theft, murder and arson descend upon the peaceful communities of California? Why was the atmosphere of the State darkened and befouled with every misdeed great and small, from highway robbery to official corruption, from banditry and gangsterism in their most truculent forms to that petty chicanery which hides behind the skirts of apparent decency and order? Why was California all at once the paradise of rowdies and cutthroats, of professional disturbers of the peace, and of vampire drainers of the life-blood of society?

Let us attempt, as briefly as possible, to answer these questions; and having reached some understanding of the causes that bred crime somewhat as a stagnant pool breeds mosquitoes, let us proceed to consider some of the actual manifestations of lawlessness, and some of the first measures taken *in defiance of the law* for the suppression of the criminal elements.

The reasons for the sudden outburst of ruffianism were many and varied, and yet strangely intermingled. To begin with the most obvious, there was the fact that the call of gold in California was a call to the reckless, the unchastened, the evilly disposed individuals in all lands of the earth. While many were drawn by forces no more sinister than youthful ambition and the allurement of adventure, many others crowded to California, it is to be feared, simply because it offered unparalleled opportunities for a wolfish career. The scum and refuse of the earth; scoundrels from the British penal colonies, rogues from Sydney and Van Diemen's Land —these touched shoulders on the streets of San Francisco with the most sturdy and honest of the argonauts; and these were not easily to be weaned from their old habits of throat-slashing and pilfering. From our own Eastern states, moreover, came some of the dregs of society, who were to form the basis of the organization of Hounds, which we are soon to consider; and from every land in the globe poured men who had not lived in agreement with the authorities, men who were irked by the restraints of civilized life, men who were wanted by the police or feared that they might ,be wanted, men who had lost both fortune and reputation under conditions they preferred not to recount, men who, freed from jail or suffering beneath some shadow of social disapproval, chose to risk all and forget all amid the free and open atmosphere of the West. For was there anywhere a safer refuge than in this new land, where little was to be dreaded from juries or courts? where a man might discard his former name, and be known merely as "Squint-eyed Tim," or "Missouri Pete," or "Six-Shooter Al," or something equally colorful and unrevealing? Was California not an offering of heaven itself to him with a past to conceal? And would it not be shameful ingratitude to refuse this gift of the gods and not to become a citizen of the Golden West?

But even aside from the hardened scoundrels, there were many who went astray and yet who, under more normal circumstances, might have led unexceptionable lives. For one thing, there was the contagion of contact with the baser elements, which, like rotten apples, could not mingle with the sound fruit without spreading contamination. It is well known that association with vile and immoral men, in the slums of our great cities no less than in reformatories and prisons, has often tended to work irreparable ruin to youth; and, in the same way, many an adventurer was corrupted amid the licentious environment of the early west. By the very nature of the case, such tragedies do not ordinarily leave any written record, but we can easily conjure up the sort of situation that repeated itself times without number. Let us suppose, for example, that Johnnie Jones, a callow stripling of amiable enough intentions but weak will, has just landed amid the hustle and bustle of San Francisco; and let us imagine that among his neighbors, as he pitches his tent beneath the crags of Telegraph Hill, are some assured looking older men, who instantly strike up an acquaintance, and after a time, having gained his confidence, whisper to him of alluring means of getting rich quick, and, by way of added enticement, display several bags full of bright coin and gleaming gold dust. True, the man of strength would not succumb—but, among the thousands that made their way to California in search of quick fortune, not all could have been above temptation. It is safe to say that many a one, who in his native New York or New Jersey might have made a respectable grocery clerk or hardwareman, was drawn by scheming companions into a course that led directly toward the hangman's noose.

Similarly, the extravagant atmosphere of the West, where money was gained and expended with a freedom to awaken Midas dreams even in the least susceptible, must have been as an irresistible poison bait to many a young hotblood who, in his home town, would have grown to be a pillar of the community, a director of church and school. And—even more tragically—the fact that not all could succeed, that many must come back from the mines broken in hope and in fortune, would appear to be the explanation of many careers of crime, since he who cannot gain his ends legitimately may not scruple about gaining them illegitimately.

A somewhat less obvious, but a deeper underlying reason for lawlessness, is to be found in the violent contact of two opposing cultures,—a contact of a suddenness probably without parallel in history, if we overlook the cases of military conquest. We have, to begin with, the somewhat dreamy, genial, pacifically inclined, unambitious civilization of the *padres* and the *rancheros,* who live contentedly in a land of little work and little money but with a sufficiency of all essentials; then, almost overnight, the scenes are shifted, and a swarm of strangers swoop down upon the land like a barbarian horde, greedy to seize, to devour, to reap, to profit. Energy and adventure, daring and hardihood, envy and competition, the swaggering of the bully and the recklessness of the gold-seeker, have all at once become the law of the land; all codes and traditions are tossed to the four winds; neither the power of justice nor the sanctions of morality retain any efficacy; the rule is, *Each for himself, and the world be damned!*

And what, then, of those who represent the old order? What of the Indians and the Spaniards? Shall they not be pushed aside, shoved to the wall, trampled upon as impediments in the way of the newcomer? Observe, then, one prolific source of crime—of violence that can but breed further violence. It is well known how the redman was abused, mistreated, and even murdered, in California no less than in other parts of America; the record of the innumerable massacres is a sad and disgraceful one. By way of example, one case will suffice: on March 16, 1850, a letter appeared in the *Alta California,* mentioning "an armed body of Americans, who publicly organized themselves in the village of Sonoma, for the avowed purpose of exterminating the Indians in this valley and burning the ranches and lodges where this innocent and laboring people lived." It was said that, on this occasion, ten dead natives were found in a single place.

But if the attitude toward the Indians was not only arrogant but bloodthirsty, the feeling in regard to the Mexicans or greasers can hardly be regarded as humane. One of the mildest expressions of opinion concerning these and other aliens appeared in the *Panama Star* (published on the Isthmus). "If foreigners come," suggested this journal, "let them till the soil, and make roads, or do any other work that may suit them, and they may become prosperous; but the gold mines were preserved by nature for Americans only, who possess noble hearts."

In accordance with this sentiment, which they were not always able to express but which undoubtedly they felt to the depth of their magnanimous souls, the new arrivals from such points as Missouri, Louisiana and Pennsylvania would take pains to demonstrate their own inalienable right to the soil of California. Let no mere greaser dare to stake claims at the golden diggings, even though he may have been in the country long before its present possessors; the noble-hearted brotherhood would take good care to protect their natural rights in Eldorado! To be sure, there might be some shooting as the result; the ousted greaser might be so insolent as to seek vengeance, or even take to robbing honest folk, now that he was kept from competing with his betters at the mines—but such, alas! are the risks that the noble-hearted must undergo in defense of their principles!

As an example of crime directly stimulated and inflamed by the conflict of races, the case of Joaquin Murieta instantly comes to mind,—Murieta, one of the most dangerous, indomitable and dreaded bandits that ever harried the face of this continent. This youth (he was little more than twenty-one when his crimson career was over) is said to have been a Mexican of good family, who toiled honestly enough among the gold mines of the Stanislaus, where in the spring of 1850 he was prospering—until adversity met him in the shape of half a dozen of the natural lords of the land. These gentlemen—somewhat rough-looking individuals, one gathers, in spite of the nobility that swelled their bosoms—visited Joaquin uninvited one evening, as he sat with his wife Rosita, resting from the day's exertions; and, as befits the masters of the country, they lost no time about informing him that greasers were not allowed to work "American gold." "Git!" cried the leader of the party, with more force than elegance, and motioned toward Rosita with a gesture that was anything but complimentary. Joaquin leapt up in her defense; one of the men struck him sharply in the face; and only the girl's desperate interference restrained the Mexican from retaliating by means of his bowie-knife—with consequences that might have been fatal to more than one party. As it was, Murieta was beaten into insensibility before his guests departed.

After abandoning his home by the Stanislaus, the fugitive sought refuge on a rancho amid the recesses of the Calaveras mountains; but again some of the noble-hearted fraternity appeared with the imperative command, "Git!" And again he took to his heels. But once more prosperity seemed to beckon, for he found lucrative and congenial employment as monte-dealer at Murphy Diggings,—short-lived employment, however, terminated by a false accusation of horse-theft. No use to protest his innocence! Acting upon that well-known principle, "Punish him first, try him afterwards!", the mob stripped him, lashed him to a tree, and stood by while the rawhide descended upon his quivering, bleeding flesh. And, at the same time, they seized his half-brother and hung him for the theft of the same horse.

But no longer was Joaquin to submit to abuse by the "noble-hearted." More than one of those who flogged him and killed his brother were to feel the thrust of his avenging knife. From that time forth, he was an outlaw, a sworn enemy of society; and for the better part of the next three years, until he came to the inevitable violent ending, he was to head a gang which, by its lightning movements, rapine and murders, was to be the terror of a large part of California. It has been claimed that at first Murieta admired the Americans, and that only because of their deadly injustices had his liking turned to hatred; and, whatever the facts may be in this regard, it is easy to see how the mistreatment he received would have sufficed to turn even a less fiery spirit toward vengeance and crime. In this connection, I am reminded of a statement by D. S. Richardson (in the *Overland Monthly* for August, 1888) to the effect that to the lower class of Mexican "the murder or robbery of a hated gringo was not a crime, but an act of vengeance. It was even exalted to the plane of patriotism, and was looked upon as an incident only of the strife for supremacy between two antagonistic races." May this not have been the attitude of mind that dominated Joaquin in the perpetration of his innumerable outrages?

It will be argued in reply that Murieta was not justified in striking at the heads of all Americans in return for the misdeeds of the few; and, while this must be granted, we should remember that in the philosophy of many half-civilized peoples, including the Indians, it is deemed legitimate to make any member of a clan pay the toll for the offenses of any other member. And Murieta, like scores of the bandits that harassed early California, was the heir to Indian traditions. Hence his case shows one clear source of crime in the conflict of races, cultures, and philosophies, and in the arrogance and bias of the dominant class and their summary methods of punishment, no less than in the certainty that any individual, denied the normal outlet for his activities, will seek expression through abnormal channels.

We have therefore every reason for suggesting the probability that, had there been no gold rush, Murieta would have lived out his days in peace and honor, and would never have found cause for unsheathing the more ferocious forces of his nature, and never have organized his audacious raids, nor galloped over shuddering countrysides, nor slashed at palpitant throats, nor had a price put on his head, nor been known as a prince of bad men, nor been hounded to a bloody death when he had barely reached what other men would call their majority.

One of the ramparts that Joaquin encountered, one of the rocks against which and for which he beat out his life, was that spirit which has long been among the underpinnings of occidental life. This was the power of Mammon. It was Mammon —that fomenter of feuds, rebellions, brigandage and warfare throughout the ages—whose stamp had been set upon the brows of thousands of gold-seekers; it was Mammon who, sometimes disguised but never wholly invisible, was responsible for a large percentage of the crimes that disturbed the western border. Note that the quarrels which involved Murieta, and which sent him off in fury and bitterness upon the bandit's career, were always quarrels involving property: first, he must not be allowed to interfere with the vested interests of the Americans in the gold-bearing dirt of the Sierras; secondly, he must be punished for having supposedly stolen a horse. And, in the same way, if we will look further into the records of early California, we will find the continual interdependence of property and crime; we will observe how, with monotonous frequency, men burn and murder for the sake of wealth, and how the penalties dealt the offenders are often proportionate to the gravity of their assault upon the rights of ownership. It is significant that he who stole a man's goods was likely to be treated more severely than he who killed the man himself; that horse-stealing and cattle-rustling were commonly capital offenses, and that infuriated mobs—not waiting for the slower processes of the law—would often seize the man who had taken his neighbor's steed, and leave him dangling from the limb of the nearest tree.

Even after making all allowance for the element of high youthful spirits and adventure, we must acknowledge that many of the argonauts arrived with the primary motive of enriching themselves, and cared little how this end was accomplished. Gold in the literal sense of the term was their objective; and, having reaped a harvest of this desirable commodity, they intended to leave the country—hence it was of small

account to them whether or not the land was wrecked and de-
spoiled, by themselves or by others. So long as their own toes
were not trampled upon, why bestir themselves to see that
justice was administered? And, so long as they had a reasonable
chance of success, why hesitate at any methods of self-aggrand-
izement? Something of the spirit of the pirate—"Loot the
ship, and let her sink!"—seems to have actuated many of these
young gallants, to whom, indeed, all California was little more
than one great golden vessel made for their plundering. Under
such circumstances, only the sternest and most remorseless execution of justice could exercise any restraint.

Yet a stern and remorseless execution of justice was what the
new communities most decidedly lacked. There were, it is
true, the Miners' Courts, which attempted to organize justice
in a rough-and-ready fashion, and which, for all their crudity,
did lay down many sound rules and reach many reasonable decisions; and there were those numerous cases in which the grim
personage of Judge Lynch presided, and irate mobs of citizens, as we have just remarked, would take the law into their
own hands,—sometimes hanging the right man, and occasionally executing the wrong one, and in one or two recorded instances discovering their error in the nick of time and cutting
down and apologizing to the individual whom they had all
but strangled. But little was to be expected, in the early days,
from the regularly organized tribunals; partly because of their
inherent weakness; and partly because, as we shall see, they
were often so invaded by the power of money as to be a shield
rather than a terror for the criminals. In 1849—when the outburst of violence began—there was no legitimate State government to exercise control, for the politicians at Washington, concerned then as now with petty squabbles that went scarcely further than their own vote-getting, were so absorbed in the slav-
ery issue that they could pass no measures for the protection of

the remote Pacific frontier. And, at the same time, recognized municipal authorities were almost non-existent, even in the growing metropolis of San Francisco; the old Mexican system of the alcalde had lost its efficacy, and there was nothing to supplant it; there was no police force to care for the existing population, and none to make provision for the rapidly augmented crowds of strangers, some of them of the most vicious and desperate type. Accordingly, chaos ruled, crime began to run rampant, and the professional marauder was in his heyday.

One of the consequences—itself a fruitful source of crime—was that every man went heavily armed, for the purpose of self-defense if with no more sinister motive; pistols and bowie-knives became as much a part of the recognized masculine equipment as boots and hats. And what followed is what always follows from preparedness, whether among individuals or among nations: heavy armaments could not exist without being used: these cartridges could not be worn without sooner or later scorching human flesh; these daggers could not be dangled without sooner or later finding their way to a human heart; for, like all instruments of defense, they could be employed, at any whim or passion, for ends of aggression.

Even where courts existed, they were often arbitrary in their decisions. Witness, for example, the court of Judge Almond (a former peanut vendor) which was opened on December 12th, 1849, for purposes of civil administration, in the old school-house on the Plaza. Although, according to Frank Soulé (*The Annals of San Francisco*) he rendered more "just and equitable" decisions than many later jurists, his methods were not such as would generally be considered to conform to the dignity of the law. Picture him engaged in the interesting pastime of paring his corns or scraping his nails, while seated on a dilapidated old chair, with his feet on a higher level than his head as they reposed on a small mantle above a smoking fire. Occasionally he might delay proceedings in order to squirt tobacco juice or to satisfy his thirst by means of something other than water, while he was generous in supplying writs and injunctions at an ounce of gold-dust each. Moreover, although he had never studied jurisprudence, he had decided ideas about the law and its execution. "He was a man of quick discernment and clear judgment," state the *Annals,* "and his opinion once formed, and that sometimes occurred before even the first witness was fully heard, his decision was made. Nothing further need be said."

Perhaps an even more typical representative of the early San Francisco judiciary was Ned McGowan—justice of the peace, and later associate justice of the Court of Sessions and holder of various other offices. He hailed from Pennsylvania, where he had practiced on the wrong side of the bar, having been in trouble with the authorities for various offenses, such as stabbing, or conspiracy to pass stolen money,—but none of these blots on his escutcheon seem to have hampered his later career as a dispenser of justice. His methods, it appears, were more lucrative to himself than to the community, as is indicated by the case of the lawyer who had just landed in San Francisco after a passage around Cape Horn, and had been chosen to defend his fellow passengers against a charge of disorderly conduct. Lo and behold! whom should he recognize on the bench but his old acquaintance Ned McGowan? Dismay filled the attorney's countenance; he realized that all his eloquence would avail him naught. And so, making the best of a bad position, he turned to his clients, and advised, "Gentlemen, you have no use for me. You may as well come down heavy with the coin first as last; it is your only chance."

Another suggestion of the calibre of the justice dispensed by

McGowan is to be found in the following paragraph, from the *Evening Picayune* of August 20, 1850:

"Justice McGowan's court—An interesting case came off this morning, interesting because several interesting young ladies appeared as witnesses. Thomas Jackson claimed $200 for wages . . . and presented as evidence in his behalf Miss Maloney and Miss Margaret Waring, two young ladies of rare attraction and fashionable apparel. The judge, of course, could do nothing less than render a verdict in favor of the plaintiff."

Considering the standards of the courts—such courts as there were—it is small wonder that there was little if anything in a legal way to restrain the ruffians from the full and unimpeded practice of their profession. Conditions were complicated, furthermore, by the fact that there was not even a jail until August, 1849—and even then only a poor and insufficient prison in the shape of the dismantled brig *Euphemia*.

Consequently, there grew up what may be called a city within a city—*Sydney town,* the home and citadel of some of the lowest knaves and rascals that ever settled down to prey on any community. Let us glance at it, as it sprawls near the base of Telegraph Hill, composed of tents and minute hovels scattered helter-skelter on the level and in tiny ravines, with a sprinkling of drinking saloons, dance-halls and other dives; while overhead looms the shadowing slope, rough and irregular and broken by numerous spurs. In this inviting vicinity, one may encounter the members of the fraternity of Sydney coves or Sydney ducks, who, having served out their penal sentence in Australia, are now free to apply themselves in a new sphere, and prove their skill by ranging the unlanterned streets at night, stealing or destroying whatever suits their fancy, and striking down any unfortunate citizen who may chance to be in their way; or else, decoying their victim to some cliff above the bay, harry him to his death on the rocks below. How many are thus slain is a matter beyond computation, for the Sydney ducks prefer to leave no records of such transactions; yet, in testimony to their activities, innumerable human bones have been washed up by the waves around North Beach.

But proficient as the Sydney ducks were in crime, they were not responsible for the particular demonstration that aroused the community in the summer of 1849, and that led to the first popular demand for justice. It would not, indeed, be out of place to suggest that the example of the gentlemen from Sydney may have proved a stimulus and an incentive, since in felonies, as in other things, there is nothing like the power of a good teacher; nevertheless, the fact remains that the credit for the affair of 1849 belongs to a group of native Americans: a regiment of New York volunteers, who, some time before, had been disbanded, and had been sent to California in the hope that they would help to people the land with a high class of settlers.

It was these who, at a time when the police force was non-existent, formed themselves into what was perhaps the first organized group in the city of San Francisco. It was these who, with that genius for the proper appellation which distinguished them throughout their career, entitled themselves The Hounds—although later, feeling that this name did not do them justice, they called themselves The San Francisco Society of Regulators: an equally appropriate designation, since their one object in existence was to regulate San Francisco for their own benefit. The headquarters of the tribe—a canvas structure on Kearny Street—was fittingly known as Tammany Hall; and from this tent, so touchingly named in memory of a certain Wigwam in Manhattan, the members of the intrepid brotherhood would sally forth on their tribute-collecting expeditions—which, since they had nothing to fear from any power on earth, were often conducted in broad daylight and with that manner of bluff assurance befitting the lords of the land.

Let us follow a party of these almighty Hounds as they strut through the streets on one of their foraging tours. Perhaps it is Sunday; and, feeling in a good mood, they proceed to the music of fife and drum, accompanied by such howls and groans as they feel necessary to punctuate the ceremonies; while their leaders walk in military uniforms, and beneath the colors of flying flags. Or perhaps it is a mere week-day, and they go about their business in a more matter-of-fact manner. In any case, they enter a store—let us say, a clothing store—and having calmly collected such hats, socks, shirts and other articles as suit their whim, they as calmly take their leave; while the proprietor, who sits cowering in a corner, does not dare to lift his voice and offer the insult of suggesting payment.

Next the Regulators visit a restaurant, and, making a loud noise and clatter, call for food and drink—which the alarmed proprietor and waiters know better than to refuse, though they may leave other customers unserved while the demands of the newcomers are satisfied. Should the Hounds become impatient or aroused, they are capable of manifesting their wrath by kicking over the tables, and spilling decanters, glasses and plates unceremoniously upon the floor; nor is their mood likely to be improved by the gin cocktails and similar "refreshments" which they consume. Hence the restaurant owner may throw up his hands with a thankful sigh if his patrons leave his place undemolished.

But it is only toward the close of their career that the Hounds commit their depredations on a really generous scale. Success breeds confidence; and, meeting with no opposition in their earlier raids, they gradually extend their operations, with a manner increasingly more brazen. However—as befits good loyal native Americans—they are partial to foreigners when looking for victims; they share to the full the hearty Anglo-Saxon contempt for the greaser; and they make it their self-assumed patriotic duty to protect their fellow citizens from the alien elements—and particularly from the Peruvians and Chileans. It is not recorded that the latter are an especial menace to the Americans; nevertheless, the Regulators, with a true crusading spirit, consider it a matter of principle to harry these defenseless foreigners; to terrorize them, to tear down their huts, and, incidentally, to take anything of value that may happen to be contained within.

It is on the fourteenth of July, 1849, that matters come to a climax. The process of "regulation" now goes beyond anything previously attempted; in broad daylight, and with an insolence that puts to shame their own by no means timid record, they launch an attack upon the Chilean quarters. And how the sticks and bullets fly! How the pistol-shots ring out! How the shrieks of women rend the air! the groans of men, the wails of children! How the thudding clubs descend upon the Chilean tents, lashing them to fragments! How the marauders rush in with hoots and howls, kicking and cuffing the dark-skinned foreigners as they scramble to escape! With what savage yells the invaders fling stones at the retreating, blood-smeared shapes! With what fury they trample on prostrate bodies! What mutterings and foul-mouthed blasphemies mingle with the roars of excitement and the moans of the beaten! Here some mounted men gallop wildly about, chasing the terrorized Chileans and firing upon them; there the looters avidly gather up the jewels and money found in a ravaged tent, while dashing to bits such articles as they think unworthy of capture. To theft and vandalism, they add rape and murder; a Chilean woman and her daughter are seized and assaulted;

the former dies, and the latter escapes only after slashing at one of her assailants with a bowie-knife. Truly, it is a spectacle of madness, a scene reminiscent of wartime horrors! an outrage such as has rarely been perpetrated upon an unoffending people in a day of peace!

But on this occasion, it would appear, the regulation has gone a bit too far even for the taste of a pioneer community. All during the afternoon and night of the fifteenth the chastisement of the Chileans continues, being carried to every part of the city where one of the unfortunate South Americans can be found; and there is no citizen who dares to lift his hand against the redoubtable gangsters. Patience, however, has its breaking point; and that point has now been reached. If the brawlers and ruffians can organize, why not the more respectable elements?

So reasons that well known resident, Sam Brannan, whom we last saw sailing through the Golden Gate not quite three years before at the head of a company of Mormons. Hence on the following day, while the Regulators are resting from their hard night's exertions, Brannan takes his perch on a barrel at the corner of Montgomery and Clay Streets, and begins to exercise his oratorical gifts. One can picture him as he stands there, his hands waving excitedly and a crowd gathering to drink in his words: a stalwart-looking man of thirty, with broad chest, shaggy hair and side-whiskers, blazing black eyes and a resonant voice. His speech is not elegant, but it is such as the people understand and find it good to hear; consequently, the crowd grows as if by magic, until they form a dense surging mass and it is impossible for the newcomers to get near the speaker. A motion is therefore in order to adjourn to that acknowledged center of town, the Plaza; and Sam and his enthusiastic cohorts lose no time about making the migration; after which, as if with deliberate irony, he makes a rostrum of the roof of the only agency of established justice: the one-story office of the alcalde, Leavenworth.

With the legal authorities thus beneath his feet, Sam waxes fiery to an ever-increasing crowd: which fact, it would seem, does not meet with the approval of the Hounds, who have no relish for regulation of the type he is advocating. Accordingly, word is brought to him, Beware! the Hounds are on the alert, and retribution shall be swift and sudden. There is, to be specific, a little house on a hill, known as the residence of one Samuel Brannan, Esq.—in fact, his most precious possession! —and an application of fire to this particular domicile will be most timely, if the said Samuel Brannan does not forthwith cease his attacks upon the inoffensive Regulators.

Such is the import if not the precise wording of the message brought to Mr. Brannan as he stands there on the roof of the alcalde's office, warming the emotions of the crowd. But is Mr. Brannan daunted? Far from it! For a moment he stands before the multitude pale with anger, quivering in every limb; then, like a boomerang, the threat of the Hounds reacts upon themselves, and arouses their foe to more furious denunciation. Down with the Hounds! Down with them! They are a law unto themselves, a peril to the community! Wipe them out, exterminate them, like the vermin they are! One can almost hear Brannan hurling out these words, and others still more severe, while the crowd stands spellbound, aghast, the hundreds of straining faces intent upon the speaker, the hundreds of minds moved as by a common throb of indignation.

But no! not all the hundreds of minds! From amid the multitude, protesting voices arise; and pistols are waved in air. Let Sam take heed! In another moment, he may topple and fall, clutching at a crimsoned breast.

But defiantly he opens his shirt, as if to invite doom; defiantly he thunders on, growing constantly more abusive of

WILLIAM TELL COLEMAN

the Hounds. And the members of that fraternity, doubtless aware that if they attempt to make good their threats, they will be torn limb from limb by the mob, quietly slink away and disappear. It is one thing to swoop down upon the defenseless Chileans! but quite another thing, they perceive, to challenge an aroused rabble of their own countrymen, most of them armed to the teeth!

From words to action, as it turned out, was no great distance for Brannan and his compatriots. As soon as the speaking was over, the hearers formed themselves into companies of one hundred men each, with duly appointed commanders; and they decided by lot which company should first stand guard, with the object of hunting Hounds.

This not being considered sufficient, a mass meeting of citizens was convened on the Plaza at three o'clock that afternoon; and, thanks to this assemblage—the largest yet known in California—a subscription was taken up to aid the sufferers from the preceding day's "regulation," and two hundred and thirty citizens were enrolled for immediate police service.

It is at this point that the Hounds virtually disappear from history. Strange to say, considering the assurance and effrontery of their previous maneuvers, they began to scatter like rats; and, before evening, seventeen of them had been caught and placed in an improvised prison on the United States vessel *Warren*.

The rest may be swiftly told: at a popular meeting, two judges were chosen to assist the alcalde in the trial of the prisoners; a grand jury was summoned, and the defendants indicted; a trial was held according to legal forms, with the result that—in spite of efforts to prove *alibis*—nine of the Regulators were convicted and sentenced to various punishments, ranging up to ten years' imprisonment.

It would make a fitting conclusion to say that the penalties were actually inflicted, and that, accordingly, crime did not go unchastened. Such, however, was not to be the case; in the disorganized state of society, there was no way of executing the commands of justice; owing to the scarcity of jails and jailors, the people had to content themselves with shipping some of the culprits out of town and liberating others.

Nevertheless, the main objective of Brannan and his colleagues had been attained; the Society of Regulators had been broken up once and for all—and that without any resort to lynch law; and more than a year and a half was to pass before the people would again feel obliged to take the administration of justice and the punishment of offenders into their own hands.

CHAPTER III

Exterminators of vermin have often observed that a single dose of poison is insufficient to annihilate the pests. Somehow, the vile little creatures will survive even the most deadly spray, and, at the first opportunity, will crawl forth from their nooks and crannies to perform their old antics as obnoxiously as ever. And as it is with insects and other lowly members of the animal kingdom, so it is with those humans who crawl amid the rubbish heaps of crime. By a determined effort, they may be repressed for a while; but it requires more than one cleansing application to drive them entirely from the premises.

Such, at least, is what the citizens of San Francisco learned to their regret after the affair of the Hounds. Although the society of Regulators was no more, crime was to be no stranger to the city by the Golden Gate. And for this there were several reasons. For one thing, the men of Sydney had not left; had not even been intimidated by the maltreatment of their brothers, the Hounds. And, for another thing, the old, reckless, intemperate spirit of the city remained; the gambling halls survived, the drinking saloons still flourished, men still brandished slung-shots, rifles, and knives, and regarded life lightly and adventurously, as a thing to be tossed away as heedlessly as the bags of gold-dust they risked at the card-tables.

Hence it was perfectly possible that you would be standing some evening as an innocent onlooker at a game of monte or faro, and that, of a sudden, loud oaths would be heard, pistols would be lashed out, and, amid shouts and yells, the crowd would scurry for refuge under the tables and behind the counters. Then would come the flashing of gunfire and the report of shots—one of which might lodge in your breast, although you had had nothing to do with the altercation. . . . Or, again, you might be walking calmly in the sunlight down one of the main thoroughfares, when two men, springing alertly into view from opposite sides of the street, would draw their guns, take aim, and fire at one another—and well for you if you did not stop a stray bullet from this vendetta! In any case, if you were accidentally hurt during a feud between your fellow citizens, you could look for no recourse in the law; your injury would be considered regrettable, no doubt, but was too common a sort of occurrence to arouse much comment—besides, whose fault was it if you had not been quick enough to keep out of the way?

At a time when killing affrays were so abundant even among the so-called respectable elements, what could one expect of the professional criminals? Would they not merely feel themselves to be in fashion when they now and then claimed tribute of a life? And is it surprising if organized villainy, a short while after the dismemberment of the Hounds association, became more aggressive than ever? Let no citizen now feel safe even in broad daylight! there was no telling when a party of highwaymen, swinging guns and knives, might not come galloping down upon him! Let no citizen venture alone into the streets at night! the thoroughfares were haunted with prowlers, who might relieve him of his valuables and put an end to his earthly career! And let no citizen take a house in an isolated district; for, unless he have a sufficient guard, he will never be able to close his eyes without the dread of loot and murder!

So bad did matters become—and so free and easy was the way of the despoiler—that a new criminal organization arose, more secret than the Hounds and less blatantly demonstrative, but for that reason all the more sinister and difficult to extirpate. Operating by means of spies and agents, who disguised themselves as peddlers while engaging on their reconnoitering expeditions and marking the houses intended for plunder, this new criminal fraternity was as systematic in its activities as the Regulators had been casual and haphazard. It adopted what one may call "business methods" in wrong-doing; it classified the various offenses into categories, and apportioned them out to its disciples according to their capabilities, thus taking care always to make the criminal fit the crime; moreover, it provided a scholastic training for young hopefuls in housebreaking and murder, and offered courses under the skilled supervision of more than one Fagin, for the benefit of promising youths of from ten to sixteen, who desired to distinguish themselves in anything from ordinary swindling to the higher varieties of brigandage.

It is little wonder, therefore, that the production of felons became one of the established local industries. It is little wonder if we read of misdeeds of all types and flavors, from the shipment of spurious gold dust from Mexico (reported in the *Alta California* for April 1, 1850) to the deliberate burning of the city. There is, in fact, good reason to suppose that incendiarism was not the least common nor the least effective of the methods employed by the plunderers; there is evidence that it was not merely by accident that the city was six times devastated by fire within a period of about a year and a half. For example, Frank Soulé (a contemporary writer) has this to say regarding the conflagration of June 22nd, 1851, which destroyed some fourteen or fifteen square blocks:

"There was no doubt that the fire was the work of an incendiary. No fire had been used in the house in which it commenced for any purpose whatever. As it progressed, the flames would suddenly start up in advance, and in one or more instances persons were detected in applying fire. It was anything rather than a consoling thought that three or four millions of dollars should be destroyed, and thousands of people turned houseless into the streets, merely to gratify the hatred or love of robbery of a few scoundrels."

Months before the occurrence of this particular outrage, the newspapers had been filled with warnings of arson, and had occasionally uttered their indignation in terms that were the natural prelude to the formation of vigilance committees by the long-suffering citizens. Thus, in the *Alta California* of January 24th, 1850, we read the following in regard to a fire a short distance above the newspaper office:

"From the appearance of the fire when discovered, and from the character of the materials of which it was composed, there is not the least doubt that it was the work of an incendiary. . . .

"It is a well known fact that some of the most desperate scoundrels of England who have been serving the Queen in Sydney are in this city, and that they would stick at nothing in the attempt to obtain money by any diabolical crime. Our merchants must organize some system of private watchmen . . . and take every measure to put as many checks as possible upon the incendiary, for there is no question but that the attempt of last night will be repeated."

Even more outspoken was the *Herald* following a fire which occurred on the fourteenth of December of the same year, and which had evidently been deliberately started in order to burn the office of the Pacific Mail Steamship Company and rifle it of treasure. Cannot one see the Vigilance Committees already girding on their arms as one reads the following words?—

"We do not advocate the rash and vengeful infliction of summary punishment on any person against whom the proof is not positive . . . but although opposed to capital punishment in old communities, where the execution of the law is so perfectly

systematized that justice seldom fails of its victim, we nevertheless believe that some startling and extraordinary correction
is necessary in San Francisco to arrest the alarming increase of
crimes against property and life, and to save the remainder of
the city from destruction."

"Startling and extraordinary" was the correction eventually
to be meted out by the citizens of San Francisco—perhaps more
so than even the able editor of the *Herald* could have foreseen.
Nevertheless, it is highly improbable that the people would
have had any recourse to such unusual means if they could have
been assured of protection through normal legal channels.

But the normal legal channels, unfortunately, continued to
be virtually non-existent.   Even after the establishment of local
and state government, the citizen seeking refuge in the law was
a little like the sheep looking for shelter in a den of wolves.
What else could one expect, when the office-holders were the
very scum of the community? The lesser positions did not offer
sufficient in the way of emoluments to attract able men at a
time when money might be made prolifically in private enterprise; while the higher offices, likewise, were in the main a
magnet for rogues: witness the fact that John McDougal, one-
time governor of the State, was arrested for election frauds in
September, 1856. Or witness, again, the behavior of the aldermen of San Francisco, who, with unbounded generosity, award-
ed themselves enormous salaries, voted themselves each a handsome gold medal at public expense, took care of their friends
by granting contracts at inflated prices, connived in relieving
the city of its lands, and piled up a burden of taxation beneath
which the community fairly staggered.

In more ways than one, the citizens themselves were unquestionably responsible for this condition, since then, as now, the
voters cast their ballots with anything but logic—as is indicated

by the case of Bryant and Hays, who, at the first county election
of officers in San Francisco in April, 1850, were rivals for the
position of sheriff. It is said that the former, thanks to the free
distribution of lunches and drinks at the hotel he conducted,
was on the point of winning the election . . . when lo! Hays,
who was a "colonel" from Texas, conceived the idea of appear-
ing on the Plaza in the character of a Texas ranger, dashing
back and forth on a black horse amid the tumult of drums and
trumpets, and treating the dazzled throng to an exhibition of
daring feats of horsemanship. Alas for Bryant! What after
all were his free meals and whiskeys beside the qualifications of
his adversary? Let Hays, having shown his equestrian abilities,
be elevated at once to the sheriff's office!

The professional politicians, however, took care that the will
of the people should not too often assert itself, whether to elect
a Texas ranger or any other idol of the day. The fact that a
given candidate had received a majority of the votes was by no
means a guaranty that he was to take office: the bosses saw to
that by counting the votes according to a process of arithmetic
all their own. The stuffing of the ballot-boxes was soon to
become an established practice, as was also the less subtle
method of hiring supporters of the vote-repeating variety, and
brawlers to intimidate or maul persons suspected of wishing to
vote for the opposition. If necessity required, inconvenient ballots might even be burned: for example, in the *Alta California*
for April 8th, 1850, we are told that all the ballots cast in the
recent election had been given to the flames, with the consent
of the judge and the board of inspectors—and while no specific
charges are made, the implications are clear enough. In view
of the fact that elections were frequently in the hands of the
most corrupt elements, it is not surprising if political life remained at a low estate.

But what was the precise effect of the election frauds upon the more bloody varieties of crime? The connection is easy, enough to see; for when the officers of the law are corrupt, there may be safety for scoundrels, but none for ordinary citizens. Suppose, for example, that you have been assaulted and robbed, but that by some stroke of fortune you have survived, and are even able to identify your assailants. Naturally, you hasten to court, and swear out a warrant for their arrest—and what then? You are confronted by the cutthroats who have your money and who came near to taking your life; and they merely grin and deny the offense. Even though ordered held for further examination, they are released on bail, following the sacrifice of some worthless security—and this may be the last you will ever see of them. But possibly they consider it not worth while to disappear; far easier to face trial—a procedure by no means unique in their experience. So a jury is chosen, largely from the professional hangers-on at court,—a genial crowd, constitutionally indisposed to work, their faces a little dull and besotted, their noses red from excess of alcoholic refreshments, their minds perhaps not inelastic when it comes to doing a little favor for a "friend." By this company of their "peers" the members of the robber gang are tried; and, strange to say, it turns out that you have done your assailants an injustice. They are not robbers at all, but respectable, honest citizens! This is proved by no less than four or five witnesses, who, though their brows are suggestive of anything but innocence and candor, are none the less believed when they testify that the accused men were all in Benicia, or San José, or Stockton, or some other remote point, on the day when the crime was committed. Hence, though you foam at the mouth in protest, the prisoners are released.

You are subsequently told—and are given convincing proof—that the police are in collusion with the despoilers, and receive their share of the loot; and that the judge who tried the case, even if not actually bribed, is inclined to look with a lenient eye upon the law-breakers, since it is upon their support that he depends for re-election.

Under such circumstances, is it surprising if you go away nursing your grievance? if you feel a sore spot in your heart at the very mention of the law and its administration? and if you lend a willing ear when subsequently some one speaks to you of forming a people's committee to take the execution of justice and the punishment of knaves into your own hands?

The extent of the degradation of the courts, the depth of their venality, is indicated by the extreme scarcity of convictions in cases involving assaults upon life and property. According to a statement of the district attorney of San Francisco (as reported by Bancroft), there were twelve hundred murders in the city in the four years beginning with 1850; yet the only legal execution was that of a Spaniard, José Forni, who was hanged on December 10, 1852, for the slaying of a Mexican. Even though these figures are not authenticated, there is no question at all as to the general conditions which they indicate, wherein the chances were better than several hundred to one that the perpetrator of a major crime would not be brought to justice. Murder, it would seem, had come to be safer than snipe-shooting.

Nevertheless, it would appear to me—although, as one who writes long after the event, I may be in error—that had the people been more seriously interested in the frustration of crime, they might have succeeded without resort to the extreme measures afterwards adopted. Had public spirit outweighed private interest, capable men might have been found to make up the juries and occupy the lesser offices in spite of the small salaries; had anxiety for the public weal been uppermost in the minds of the majority, means could have been devised for safeguarding elections, and for eliminating corruption and gangsterism. That vast outburst of popular energy and righteous indignation, which subsequently went into the formation of the Vigilance Committees, might at the outset have sufficed to sweep the fraudulent officials from their thrones and to establish a reign of purity and justice. But at a time when a philosophy of savage individualism was rampant; at a time when the eyes of the masses were fastened upon a goal of personal acquisition, it was not to be expected that a moral wave would arise to sweep the corruptionists out of power. And so, although the people were occasionally to express their fury, and eventually were to band themselves into an organization of unprecedented power, it is significant that the force of their earlier attacks was directed against the mere outcroppings of wrong rather than against its underpinnings; against the perpetrators of certain base and violent crimes, but not primarily against those vicious officials and that vicious political system which their own indifference and self-concern had made possible.

But let us not criticize too severely. It is impossible to say what we ourselves would have done had we been present in that crime-harried city, knowing that scores of assaults and robberies were committed each day with impunity, knowing that the firebrands of the plunderer were constant menaces in the dark, knowing that many a "good man and true" had been struck down by the assassin, knowing that the desperadoes enjoyed such security in Sydney town that even the police dared not venture there except in large parties. Under such circumstances, we would probably have succumbed to the natural human tendency to pick a "villain" or set of villains as the reason for all the iniquities, rather than the forces that had made it possible for such wretches to function; and it is most unlikely that, in our counter-thrusts, we would have done anything more thoroughgoing and incisive, more sane and coolly controlled than the measures taken by the citizens of San Francisco. It may be said, indeed, that whatever we think *might* have been done to meet the emergency, they did actually confront an unparalleled situation in an unparalleled way.

But before the day arrived for them to act systematically *outside the law,* innumerable fits and spasms of popular frenzy were to indicate which way the wind was blowing. There were, for example, the indignation meetings held in 1850 as a protest against the rapacity of the local authorities; there were the individual cases in which thieves were caught and roughly treated by the mob, as when William Wilson was beaten with fists, clubs and iron hoops for stealing a shirt and vest, in February, 1851; there was the attempt at lynching, when twenty horsemen from Mission Dolores bore down upon the officials in charge of the murderer William Slater, and attempted to seize the culprit; there was the episode of William Walker, an editor of the *Daily Herald*, who was committed to prison by Judge Levi Parsons for his fulminations against the "masterly inactivity" of the courts, and who was visited in jail by a crowd of four thousand sympathizers—with the result that he was liberated under a writ of *habeas corpus,* while the judge not long afterwards resigned beneath the pressure of public condemnation. And—even more significant of the temper of the times—there was the case of Benjamin Lewis, who was being examined in the Recorder's Court on a charge of arson, when the courtroom began to fill amid scenes of wild turbulence, and three or four thousand persons surged outside the building in an impassioned mob, with yells of "Hang him! Hang him! Lynch the villain! Hang the fire-raising wretch!" Fortunately for Lewis, the rabble listened to the advice of Sam Brannan that the prisoner be given over to the volunteer police, which had been formed not long before. But it was small satisfaction to the multitude to learn that the accused had meanwhile been spirited away by the regular police, no one knew where; nor was the popular ire appeased when, some time later, Lewis was brought to trial, and on two successive occasions escaped because of a "flaw" in the indictment.

While legal technicalities thus conspired with the apathy and cynicism of the officials to make a travesty of justice, it was only a question of time when some more vigorous outburst of popular feeling should occur. Chance might play the deciding rôle as to just what event or series of events should ignite the spark; but so fitful and disturbed was the public mood that the certainty of some eventual eruption might have been taken for granted.

It was by no means inevitable, although it was entirely appropriate, that the way to the Vigilance Committees should have been opened by the robbery of the dry goods store of C. J. Jansen, on Montgomery Street near Washington. This event, which took place on February 19th, 1851, arose under most aggravating circumstances. It occurred in the heart of town, and at the early hour of 8 P. M. (then considered a normal time for conducting trade); and its victim—a well-liked local merchant—had not only been robbed of nearly two thousand dollars, but had been knocked senseless with a slung-shot, beaten on the head, trampled, and apparently left for dead by his two assailants.

Gross as the outrage was, it was by no means of an unusual nature in that thug-infested city—yet it was sufficient to light the long-awaited fuse. Take note, for example, of the inflammatory editorial that appeared in the *Alta California:*

"How many murders have been committed in this city within a year! And who has been hung or shot or punished for the crime? Nobody. How many men shot and stabbed, knocked down and bruised; and who has been punished for it? How many thefts and arsons, robberies and crimes of less note; and where are the perpetrators? . . . "

A plea like this, furiously emotional yet based on well known facts, could hardly fail of its effect. The people, already at a fever-pitch of indignation, were roused almost to hysteria when, on the second day following the crime, it was known that the two supposed brigands had been arrested. About the identity of one of them—who gave his name as Windred—there was some slight question; but the other had been positively identified by the victim of the assault as none other than James Stuart, a noted outlaw who had been held some months before for the murder of the sheriff of Auburn, and had subsequently broken jail at Sacramento. Of what avail for the prisoner to protest that he was not Stuart at all, but Thomas Burdue? that he had a wife and children in Australia? that he was innocent of all crime, though he had everywhere met with misfortune and had thrice been arrested for misdeeds committed by others? Let the man rave on! he convinced no one by his preposterous tale! was it to be supposed that a rascal who could commit murder without flinching would hesitate at lying?

Yet the strange fact is that the man was not lying. He really was Thomas Burdue, and not the redoubtable James Stuart. But nature had played him the meanest of tricks: it had made him of about the same height and complexion as Stuart; it had given him the same black beard, the same bald spot at the crown of the head, the same long wavy brown hair reaching below his collar, the same glittering uneasy black eyes; while, as if to baffle the most adroit, he had acquired a scar on the left cheek, a ring of India ink about one of his fingers, and a stiff appearance on another,—all of which served to identify him the more positively as Stuart. Witnesses were not hard to find who would testify—and testify in all sincerity—that the alleged Burdue was in fact the Auburn murderer.

Another irony of the case is that the second prisoner, Windred, was likewise an innocent man. And so we find a popular tribunal setting out to vindicate the ends of justice, with two guiltless individuals as the prospective victims.

But as yet there was no popular tribunal. There was only an infuriated mob, which gathered about the building containing the supposed criminals. "Hang them! Hang them!" rang out the cries of threatening hundreds; and these shouts, "Hang them! Hang them! Lynch them! Lynch them!", were taken up and repeated when the prisoners were escorted out of their cells to visit the disabled Mr. Jansen, for the purpose of being identified. There was even an attempt at lynching when some members of the distracted rabble made a dash for Burdue— only to be driven back by the revolvers of the guard.

The worst, however, was still to come. While the defendants were taken to court for examination, and were being held over for further questioning the following week, a crowd of five thousand men collected about the city hall, with angry mutterings and ugly scowls that boded no good for Burdue and Windred.

"Now is the time! Now!" exclaimed some one, when the judge announced that proceedings were over for the day—and, to his consternation, he found that proceedings were only beginning. Once more the mob lunged forward to secure the prisoners—and then what pandemonium! One could hear the sound of oaths and scuffling bodies, the crash and clattering of splitting railings and broken tables and chairs, the yells of confusion, of terror, of dismay; one could see the black mass of assailants as, thickly wedged together, they pressed forward with brandished fists and frenzy-lighted eyes; one could observe the sheriff and his men as, seizing the prisoners, they were forced backward while lashing out violently at the crowd. Then, from the armory of the Washington Guards next door, an armed company rushed upon the scene, and drove the throng from the beleaguered court-room, while shrieks, groans, and hisses filled the air, and cries of "Shame! Shame! Shame!"

But by degrees the frustrated multitude was pacified, thanks to some of the more sober of their own number; and they peacefully separated and returned to their homes, after appointing a committee to guard the prisoners during the night, and to report at a mass meeting at ten the next morning.

Ten o'clock arrived, and a dense crowd—eight or ten thousand strong—were waiting in the Plaza. To this eager gathering the reports of the committee were read, the majority recommending that the accused be tried that afternoon by a judge and jury selected from among the people; the minority, headed by Sam Brannan, being in favor of the immediate application of lynch law.

"I am very much surprised," declared the excitable Brannan, "to hear people talk about grand juries, or recorders, or mayors. I'm tired of such talk. These men are murderers, I say, as well as thieves. I know it, and I will die or see them hung by the neck. . . . The law and the courts never yet hung a man in California; and every morning we are reading fresh accounts of murders and robberies. I want no technicalities. Such things are devised to shield the guilty."

Fortunately, however, Brannan's impetuous suggestions were vetoed by his colleagues; and the meeting, after appointing a party of twenty men to stand watch over the prisoners, adjourned until the following day.

Meanwhile, as if the temper of the mob needed to be still further inflamed, handbills of a radical nature had been printed and distributed throughout the city:

"CITIZENS OF SAN FRANCISCO.

"The series of murders and robberies that have been committed in this city seem to leave us entirely in a state of anarchy.

When thieves are left without control to rob and kill, then doth the honest traveler fear each bush a thief. Law, it appears, is but a nonentity, to be scoffed at; redress can be had for aggression but through the never-failing remedy so admirably laid down in the code of Judge Lynch. Not that we should admire this process for redress, but that it seems to be inevitably necessary.

"Are we to be robbed and assassinated in our domiciles, and the law to let our aggressors perambulate the streets merely because they have furnished straw bail? If so, let each man be his own executioner. Fie upon your laws! they have no force.

"All those who would rid our city of robbers and murderers will assemble on Sunday, at two o'clock, on the Plaza."

Here was a proclamation which, in an older and better established community, would have been considered revolutionary. Here was defiance that, in more lands than one, would have earned the author of the handbills a long term in a penitentiary. In what city of what country today, one may ask, would any citizen dare to fling such an open challenge in the face of constituted authority? Yet in San Francisco in the year 1851 it represented no more nor less than the simple expression of public opinion; it represented no more nor less than what thousands had been thinking and saying; it was but a virtual repetition of the ideas uttered in private homes and from the pages of the press. "There is clearly no remedy for the existing evil but in the strong arms and stout souls of the citizens themselves," declared the *Herald* on February 22nd, so expressing the same point of view more concisely—and that "strong arms and stout souls" were ready, was to be amply demonstrated in the days to come.

It was on Sunday the 23rd that matters reached a climax. Then great crowds began to gather about the Graham House, at Pacific and Kearny Streets, where the prisoners were quarter-ed; dense masses of men began to pour in from all sides, many with their side-arms showing; and the evidences of determination and anger were apparent not only in the aroused eyes and excited glances of the multitude, but in their clenched fists, their nervous, hasty movements, their sullen resistance when addressed by the mayor and asked to disperse, and their resolute manner of packing themselves solidly about the building, until all entrances were blocked. It now seemed as if no power on earth could save the unfortunate Burdue and Windred from the wrath of the rabble.

At this point let us introduce William Tell Coleman, a merchant of the city at whom we glanced casually as he rode into California on the crest of the Gold Rush in August, 1849. Twenty-seven years old and of a stern, determined appearance, with a tall, well-formed frame, and clear, deep eyes beneath an imposing breadth of forehead, Coleman was instantly to spring into control of that leaderless mob; and, by a process wholly unforeseen yet altogether natural, was unwittingly to pave the way not only for his rôle in the Vigilance Committee of 1851 but for his fateful ascendancy in the greater movement five years later.

On that eventful Sunday morning late in February, Coleman observed the multitude gathering about the Graham House; and, realizing that grave happenings were in store, he prudently went home and exchanged his Sunday suit for workaday garb. Returning, he found that matters had not improved; the prisoners were still in imminent peril of being lynched. "I always had had a horror of a mob and its wild and hasty excesses," he declared years later (in the *Century Magazine* for November, 1891), "and it occurred to me that a middle course might be adopted, and a fair and speedy trial be secured by a court of the people, organized on the spot."

Acting upon this impression, he forced his way into the building and up to a front balcony, from which he managed to catch the ear of the people. Let them all form themselves into a court inside the building! proposed Coleman. Let the prisoners be brought forth, and counsel be allowed on both sides; let testimony be taken, and judgment passed after a fair trial; and let the accused be hanged if found guilty.

"Never in my life," Coleman records, "had I heard a more instantaneous and tumultuous shout of applause. It was light breaking through the dark overhanging cloud. It solved the problem and satisfied the longings of the people. This note had struck the chord and every nerve seemed to vibrate in harmony."

The decisive point having been reached, all citizens who could pack themselves into the building were invited in, while the rest remained outside as a guard. And now for the immediate selection of judge and jury, followed by a trial with no legal technicalities or delays! J. R. Spence, a well known local merchant, was appointed judge; two associate justices were chosen to sit at his side; twelve citizens were promptly picked to serve on the jury; three prominent lawyers volunteered to act for the defense; while Coleman himself, responsive to popular demand, was enlisted as prosecuting attorney.

And now, for about six hours, the strangest of trials was conducted. All around the building stood a compact, eager mass of men, about ten thousand of them, all tensely, grimly waiting; while within the hall the crowd was so dense that, on making his way to the front, according to his own testimony, Coleman was "literally forced to walk over the heads and shoulders of the thickly packed mass of people." Meanwhile the audience manifested extreme impatience, from time to time breaking out in clamorous demonstrations, in their fear lest the prisoners escape; and on each occasion Coleman had to leave the courtroom and make a short speech, which always succeeded in cooling the emotions of the throng.

When finally the witnesses had all been examined and the jury had retired, another long wait ensued. The minutes wore into hours; the clock ticked away until it was nine in the evening; but still there were many who, braving the chill winds of the February night, remained massed against the building, waiting, waiting, waiting . . . unwilling to go home until they had learned the verdict of the tribunal.

And how intently the spectators hung upon the foreman's words when finally the jury filed back! But what an uproar of rage, of disappointment as the decision was announced! The jury had disagreed! The accused were not to be hanged after all!

Yet the spectators, in their indignation, would not permit themselves to be so easily cheated of their prey.

"Hang them! Hang them anyhow!" a chorus of cries sounded to the heavens. "They deserve it! They deserve it! Hang them! Hang them!" And it would have taken no more than the whisk of a breeze to have converted that tired gathering into a howling lynch-bent mob that no earthly power could have checked. There came the crash of breaking windows as the crowd outside surged toward the building; there was the sound of rushing forms as the rabble burst through the door; there was the smash and crackling of splitting timbers as the rail around the bar was demolished; and firearms were flashed in air as the jurymen, threatened by the onsweeping rout, drew their revolvers and forced their way back to the safety of the jury-room.

Nevertheless, wiser counsel prevailed. Addressing the inflamed multitude, Coleman once again brought back something like calm. "No, a thousand times no!" he protested, in response to the suggestion that the prisoners and one of the attorneys for the defense be strung to the nearest crossbeams. "We cannot afford to make a mistake, and surely we cannot afford to have innocent blood on our hands."

According to Coleman, one of the counsel for the prisoners had secured admission to the jury-room and forced a disagreement. But according to G. E. Shenck, a member of the jury, some serious doubts were actually entertained as to the identity of the defendants, resulting in the verdict of nine for conviction and three for dismissal.

In any case, this verdict stood. It speaks something for the self-control of the crowd that the prisoners were not lynched, as they undoubtedly would have been in some communities. Although both men had to be kept out of the courtroom and carefully concealed for several days after the trial, they were duly turned over, unharmed, to the regular authorities, who subsequently sentenced them each to fourteen years' imprisonment. But Windred, thanks to the connivance of some of the real culprits, avoided the penalty by cutting his way out of jail; while Burdue, sent to Marysville to stand trial for the murder of the sheriff, was found guilty and condemned to be hanged . . . to be released in the nick of time, however, after the apprehension of the real culprit, his double, James Stuart.

Yet public opinion remained unsatisfied—and it would have been evident even to the most casual observer that other outbreaks were in store. The following, from the *Evening Picayune* of Monday the 24th, may be taken as indicative of a certain element in the sentiment of the day:

"While mingling with the crowd before the City Hall yesterday afternoon, a tall, gaunt individual, with black eyes and an abundance of hair, broke out indignantly in this fashion: 'Cuss me, what a country this here is for regulating things! Where I come from those chaps in thar would have swung long ago, and no speechifying and humbugging thought of . . . Cuss me, but I'm clean sick of this country, where they let cussed red devils and white wolves run over them without so much as slipping the wind on one of them when he's caught! It's a weak country—an unnat'ral place, and fit only for greasers.' "

In these words one can perhaps gather some hint of the difference between San Francisco, lawless as it was, and those more primitive communities where a suspect was hanged first and tried afterwards, under the almighty sway of that grim jurist, Judge Lynch.

CHAPTER IV

IT was not only the more bloodthirsty and vengeance-hungry citizens that had cause for disappointment in the outcome of the Burdue-Windred trial; every inhabitant of San Francisco who valued peace, life and property had reason for discontent. None but the criminal elements, in fact, took encouragement from the verdict. It was as if a proclamation had been published, to the following effect:

"Incendiaries, thieves and assassins! may you prosper! You are the masters of the city; there is nothing that can be done to control you. The ordinary processes of law are powerless, and even shield you; the extraordinary processes, like last Sunday's trial, are equally ineffective. So go your way! Burn, loot, destroy and kill! There is none that can stop you!"

Precisely as if they had received some such license to commit new outrages, the denizens of Sydney town and other miscreants waxed bolder and fiercer following the unsuccessful effort of the people to take the law into their own hands. Many and woeful were the deeds of violence now committed; it became less safe than ever to venture forth at night, less safe than ever to possess anything which the professional prowlers might want. An average of twenty cases a day were brought before the Recorder's Court—very few of them, unfortunately, resulting in convictions. Men were knocked down on the streets, and robbed of their valuables; men were stabbed in the dance-halls and saloons; men were shot, or beaten insensible; men found their stores ransacked, their houses invaded—and all without the possibility of striking back.

As an indication of the extent of the evil, let us consider the record of a single day (June 9th, 1851). On this date, according to the *Annals of San Francisco,* thirty-six cases appeared before the Recorder's Court for one district alone, "six for drunkenness, six for fighting, six for larceny, three for stabbing, one for burglary, four for fast riding, three for assaulting officers, three for keeping disorderly houses, one for an attempt at robbery, etc." Yet the day on which these crimes had occurred, a Sunday, "had been remarked by the presses as having been unusually quiet and decently observed—without any noise or crime worth noticing."

It was at about this time that the first Vigilance Committee originated. Since the public agencies were unable or unwilling to offer protection against the marauders, the citizens by degrees developed the idea of an association whereby to practice the gentle art of self-defense. The beginnings were to be seen in the Burdue-Windred affair, which we have just considered; in fact, the roots can be traced as far back as the episode of the Hounds; but it was not until June, 1851, that the new movement really took shape. As a preliminary, however, there had been a night patrol organized by the merchants somewhat earlier in the year,—an association of about a hundred citizens, who contributed not only their money but their time, and took turns standing guard in the various districts of the city, each member serving four eight-hour periods a month. From such an organization to the formation of a Vigilance Committee was by no means an unnatural step; for, now that the citizens had formed a private police for protection against the despoilers, was it illogical to consider the creation of a tribunal in which the criminals might be tried?

Nevertheless, the measure was not to be indulged in lightly; the possibilities were altogether too ominous. Consider the situation: you are a citizen of San Francisco, and have led an honest, peace-loving life, without any desire to interfere in the administration of public affairs. But for many months your nerves have been frayed, and dread and anger have clutched at your heart; you have been driven through increasing stages of exasperation, anxiety and terror as you have seen the buildings of your friends and neighbors rifled, and have felt a well found-ed alarm not only for your own safety but for that of your family. Dismay, indignation and horror reach a climax when, with monotonous frequency, the city is swept by devastating fires that claim a heavy toll not only in property but in life, and that apparently were caused *deliberately*. What is to be done? A neighbor takes you aside, and whispers, "If the law doesn't clean out the wretches, we've got to do it ourselves. Otherwise, we might as well pick up our baggage and leave them the whole city." You nod agreement; but, even so, you hesitate. Not easily can a respectable, law-abiding citizen rise in defiance of the law. Not easily can he take upon himself the commission of deeds which, if given their legal penalty, might bring him to the scaffold. Not easily can he rise up in matters involving life and death, make himself a court of final appeal, and slip the constricting noose about the necks of fellow beings no matter how base and despicable. Yet what when there is no choice? What when it is their blood or your own? What when it is their lives or those of your own friends, brothers, or children?

Through some such course of reasoning; through some such waves of sentiment and counter-sentiment, the citizens of San Francisco were tossed before they could agree to the drastic measure of a Vigilance Committee. Had they not been both patient and undecided, they would surely have formed such a Committee much sooner.

Quite different had it been in the mines. There, where the population was even more fluctuant and unstable; there, where the sober merchant and professional classes were not in evi-dence; there, where man faced nature amid all the savagery of his original environment and had scarcely even the shadow of normal law, all ordinary rules and traditions were thrust aside, respect for human life was at a minimum, and little question was asked as to how far a particular crime had been justified. Let the thief, the murderer die! So decreed the miners; and many a rampaging mob, sometimes besotted with whisky, often inflamed with passion, not infrequently lusting after revenge, seized the suspected miscreant and held him until his struggles ceased at the end of a rope. Even women were not immune— as is indicated by the case of the negress who was whipped to death near Stockton; and by the example of the young Mexican woman, Juanita by name, who was seized by a mob at Downie- ville in 1851 and hanged for stabbing a drunken miner in de- fense of her honor.

But this reign of the rabble, this rule of violence—so uncon- trollable, so brutal, so repugnant to all civilized sensibilities— was not what the citizens of San Francisco desired. This they abhorred; but doubtless they realized that any extra-legal pro- ceedings, however well organized and directed, might lead in this direction; and doubtless the dread of offering aid and en- couragement to lynch law was one of the factors that delayed the creation of the first Vigilance Committee until June, 1851.

Meanwhile forces not only within the city but outside were propelling the people of San Francisco in the direction of Vigil- ance. Crime was by no means confined to the region of the Golden Gate; murder, robbery and incendiarism were scatter- ing terror throughout the State; the business section of the city of Stockton (at that time one of the leading towns of Cali- fornia) had been destroyed on May 6th, 1851, presumably by the fire-fiends; and shortly afterwards the same community was thrown into a tumult by the discovery of an organized gang of horse thieves, which was none other than that of the notori- ous Joaquin Murieta, who at that time was just beginning his career. The movement toward Vigilance was undoubtedly stimulated by disclosures regarding this band, by the disquieting confessions of one of the company, and by the firebrands in the shape of editorials, which appeared in the Stockton *Journal*. "Without war cry," declares that paper, "we have an enemy in our midst whose signal is theft! murder! fire! If an enemy should attack us from without, all would rise and repel him. The laws are good for peaceful times, but for such turmoil as we now endure stringent measures are necessary." Martial rule, in fact, was advocated; and also a committee of citizens to take justice into their own hands and ship the desperadoes out of town.

Yes! Vigilance was in the air; and if one particular incident had not given rise to it, some other incident would certainly have brought it into being. As it happened, the specific starting point appears to have been a conversation between James Neall and George Oakes, two respected business men of San Francisco, who lived south of Market Street in the region then known as Happy Valley. Chancing to meet on Sunday, June the 8th, they discussed the necessity of doing something to combat the perilous state of society; and it occurred to them to pay a visit to Sam Brannan, with the object of enlisting his cooperation. They therefore walked over to Brannan's office at Sansome and Bush Streets, found Mr. Brannan in a receptive mood, and, after talking the matter over with him, decided that each would supply the names of some reliable persons to meet next day at twelve o'clock at the California Engine House. At twelve on Monday, accordingly, there was a gathering that jammed the room to the doors; and, after much discussion, they adjourned to meet again that evening; following which they met once more on Tuesday evening, and at that time completed the organization of the first Committee of Vigilance.

One has only to glance at the early documents of the Committee in order to perceive how deadly in earnest were its members, and how grave was the atmosphere that surrounded them. Its avowed object, according to a statement of William T. Coleman, was "to vigilantly watch and pursue the outlaws who were infesting the city, and bring them to justice, through the regularly constituted courts, if that could be, through more summary and direct process, if must be. Each member pledged his word of honor, his life and fortune if need be, for the protection of his fellow members, for the protection of the life and property of the citizens and of the community, and for purging the city of the bad characters who were making themselves odious in it."

In the constitution of the society, dated June 9th, 1851, this position is stated emphatically:

"Whereas it has become apparent to the citizens of San Francisco that there is no security for life and property either under the regulations of Society as it at present exists or under the laws as now administered,—therefore, the Citizens whose names are hereto attached do unite themselves into an association for the maintenance of the peace and good order of Society and the preservation of the lives and property of the Citizens of San Francisco and do bind themselves unto each other to do and perform every lawful act for the maintenance of law and order and to sustain the laws when faithfully and properly administered but we are determined that no thief burglar incendiary or assassin shall escape punishment, either by the quibbles of the law the insecurity of prisons the carelessness or corruption of the Police or a laxity of those who pretend to administer justice."

Here was challenge, and with a vengeance! here was the gauntlet flung directly in the face of the law, the courts, and all the regular authorities! Here was a declaration of war! the promise of a fight without quarter! Here was an insurrection of the people, but an insurrection of a unique kind, since it did not undertake to supplant mayor or police, judges or governor, but merely to take over the work in which they had so lamentably failed.

But let us read on in the Constitution. The Vigilance Committee proposed to have a room for its meetings, with one or more members in constant attendance, so that they might be notified of acts of crime, and, if need be, assemble the Committee; it established a signal for convoking all the members; it pledged the honor of the members in sustaining one another in their mutual undertakings; it arranged for the appointment of officers and of a standing Committee of finance and qualification; and it decreed that "no person shall be admitted a member of this association unless he be a respectable citizen and approved of by the Committee on qualification before admission."

Within the Committee itself, the greatest secrecy prevailed. For it had a dual organization: an executive committee of twenty, by which plans were weighed and decisions taken; and a general committee, eventually of more than 700 members, which endorsed and executed the plans, yet knew nothing of the deliberations of the ruling group. But the secrecy went far beyond this: except for a few recognized leaders, the public could never be certain which man was or was not a member of the Committee: the housebreaker, the thief, could not know whether or not his next-door neighbor were a Committeeman, waiting to ferret out his evildoing and report him; the swindler, the ruffian looking for henchmen in crime could not be sure when he might not confront one of the Vigilance spies, and be summoned for examination by the redoubtable Committee.

Yet the Committee was composed, in the main, of the most substantial, respectable, and prominent men of the community.

There was, of course, Sam Brannan, then a well known and well-to-do real estate operator; there was William T. Coleman, a serious-minded man of business, who was to play the leading rôle in the committee of 1856; there was Isaac Bluxome, Jr., a successful commission merchant, who had organized a military company following the affair of the Hounds; there was Selim E. Woodworth, explorer, adventurer, and business man; there was Frederick A. Woodworth, afterwards to be a member of the State Senate; there was Garrett W. Ryckman, printer, brewer and politician, who had already arrived at the sedate age of fifty-three; there was pugnacious little George Ward, a somewhat dandified individual with a penchant for flourishing firearms; there was Stephen Payran, a professional copyist from Philadelphia; there was James King of William, a banker, of whom more later; and there were sailors, merchants, colonels, boatmen, physicians, dentists, lumbermen, and representatives of practically every trade and profession in San Francisco. Quite in contrast to the parties that made up the lynching-bees in the outlying districts, the Vigilance Committee was emphatically not composed of the more disorderly and ruffianly elements. It is safe to say that, had they dwelt in older and more settled regions, the vast majority would never have been known as other than peaceful, law-abiding citizens.

Practically on the eve of the Committee's organization, it was faced with a crucial test. The opportunity was provided by one John Jenkins, a Sydney duck, a man of evil reputation, who had owned a lodging house of the lower sort, which he had sold shortly before.

At about dusk on the evening of June 10th, just as the Committee was completing its plans for chastising rogues, Jenkins helped himself to a portable safe in the office of George Virgin on Long Wharf, threw it into a small boat nearby, and started off into the bay. But apparently he had been incautious; or perhaps he had not deemed it necessary to exercise caution regarding so slight a crime. In any event, he was detected, the cry, "Stop, thief! Stop!", was raised, and a dozen citizens set out after him as he paddled off across the bay. Alas now for Mr. Jenkins! He was a strong man, and an audacious one, but his pursuers were too many for him! Perceiving that he could not escape, he threw the safe overboard; and while some of his enemies fished for the lost article and recovered it by means of grappling hooks, others surrounded him and took him prisoner.

At first it was thought of turning him over to the regular authorities. But no! some one suggested. Why not try the newly organized Vigilance Committee? So into the hands of the Committee the unfortunate Jenkins was delivered,—a protesting giant, tall, well-formed, of Herculean frame, but snarling defiance like a caught grizzly, and growling blasphemies that repelled even the hardened men of that frontier community.

Little did that safe-robber know how soon he was to meet his fate! But the people of San Francisco, early that evening, realized that strange, grim doings were afoot. From the bell of the California Engine House, at Market and Bush Streets, there came an ominous signal: tap, tap . . . tap, tap . . . tap, tap. Then, after a short interval, the bell of the Monumental Company, blocks away near the Plaza, echoed the summons: tap, tap . . . tap, tap . . . tap, tap.

Instantly the city was alert. Men ran into the streets. "What's up? What's up?" cried those who were not partners in the secret. But the members of the Vigilance Committee wasted no time about answering futile queries. For them but to harken and obey! They had recognized the signal for the meeting of the General Committee, and they hastened to the agreed meeting-place at Sam Brannan's office. Within this building, one might have seen a guarded door; men approached, whispered a pass-word, and were admitted; while others, not knowing the magic syllables, knocked in vain outside. Only the initiated might participate in the trial about to be enacted,—the trial to determine whether John Jenkins were to live or die!

No time was wasted on delays or technicalities. A jury was selected, a prosecuting attorney was appointed, witnesses were heard, and, after all the evidence was in, the sentence was passed: GUILTY. And the penalty was: DEATH!

Even so, the Committee hesitated. It was one thing to render judgment; it was another thing to execute it. It was one thing to proclaim a human being unworthy to live; it was another thing to assume the dreadful responsibility of taking his life. And so, despite the swiftness of the trial, an interval of vacillation followed; during which the condemned Jenkins stood confronting his captors with undaunted insolence, denying that he was to be executed, and promising that his friends of Sydney town would band together and rescue him. Even the usually over-hasty Brannan appeared to waver . . . until one of the Vigilantes, William A. Howard, stepped resolutely forward, threw down his cap, and declared: "Gentlemen, as I understand it, we came here to hang somebody!"

From that time forth, it seemed certain that "somebody" was to be hanged. Immediate execution was decreed; a minister, called in to administer "spiritual consolation" to the condemned, admitted that the man was "incorrigible"; and the only one to object was Coleman, who declared it to be cowardly to execute the victim at night. Why not wait until morning, he argued, and let the action occur in the light of day?

But no! further delay would be perilous! The Committee had been warned that Jenkins' confederates in crime were organizing; that an attack from them was to be expected, in an attempt to free the prisoner. Is it to be wondered, therefore, if

THE HANGING OF STUART BY THE VIGILANCE COMMITTEE

the nerves of the Committee members were somewhat shaken? and if, having resolved upon action, they were anxious to get the grisly deed done as soon as possible?

Then away with Jenkins! Forward march to the gallows! It was not quite two in the morning when the Vigilantes emerged in solid ranks from the building that had witnessed their grim deliberations. In their center walked the handcuffed prisoner, between two guards, and surrounded by a circle of rope. All the men were armed; while behind the unhappy Jenkins strode diminutive George Ward, brandishing a pistol and warning the captive against any attempt to escape. Weird and sepulchral the scene must have been, as the men in orderly companies marched down the dim-lighted streets; while the bells of the engine companies tolled a dirge for the soul so soon to depart.

But not all was to be completed without incident. The police appeared on the scene, but preferred not to resist the drawn pistols of the Vigilantes; the henchmen of Jenkins arrived, and vainly attempted to rescue their comrade at the corner of Clay and Kearny Streets; while once again, just before the execution, the friends of the doomed man returned to the assault, made a dash for the prisoner, and went so far as to take hold of his legs—but without result, for, by sheer muscular strength, the Committee retained its prey.

It will be best to draw a veil over the scene that followed. Even though the victim was a man of depraved character, one cannot contemplate without horror the deliberate stoppage of life, the premeditated strangling of one in the prime of his strength and health. Something of the uncanny, terrorizing atmosphere of that night is preserved for us in the account of an eyewitness (which I find in T. A. Barry and B. A. Patten's "Men and Memories of San Francisco"):

"There is something indescribably awful . . . about a silent crowd of men in the darkness of night. Loud words of jest and laughter, or angry altercation, give explanation; but a dense crowd of silent men, standing mysterious and alarmingly suggestive, or moving on, with that muffled tramp, so terrible and never to be forgotten, when heard from the feet of hurrying men with silent tongues, chills the listener's blood with dreadful apprehension."

The night is described as having been moonlit, with passing cloud-shadows; but as a silent, dangling form was by turns bathed in a serene lunar radiance and steeped in utter blackness, the lamps of the gambling saloons about the Plaza still shone undisturbed, and thousands still went their mad, laughing, reckless, quarreling way, unaware either of the eerie illumination of the night skies or of the darkness of that drab, helpless, grewsome figure with its neck stretched beneath the coils of a rope.

CHAPTER V

A REAL VILLAIN CORRALLED—ANTI-VIGILANCE AWAKENS

THE execution of Jenkins, foul-mouthed and graceless ruffian though he was, inevitably arouses some provoking questions. Why should this particular individual have been the first target for the Committee's vengeance? Was it that he was an especially infamous lawbreaker? that his crimes were of an unusually flagrant nature? Obviously not; for he had merely been caught in the theft of a safe—which, at a time when incendiaries and assassins were legion, was an offense of the second order. True, under the State law, this act was punishable with death; true, unsavory rumors were attached to Jenkins, hinting (but only hinting!) at more vicious deeds; true, the manner of the man was repulsive and antagonistic; true, his robbery was committed on the eve of the formation of the Committee, and therefore constituted, in a way, a challenge to its very purpose in being. Yet these reasons in themselves are not sufficient to explain why Jenkins should have been the first victim of the Vigilantes when more dangerous villains remained at large. To find a complete solution, we must note that the trap of Vigilance had just been sprung, that the Committee was lying in readiness for its prey, and that Jenkins merely happened to be the first to walk into its clutches. Had it not been he, it would have been some other —some unheard-of Smith or Brown or Jones who, as it turned out, may actually have ended his career in jail, or in exile, or in opulence. And Jenkins—had he but had the discretion to commit his theft a little earlier, or some time later, might have gone on stealing safes with impunity till the close of his days.

However, it did not matter much—not, at least, to the Committee. To the rat-catcher, what difference which rodent he traps?—so long as it be a good, hearty specimen of its species! The Vigilantes had vindicated their right to exist; they had rid the city of at least one rascal—and they had put a wholesome terror into the hearts of all members of the cutthroat fraternity, with the result that a satisfying diminution in crime was observed.

Jenkins, of course, marked but the beginning of the Committee's activities. Having disposed of this gentleman, they devoted themselves with great care, precision, and thoroughness to various other matters connected with crime, its punishment and its prevention. They arranged to keep five members on constant duty, in three-hour shifts, and likewise arranged to have every member report daily at the Committee rooms for possible instructions. They established a guard both ashore and on the water; they sent a boat to every vessel arriving from Australia, to look for ex-convicts and prevent their landing. They policed the city during the great fire of June 22, and patrolled the bay for plunder-laden craft; they offered an award of $5000 for the arrest and conviction of any person guilty of arson; they tried several "dangerous" aliens, and deported them to Australia; they decreed that a Mexican caught with stolen property be publicly given twenty-five lashes, though this is the only known case in which the Committee ordered a man to be whipped. They asserted the right of forcible entry of private premises, invading the home of one Metcalf and searching for stolen goods even among the personal belongings of his wife and daughter, whose slumbers they interrupted for this purpose. They sent peremptory warnings to suspicious characters to leave town; they undertook the completion of the county jail—a badly needed structure, on which large sums had been expended by the authorities, with small results except to needy politicians; they issued a proclamation to the "order-loving portion of the citizens of

Sacramento City, Stockton, the Pueblo de San Jose," etc., urging them to form mutually cooperating vigilance committees —and, as a result, committees actually were established in Sacramento, Santa Clara, Marysville and other communities.

Even from this brief summary, it will be apparent that the activities of the Committee were remarkable—remarkable not only for their scope and daring, but for their contempt for all the previous rules and regulations of law. In boarding ships and assuming control of immigration, they were usurping the rights not so much of the local authorities as of the United States Government itself! And in invading private dwellings without search-warrant, they were maintaining prerogatives previously known only under absolute dictatorships and autocracies. Certainly, peril lay in this direction—the peril of setting a despotic precedent. Yet the members of the Committee, it is evident, were on the whole men of temperate views, who would have been among the first to be appalled at the thought of tyranny. Despite their summary methods on certain occasions, their moderation in other instances indicates that they had no idea of snatching unwarranted power; whenever they deemed it possible, they cooperated with the established authorities. They refused to exercise jurisdiction over crimes of passion, as in the case of one Samuel Gallagher, whom they turned over to the regular police for having stabbed a man in a jealous quarrel; and they did not try or sentence any of their victims by that method of storm and riot which prevails wherever the mob assumes control.

Manifestly, their intentions were good even if their tactics were questionable; and no one, not even their severest critic, will deny that their provocation was extreme. But they were launching upon a course that threatened to plunge them, literally, into deeper and ever deeper water. And the second great test of their principles and power was to be flung at them within a few weeks by the outlaw, James Stuart—one of the most notorious desperadoes of the day, for whose crimes the unfortunate Burdue was even now standing within the shadow of death.

This individual, who had left a criminal record behind him on his arrival from Australia in November, 1849, was not slow to profit from past experience after reaching California. His career—according to his own subsequent confession—was one continuous process of law-breaking during the eighteen or nineteen months before his apprehension by the Vigilance Committee. Theft after theft, robbery after robbery had lent spice and color to his days; he had led desperate crews in the attempt to steal horses, to burglarize houses, to blow up safes; he had hatched a plot to appear piously at mass in San Jose, while keeping his eye alert for certain golden images; he had been one of the gang that had shot and robbed Charles Moore near Marysville, on the theory that they "might as well be dead as without money"; he had committed the assault upon Jansen, which had caused the trial of Burdue and Windred before the outraged citizenry, and had come near to costing the lives of those innocent victims; and he and his henchmen had sworn among themselves that, should these men be hanged, the city would once more be put to the torch. On one occasion he had been caught and barely escaped lynching, and subsequently, while his case was under trial, had broken jail; while later he had been protected, as we have seen, by his extraordinary resemblance to Burdue, who was made to bear the brunt of the popular wrath against Stuart.

Yet none of this man's crimes, strange to say, was to be the cause of his arrest. He was captured when going quietly about his way, eager only not to attract attention; and the offense of which he was suspected is one which, in all probability, he did not commit. On July 1st, 1850, a party of men were searching for the looter of a trunk among the chaparral-covered hills, near the site of the present Fairmont Hotel . . . when, noticing some one slinking away beneath the scrub oaks, they thought that they had found the thief. Stuart, brought to bay beneath their pistols, told a story of being on his way from the Mission to North Beach; but as he was off the road, their suspicions were aroused and they took him with them for examination by the Vigilance Committee, while he accompanied them complacently, expressing his desire to see something of that renowned association. One suspects, however, that he was to see a little more than he would relish!

Upon his arrival at the Committee rooms, where he gave the name of Stephens, he impressed every one favorably. Here was no surly Jenkins, growling out blasphemies or shouting his insolence; here was a gentleman, in appearance and speech. The Committee members saw before them a well-proportioned man, handsome of aspect, assured of demeanor; black-bearded, quick-eyed and alert, ready and fluent of tongue, wearing a gray woolen shirt, a coat of English cut, well fitting pantaloons tucked into his high boots, and—needless to say—a bowie-knife and revolver fastened to his belt. Certainly, there was little here to suggest the redoubtable outlaw, the mere mention of whose name had made the people wild with fury to hang his double, Burdue.

One cannot help wondering if Stuart might not have achieved success as an actor had he not sought proficiency in more lawless fields. So clever was the mask that he wore, such his air of pleasing frankness and candor, that he came within inches of hoodwinking his captors and achieving his freedom. Yet all the while he must have known that his situation was desperate, desperate as though a naked sword dangled above his head. The tragedy of Jenkins must have been fresh in his mind; he must have known that he had perpetrated crimes beside which those of Jenkins would have seemed as child's play; he must have realized that he was in the hands of men who were not to be temporized with, men who had both the will and the power to exact a mortal toll. Yet, in the face of this peril, he played his game, played it with skill and courage and external calm . . . and was only frustrated, it seems, by an accident.

Strange, how chance—or apparent chance—played its part in the life of this man. First he had been apprehended through the coincidence that he and the owner of a plundered trunk happened to be simultaneously present at a certain spot in the hills; and now an even more singular coincidence was to ruin his hope of escape. So adroitly, so ingratiatingly had he spun his tale, that his immediate release had been proposed . . . when, alas for all his schemes! one John Sullivan went on guard duty for the Committee. And Mr. Sullivan, on opening the door and glancing in at his prisoner, received a most enlightening surprise. "Hallo, Jim!" he cried. "How did you come here?"

He had recognized the man who had been his employer for six months at Foster's Bar!

Useless now to attempt dissimulation! Useless to pretend not to know Sullivan! The latter promptly informed the Committee of the identity of their new captive—and all chances of Stuart's release had vanished!

Subsequently the desperado was recognized by his attorney, Frank Pixley, who had formerly defended him with success, but who now, upon refusing to answer the Committee's questions on the ground that they were an "illegal body," was threatened with cries of "Hang him! Hang him! Hang him!" and was saved only in the nick of time from the waiting rope and tackle.

Feeling it best to slip off his disguise, which had become too transparent for further service, Stuart at length made a full confession, in which he went through the entire catalogue of his crimes, incidentally implicating about twenty-five confederates—many of whom he had formerly shielded even at great personal risk. It is hard to say what motive prompted him to the confession; perhaps it was the hope that by his candor he would gain some special consideration, and possibly be spared the ultimate penalty; or perhaps it was a sort of professional pride, a glorying in the extent and skill of his wrongdoing, which made him feel that he might as well make his exit with a flourish, as a truly magnificent villain. Some color of probability, indeed, is lent to the latter supposition by the statement of William T. Coleman:

"I myself assisted, as one of the Executive Committee, in hearing and reading this confession, and sat up through the whole night, and until the morning sun shone in at the window, before it was completed. He went through the whole range of his many rascalities, gave vivid descriptions of his adventures, entering with great zest into the details, and it was curious to see his eye brighten and twinkle, and a smile play round his facile countenance when describing his best successes, and recounting his best jobs. He threw off all restraint or reservation, and felt that he was bringing to light a brilliant record that had hitherto been necessarily kept in the dark."

Great was the public excitement when it became known who it was that the Committee had arrested; and many were the discussions among the eager citizens as to what the Vigilantes would do. Would they dare to execute Stuart? Would they take another life—and take it in cold blood? Would it, in fact, be possible for them to do so, considering that the established authorities had had much longer notice than in the case of Jenkins? Here was the crucial test; for if the Committee did not hang their man, they would no longer merit the respect of the citizens or earn the dread of criminals.

Their difficulties were complicated by the fact that Frank M. Pixley, acting for the prisoner, secured a writ of *habeas corpus*—before which dread document some of the members quailed, hesitating to defy this time-honored engine of the law. Could they actually deny Stuart his constitutional rights and privileges? True, there had been nothing very constitutional in the previous proceedings of the Committee; but violation of the law in general is nothing at all, in the estimate of some minds, compared with defiance of a specific written order of a court.

Nevertheless, most of the Vigilantes must have perceived that they might as well disband forthwith as allow a mere *habeas corpus* to interfere with their plans. Not that they would challenge it openly!—why resort to direct methods when indirect ones would serve? They did not refuse obedience to the sheriff's officer when he came with the writ—not at all! They merely found that the prisoner was not at hand! there was no *corpus* to be delivered! Two of the committee members, in fact, had gone off on a little jaunt with the reluctant Stuart, first taking the precaution to disguise him with a long cloak and a slouch hat; and after driving him for a certain distance in a carriage (under cover of a pair of pistols), they surrendered him to two other members, who in turn delivered him to others . . . so that each successive set of overseers could truthfully swear, when questioned, that they were ignorant of the prisoner's whereabouts. Yes! the law might have its subtleties, but what of the sinuosities of the Vigilance Committee?

Pixley's effort on behalf of his client having failed, a meeting of the entire Committee was held on Friday morning, July

11th—exactly ten days after the robber's arrest. So long did the meeting last that the prisoner, yawning in an adjoining room, complained that the proceedings were "damned tiresome." At last, however, his fate had been decided, and with outward composure he received the news: he was to be hung that afternoon!

As two hours of life still remained to the outlaw, the four hundred waiting members of the Committee spent the interval seated impassively in their chairs, as if by the silence and gravity of their demeanor to emphasize the solemnity of their death-watch. Meanwhile a question was put to the great crowd that had assembled outside the Committee rooms— were they in agreement with the verdict? And with but three dissenting votes, they responded, "Yes!"

Still silent, the Vigilantes at last issued from their meeting place. In platoons, ten abreast, with Stuart in their center, they marched to the water-front, where a waiting derrick gave token of their dreadful purpose. For one moment, as the hitherto unflinching outlaw gazed at this symbol of his fast-approaching doom, he wavered, and shook in every limb; then, regaining his hardihood, he went resolutely to meet his end, uttered a few words acknowledging the sentence to be just, and, after closing his eyes, permitted the executioner's rope to do its ghastly work. . . . In speechless solemnity, with unbared heads, an awestricken crowd stood by to watch, impressed by the courage of the man thus rudely launched into the journey which all must make alone.

But whatever may have been the feelings of the multitude upon the execution of Stuart, there was one man who, although not a witness to the brigand's end, had every personal reason for rejoicing. This was Thomas Burdue, who was still in prison for Stuart's crimes. Thanks to the testimony of members of the Vigilance Committee, this long-suffering double of the hanged man was at length released, as we have already mentioned, and, being penniless, received a donation of about three hundred dollars subscribed by members of the Committee; following which he published a word of gratitude in the papers:

"I have kindly to thank those gentlemen for what they have done for me; for, certainly, through *their vigilance* and the *kind providence of Almighty-God,* they succeeded in capturing the criminal for whom I have suffered so much."

But although the Committee thus served the cause of mercy to the innocent at the same time as it apportioned stern retribution to the guilty, the approbation of its doings was by no means universal. It is true that, from the beginning, the public press and public opinion had been unmistakably in its favor, and that it would not otherwise have been able to function; but, on the other hand, there had been at all times an undercurrent of opposition and resentment. The criminal element objected to the Committee for reasons too obvious to require statement; the judges, lawyers and politicians, taken as a group, resisted it not only because of their conservative training but because it threatened their own work and position; while, aside from these groups, there was a body of citizens who sincerely abhorred the resort to violence and non-legal methods. Hence the opposition, while never dangerous enough to threaten the Committee's existence, manifested itself from the first by methods both direct and indirect. A week after the execution of Jenkins, handbills had been posted about the city:

"MASS MEETING TO SUSTAIN LAW AND ORDER:

The people of the city and county of San Francisco . . . are called upon to choose now, ere it is too late, which they will serve—the law and order power of our city, or the dictators and anarchists who have lately disgraced our city by their lawless and criminal proceedings. . . ."

The effort to call a mass meeting, as it happened, came to nothing. But meanwhile attempts were made to discredit the Committee by underhanded means, as by the sending of spurious orders to unoffending citizens commanding them to leave town; and a short time later David C. Broderick, one of the most celebrated politicians of early California, and a future Senator, conducted a meeting in which it was decided to ask the city officials to sign anti-Vigilance resolutions, even to the extent of defending with their life-blood the persons threatened by the Committee.

It was not, however, until after the hanging of Stuart that the anti-Vigilance forces clearly awakened. The execution of Jenkins, daring challenge to the law though it was, might have been condoned as the hasty act of an indignant group of citizens; but the same could not be said of the case of Stuart. After this bold-faced defiance, the authorities might as well have resigned in favor of the Vigilance Committee had they not uttered some word of protest. Consequently, we find various proclamations being issued against the Committee. Probably the feeblest was that of John McDougal, Governor of the State, who in a rather colorless pronouncement "earnestly recommended" to his fellow citizens "to aid in sustaining the law, for in this is our only real and permanent security." More direct and energetic, and not smacking of the pious cant of the Governor's message, was the appeal of Mayor Brenham of San Francisco, who deplored the existence of "a voluntary association of men, under peculiar bonds to each other, and assuming most extraordinary and irresponsible powers," an association whose proceedings could have "no other than an insurrectionary tendency."

But much the most severe public indictment of the Committee occurs in the charge of Judge Alexander Campbell to the Grand Jury, following the execution of James Stuart.

"The question has now arisen," he declared, "whether the laws made by the constitutional authorities of the State are to be obeyed and executed, or whether secret societies are to frame and execute laws for the government of the county, and to exercise supreme power over the lives, liberty and property of our citizens. . . . At the time when . . . the Court was in actual session and in the performance of its duties, an association of persons, of armed and organized men, have undertaken to trample on the Constitution, defy the laws, and assume unlimited authority over the lives of the community. There is no excuse or palliation for the deed. . . . Every person who in any manner acted, aided, abetted, or assisted in taking Stuart's life, or counselled or encouraged his death, is undoubtedly GUILTY OF MURDER."

Naturally, so sweeping a charge aroused bitter opposition. The newspapers immediately took up the cudgels on behalf of the Committee; and violent were the counter-bolts hurled at Judge Campbell.

"No such committee could exist in any form in this city," writes the *California Courier* of July 14th, "if the whole body of the community did not consider that necessity and policy demanded it." The courts, according to this paper, had shown no "holy horror" at seeing some of the best men in the community shot down in cold blood; hence the zeal of the coroner "to watch like a hawk the dead body of every villainous culprit executed by the people" must amount to nothing "so long as he can take his time with the corpses of unoffending men who are murdered in cold blood by notorious criminals."

To similar effect is an editorial in the *Herald* for the same date:

"We remember in this city many instances within the last year when good worthy citizens . . . were foully murdered for gold; we remember when Captain Jarvis, than whom a more manly, honest, kind-hearted man never lived, was struck down by the knife of the assassin at his own door, with his infant in his arms and his wife by his side; the murderers were never stigmatized by the presiding judge with half the rigor exhibited in this charge by Judge Campbell against the Vigilance Committee for the public execution, after a fair trial, of a desperado whose life from childhood had been a long series of bold and successful crimes."

The *Herald* went on to point out the impossibility, not to say the absurdity, of attempting to enter an indictment and execute justice on the hundreds of Vigilantes even if, as Judge Campbell charged, they were guilty of murder. . . . And so the argument proceeded, with many blasts and counter-blasts, but with the Vigilance group still resolutely in power, and with nothing being done to check them except by means of words. The strength with which they were intrenched is indicated by the report of the Grand Jury on August 2, 1851. The Vigilance Committee is here described as being composed of "a large portion of our best and most worthy citizens," who have acted "at a great sacrifice to themselves," and "have been influenced in their actions by no personal or private malice, but for the best interests of the whole, and at a time when all other means of preventing crime and bringing criminals to deserved punishment had failed." In view of these facts, the jury decided to dismiss the anti-Vigilance charges, while admitting the city to be indebted to the Committee "for much valuable information and many important witnesses."

One detail which was not made public, and which may conceivably have had some effect in influencing the verdict, was that no less than seven out of the sixteen members of the Grand Jury were themselves enrolled in the Vigilance Committee, and thus, ironically, had been asked to pass judgment not only on their own actions, but on those of the associates whom they had sworn to support. Under such circumstances, how expect any results? Since the very strongholds of the law had been invaded by the enemy, how undertake any effective legal action against the Vigilantes?

CHAPTER VI

A NEST OF OUTLAWS—RAIDS AND COUNTER-RAIDS

To judge by the severity of the penalty inflicted upon James Stuart, one would have thought that henceforth no criminal's life would be worth much in the hands of the Vigilantes.

Nevertheless, surprisingly, the Committee continued to exercise moderation and restraint in the great majority of cases. Take, for example, its treatment of certain of Stuart's gang, such as "Jimmy from Town," a notorious thief with a propensity to pilfer whatever his hands could touch; instead of lynching him, as they had done with his luckless fellow robber Jenkins, they turned him over to the regular authorities, who promptly sentenced him to ten years in prison. Or consider its attitude toward Hamilton Taft, who confessed to having stolen fifteen hundred dollars in Placer county, and who, instead of being punished, was sent back unharmed to the scene of the robbery. Or note its leniency with regard to Samuel Church, a thief and a deserter from the army, whom his former officer recommended for hanging, but whom the Committee merely turned over to the military authorities, although knowing that he would probably receive no more severe penalty than a whipping. Or, again, observe its refusal to exercise jurisdiction in the case of W. G. Hance, who had been convicted of murder in Panama, but who had saved his life by escaping from prison; or, likewise, witness its respect for "the quality of mercy" when one Daniel Jenks, although guilty of the theft of a thousand dollars, was discharged on the ground that he was very young and had previously enjoyed a good reputation, and that this was probably his first offense.

It may be stated of lynch law, in general, that it rarely acquits; to be accused is, in actual practice, to be convicted, and to be convicted is to be punished. Considered from this point of view, one can hardly regard the activities of the Vigilance Committee as coming under the caption of lynch law at all; for as many as forty-one out of ninety-one persons tried were eventually released, while less than half of the remainder were actually punished by the Committee, and of these only four were ordered to the hangman's rope.

This does not mean that many injustices were not done, and many hardships inflicted. Even the sanest and longest established court occasionally commits errors and decides unwisely—how then expect that an association of citizens, hastily formed and self-endowed with arbitrary powers, would not now and then step aside from the cool reasoned line of justice? The mere fact that its sessions and its membership were secret —and that its methods were inquisitorial, its examination of prisoners conducted behind barred doors—would have made it impossible for the Committee always to secure impartial and equitable results; the surprising fact, therefore, is not that there were some flaws in its administration, but that those flaws were not more numerous and graver. It is true that, at this late date, we cannot determine whether the Committee did not err in some of its decisions, leaving victims who, either because they had been shipped out of the country or because they were terrorized by the Torquemadas of the secret tribunal, were unable effectively to protest their innocence. This, at all events, we do know: that numbers of men were deported from the country on no other ground than that they had served penal sentences in Australia. And while, unquestionably, the ex-convicts as a class constituted a vicious and dangerous element, still to be an ex-convict is not in itself a crime according to any law ever passed by any legislature of any country; nor does it follow that every man who has passed beneath the shadow of a prison is thereafter forever incapable of reform. If the Vigilantes had wished to be consistent, they would have invariably followed the rule they applied in the case of W. G. Hance, who, as we have seen, they refused to punish although he had been sentenced in Panama; for in all instances, when they meted out their penalties to ex-convicts, they were not only accepting without examination the word of foreign courts, but were superimposing their own punishment as additional retribution for crimes already legally expiated in full.

But even aside from the ex-convicts, a good deal of incidental injustice was done to innocent parties. Merely to be detained in the Committee rooms as a witness was a hardship, —a physical hardship, because of the enforced confinement and the rude accommodations, with the bare benches and straw mattresses,—a mental and spiritual hardship, because of the stigma attached to such detention, even though it were unjustified. We read, for example, of Victor Gray, a Frenchman, who was violently seized as a witness against a person falsely suspected of arson, and who, after his release, had sustained such grievous injuries to his sensibilities and to his reputation that he petitioned for a certificate clearing his character, and for money to enable him to leave the city. Again, we learn of Theodore Dahlgren, whose property was seized when he refused to appear at the Committee headquarters on a charge of stealing a sextant, and who was finally declared innocent after his arrest and a period of confinement, during which some of his goods had vanished.

But in spite of such injustices—which are, one fears, too often paralleled or exceeded by the acknowledged agents of the law—the Committee was attaining its chief objective. Within little more than a month after its organization, a vast improvement was noticeable in the administration of justice; the courts, chastised by the very existence of the Committee, were far more prompt and efficient in passing judgment than of old, there were one or two judges whose integrity seemed unimpeachable, the grand jury returned indictments with a zest previously unknown, and wrongdoers were actually sentenced with dispatch and severity. Under such circumstances, the Committee was willing to assume in part the functions of a mere detective agency, and to be content with turning over to the regular courts those captives whom they did not consider sufficiently dangerous to require their own special methods of treatment.

One of the chief activities of the Vigilantes, after the execution of Stuart, was to run down and capture the henchmen and colleagues of that renowned brigand, about twenty-five of whom had been accused in his confession. There had been, in fact, a whole nest of outlaws, among whom Stuart had been one of the reigning spirits—and it was against this den of thieves that the Committee launched its assault. Behold the Committee men, therefore, coming in from the bandit hunt, dragging their prey after them: Dab, the horse thief, and George Adams, alias Jack Dandy, a Sydney immigrant, expert in fitting keys to forbidden locks; and T. Belcher Kay, former port warden, who was to escape after being turned over to the ordinary courts; and many others, some of whom were to evade all penalties, and some of whom were to suffer heavily. Among the latter, the two most unfortunate were Sam Whittaker and Robert McKenzie, who had been among the leaders in Stuart's gang, and were accordingly listed to receive the especial attentions of the Committee whenever they should be caught—which, in the case of Whittaker, did not occur until after several weeks.

The latter character, who has been described by Bancroft as "a gentleman and prince among the convicts," was an ex-resident of the Sydney penal colony. Transported from England to Australia under life sentence, he had received a conditional pardon, and left for San Francisco, which he reached in August, 1849. After arriving, he had served as a steward in a public house, and later as a butcher, and it appears that for a time he led an honest life. But he soon conceived a contempt for the law, finding that large-scale offenders escaped scot-free, while he observed a sentence of two years administered for the mere theft of a pistol. "It seemed to me," he declared in his subsequent confession, "that a thief had a better chance than an honest man." Hence he decided to improve his chances. His first crime was the robbery of $900 from a bear hunter; but, cheated by his confederates, he only received $35 for this exploit. This, however, was apparently no deterrent; he planned numerous other robberies, including the Jansen affair, which nearly cost the lives of Windred and Burdue. Yet seemingly he had more of a conscience than one would expect of a member of his profession, for he mentions having exerted himself to prevent two of his companions from shooting a man named O'Flaherty; also, when urged to lend a hand in robbing the large gambling house, the El Dorado, he experienced a revulsion of feeling. "I got sick of all such work," he said, "and made up my mind to leave off, and took no further notice." Nevertheless, according to his own admission, the force of old habit was too strong, for he confesses having subsequently committed other robberies.

Bad though the record of the man, he was not unprepossessing of appearance. Like his associate Stuart, he seems to have made a favorable impression even upon his sworn foes. About thirty years of age, scrupulously neat in his person and manly in his demeanor, he could have taken his place in far better society than that of the Sydney ducks with whom his lot was cast. Moreover, not only men came under the spell of his magnetism; women also seem to have succumbed to his charms—or so, at least, we may judge from the case of Mrs. Hogan, a genteel-looking person of about thirty-five years, with whom he indulged in something of a romance.

This lady, who conducted a lodging house frequented by some of the roughest characters in the city, was ordinarily encumbered by a husband; but it happened that Whittaker moved in one fine day while Mr. Hogan was away at the mines; and the thief, who had had little hesitation about taking other people's gold, appears to have had no compunctions about appropriating another man's wife. It is true that he was subsequently dispossessed, upon the return of the indignant Hogan; but the little affair was not yet over. At about this time the Vigilance Committee was becoming uncomfortably active; and Whittaker, after deciding that his presence in parts remote would be advisable, arranged with Mrs. Hogan to meet her in San Diego. Traveling separately, and by devious routes, both of them endeavored to keep the rendezvous, the woman first having been detained by the Vigilance Committee, whom she skillfully combated in their effort to wrest telltale information from her. But Whittaker, after the Vigilantes had looked for him in vain in Sacramento, Stockton and other points, was so unfortunate as to be recognized at Santa Barbara, at which town his southward migration ended. Taken into custody by Sheriff W. V. Hearne, he was escorted back to San Francisco, where Hearne intended to deliver him to the local police; but, by a coincidence, a member of the Vigilance Committee chanced to learn of Whittaker's presence while Hearne was looking for Sheriff Hays of San Francisco —and that coincidence was to cost Whittaker his life. It was not long before members of the Committee had induced the captain of the *Ohio,* on which Whittaker was detained, to deliver the prisoner into their hands.

Whittaker was regarded as one of the most dangerous criminals ever brought before the Committee; and for this reason it was held unsafe to entrust him to the local authorities. Hence for him—as for his more coarse-grained associate Mc-Kenzie—the death sentence was decreed. True, it was not established that either offender had ever graduated from robbery into murder—but in a day when the theft of a horse might legally send a man to the gallows, such a consideration did not bear very much weight. To the scaffold with them both! The decision of the Committee was inexorable, and would have been carried into effect without delay—had it not been for the unexpected interference of the forces of "law and order."

For once, it seemed, the officials had decided to fight otherwise than by means of words for the lives of citizens illegally condemned by the Committee. On learning of the impending executions, Governor McDougal rushed down from Benicia barely in the nick of time, and enlisted the aid of Mayor Brenham of San Francisco. Not a moment could be wasted! It was already midnight! on the morrow the two men would be hanged, unless rescued immediately! Despite the lateness of the hour, therefore, the two officials scoured the city in search of a judge who would issue a warrant for the seizure of the prisoners. Having duly found a magistrate, and made out affidavits in accordance with the forms of law, the Mayor and Governor repaired to the home of the sheriff, which they reached at about three in the morning. Let not that officer enjoy his slumbers when his services were needed in a rescuing expedition! Roused by the rapping of the highest authorities of the city and state, the sheriff at first declined to participate in the night expedition; but at length, as he gradually emerged more fully into this wakeful world, he began to see the way of duty, and reluctantly called to his deputy to join him in the raid.

It is little wonder that Sheriff Hays hesitated. His attitude toward the Vigilantes had been altogether friendly; they had been most useful to him in catching thieves; and, moreover—although this fact may not have been known to him—the Committee's headquarters were well protected that night, twenty-nine men being on guard duty. What match would the sheriff and his deputy be for this large company? That which followed, accordingly, is all the more surprising; there was an interval of confusion upon the arrival of the officers; the doorman offered some slight resistance; the sheriff's deputy dashed in and called out to the prisoners, "Whittaker and McKenzie, I have come to save you!"; the condemned men rushed away with their rescuer while Sheriff Hays held the door open —and, before any one quite realized what was happening, the escape had been accomplished. So quietly was the raid conducted that President˙ Payran of the Executive Committee, sleeping in an adjoining room, was not even awakened.

One can picture the rage and bewilderment of the Committee when they learned that their prey had escaped. Of what avail had been all their precautions? Why capture prisoners at great trouble and expense if the law could so easily snatch them away again? Why not, in fact, disband and acknowledge defeat, since their efforts were no longer of any avail? Either that or make one supreme proclamation which would stir the entire city to action! Such, in effect, was the argument of President Payran—but, fortunately, more temperate counsel prevailed, and the Committee decided to take its time.

Hence four days went by . . . and nothing, apparently, happened. The prisoners, who would by now have been exploring the mysteries of another world had the Committee had its way, were reposing peacefully in jail; and, for all the public could say, they would remain there until tried by the ordinary courts. Nevertheless, much had gone on behind the scenes.

There had been a meeting at which sheriff, mayor, governor, and Vigilantes conferred as sedately as though nothing untoward had occurred; there had been spying visits to the jail by Bluxome and Ryckman of the Executive Committee, who were admitted with the sheriff's consent, and carefully ascertained that the place was not armed; and there had been a decision of thirty of the Committee members to recapture the prisoners or die in the assault.

The plans had been laid as cautiously as for a military campaign. On the specified day—a Sunday—Sheriff Hays was maneuvered out of the way by being invited to attend a bullfight at Mission Dolores. Then twenty-nine Committee members, in three companies, marched upon the jail at a time when the inmates were known to be attending divine services; while another Vigilante was stationed at a certain point on Telegraph Hill, from which he could look down upon the jail, part of which had no roof, and see exactly what was occurring there. This observer was to fling wide his arms as a signal the moment the religious ceremonies were over—whereupon the waiting Committee men were to perform their pre-arranged rôle.

At about half past two the signal was given, and instantly the invasion of the jail began. Through the front door charged one assaulting party, while another battered down the entrance to the rear; the guard, overpowered and intimidated with pistols, made but feeble resistance; McKenzie and Whittaker, desperately struggling, were pinioned and bound; then away they were borne into a waiting carriage, which immediately began a wild dash through the streets. Crowds began to gather; the bell of the Monumental Company tolled its mournful tap, tap . . . tap, tap . . . tap, tap; while onward the carriage raced to the Committee headquarters, where telltale ropes were dangling from heavy beams. It was all swiftly over; seventeen minutes after the onslaught upon the jail, the ropes were flung about two resisting necks; and almost instantly the nooses were tightened, and the writhing victims, with coats removed and fettered arms, were hoisted to their doom. . . .

Thus did the Committee not only try and execute its victims without benefit of law; thus did it invade the very premises of established authority, snatch its prey from the arms of the sheriff and the power of the courts, and imperiously wreak immediate vengeance! If, as Justice Campbell had declared, the participants in the execution of Stuart had been guilty of murder, those responsible for hanging McKenzie and Whittaker were to be charged not only with murder but with insurrection; they were dangerous rebels, who were themselves to be cured only by means of the noose.

It is in some such fashion, indeed, that they would have been treated in many lands—but what is the law in any country except the stronger power? The Vigilantes were strong, and they knew it; their membership included some of the most influential citizens; they were supported by a long precedent of lynch law in the mines and country towns; the public press was in their favor, and so was the opinion of the masses: therefore, they were superior to law—or, rather, they *were* the law. Reckless, impetuous, violent they were in the case of Whittaker and McKenzie; savage in their resort to mere physical force, brutal in their seizure and execution of men who, for all we can say, might have been properly sentenced by the regular courts. And yet, in judging them, we must not lose account of the surging, tempestuous emotions of the times; of the nightmare of crime that caused shudders to run down the spines of the law-abiding; of the challenge to the Committee's authority in the seizure of their two most important prisoners; of the sacrifices in time, effort and

MEETING OF THE VIGILANCE COMMITTEE IN PORTSMOUTH SQUARE

money which the members had undergone in order to purge
the city of thieves and assassins; and of the drain of those har-
rowing months during which the Vigilantes had attended
long, strained meetings, had stood guard, and had been
ready to answer the summons of the Monumental bell at any
hour of the night or day. Just a little of the cruelty of the
mob was undoubtedly present—just a little of its unreason-
ableness, its arrogance, just a little of that arbitrary, lordly
spirit bred by secrecy; but compare even the most audacious
action of the Committee with the deeds of any other armed
rebellious group, and you will read the token of their laudable intentions in the fact that they usurped so much less
power than they might have taken, and were never to parallel that attack upon the law which had made the capture
of Whittaker and McKenzie an affair of such daring, melo-
drama and horror.

CHAPTER VII

TWILIGHT OF VIGILANCE—THE VILLAINS RE-ASSEMBLE

With the execution of Whittaker and McKenzie, the Committee of Vigilance reached the apex of its activities. After this daring performance, the scope of its work was gradually to decline, until, without ever formally disbanding, it was virtually to pass out of existence. Yet there was still a vast amount to be done before "Finis" could be written. There were criminals to be tried and deported; there was much correspondence with country committees of vigilance; there were troublesome financial problems to be solved, for expenses were heavy, and the members had to meet the costs out of their own pockets; there was a suit to be defended against a certain Metcalf, who charged that his premises had been illegally entered and searched; there were political maneuvers to be attempted, since the Committee endorsed certain candidates for election; and there were various other unrelated pursuits, such as the establishment of a library for the benefit of the city—surely, exactly what one would not expect a group of Vigilantes to undertake!

Among the affairs of the concluding months, several episodes stand out as showing what manner of men composed the Vigilance Committee. One was the case in which Stephen Payran, President of the Executive Committee, played the part of the gallant rescuer who single-handed delivered imperiled beauty from the dragon's den. A young girl, Mary Lye by name, had been abducted from her broken-hearted relatives, and confined in a disreputable house at Marysville; and Payran, going unaccompanied to her aid, managed to bring her away in safety even though threatened by a band of ruffians. Having hurried with her to his hotel, he informed the other guests of the whole situation, and of the danger from the girl's former captors—whereupon fifteen or twenty miners drew their revolvers, and formed an escort about Payran and Mary until they had securely boarded the boat for San Francisco.

Even more revealing is the case of Captain Waterman—an affair in which the Vigilantes played exactly the opposite rôle to that usually ascribed to them. Here, instead of acting as propagators of the mob spirit, as disseminators of lynch law, they exerted themselves to disperse the mob, and avert the return of old Judge Lynch. Toward the end of October, 1851, the clipper ship *Challenge* reached San Francisco, after a voyage marked by mutiny on the part of the crew and great severity and even brutality on the side of the captain. Several of the sailors had died; others were forced, on landing, to go to the hospital for treatment of wounds received while at sea. Among the boatmen and longshoremen of San Francisco, consequently, a fierce indignation was aroused; they gathered in a mob two thousand strong, and threatened to hang the captain and mate of the *Challenge*—and for a while it looked as if the surging, shouting, blaspheming rabble might have its way. At this crisis, the Mayor thought of ringing the bell of the Monumental Engine House—in consequence of which the members of the Vigilance Committee immediately assembled and agreed to assist the authorities. "Attend, vigilants! . . . Fall into line! . . . March!" the orders rang out; and forward the armed detachment started, scattering the angry mob and saving the lives of the two menaced seamen. Thus did the opponents of "law and order" serve the very cause they were supposedly organized to resist!

As an indication of the welcome which the Vigilance Committee met among the people at large, there is nothing more eloquent than the banner of blue silk presented on August

9th, 1851, "by the Ladies of Trinity Parish, as a Testimonial of their Approbation," in acknowledgement of "the Protection of the Lives and Property of the Citizens and Residents of the City of San Francisco." Particularly significant is the motto with which the testimonial ends: "Do right and fear not!"

But in spite of the commendation of the ladies of Trinity Parish, what was the actual accomplishment of the Committee of 1851? This question can be answered more fully after we have considered the work of the greater Committee of 1856, which was an offspring—or, in a sense, a resurrection—of the earlier association. For the present, however, we may note that, for a while, there appears to have been a marked diminution in crime—but that, as the oppressive shadow of the Committee grew more remote, the criminals gradually crept forth from their lairs again, new miscreants replaced the scattered members of Stuart's gang, and theft, fraud, and murder became as abundant as of old. Yet if we turn to contemporary sources, we will observe an almost universal approval of the Committee's activities; we will be told that the streets of San Francisco had become safe again, so that a law-respecting citizen could venture forth even at night; and we will find the credit given in large part to the Vigilantes. Thus, in the *Annals of San Francisco,* we read:

"After a few hangings . . . the social state of the city was much improved. . . . Crime was now principally confined to petty thefts, for which the 'chain-gang' was an excellent punishment; while cases of bloodshed—and they were frightfully many—arose chiefly from the rampant, unregulated passions of the people."

Reading a little further in the same work, we find how short-lived was the influence of the Committee. The gun-wielding desperado may have been a little less evident for a while; but the thief, the fraudulent official and the swindler still wove their webs in the dark. "Crime in 1852," state the *Annals,* "was perhaps not sensibly diminished; but in the increasing importance of other matters of public discussion, lower-class criminals were tolerated, or less pursued. Legalized robberies . . . more occupied the attention of the citizens. It would be unjust to individuals and to human nature, to challenge *every* public officer in San Francisco with gross peculation and corruption in office; yet it was confessed on all sides that almost every citizen, who had a *chance* of preying upon the corporation means, unhesitatingly and shamefully took advantage of his position."

Again, the *Annals* thus describe the state of public morality in San Francisco:

"The scum and froth of its strange mixture of peoples, of its many scoundrels, rowdies and great men, loose women, sharpers and few honest folk, are still nearly all that is visible. The current of its daily life is muddied and defiled by the wild effervescence of these unruly spirits. It may be said that nearly all came to the city only as devout worshippers of mammon. . . . In order to accumulate the greatest heap of gold in the shortest possible time, schemes and actions had to be resorted to, which nice honor could not justify nor strict honesty adopt. In the scramble for wealth, few had consciences much purer than their neighbors; few hands were much cleaner."

In view of the prevalence of such a ruthless, acquisitive spirit, the Committee could at most scoop a little of the scum off the surface of the social cesspool. The fetid depths remained, putrid with deep spiritual decay, vile with that grasping philosophy which places each man's desires above his neighbor's needs; and it was beyond the power of any mere group of men, however fearless and determined, to sweep away the abysmal source of the corruption. The malady was not in San Francisco alone; it was in the social system and in the age, in the strutting aggressiveness of its individualism, in the predatory might of its self-assertiveness, in the bluff gold of the pinnacles that it worshipped, and in the decline of religious and ethical restraints to misconduct. Let your Stuarts, your Whittakers, your McKenzies be throttled! other thieves and blackguards would arise in their place, perhaps more subtle, but for that reason more sinister—and there could be no cure for the malady until a spade had been sunk through the muck and mire down to its deeply entangled roots. Consequently, the work of the Vigilance Committee is to be regarded in the light of a palliative, a temporary remedy—salutary in some of its results, deplorable in others, but in any case no more than a scraper of surfaces.

After the suspension of the Committee's activities, the opinion of the time seemed to oppose a resumption of its work. So we may conclude from the *Annals,* which, published in 1855, issue the warning that the original Committee is still ready to relieve society "from the horrors of unchecked and triumphant villainy," but expresses the hope "that never again shall there need to be revived those terrible times of 1851." And so also we may judge from the newspapers, which, despite an occasional dissenting view, seem generally to regard the Vigilance Committee as the dire necessity of a stern but unregretted past. Even James King of William—who, as we shall see, was not only a member of the Committee of 1851, but the direct cause of the rise of its more powerful successor five years later—opposed the extension of the Vigilance principle in 1855, and declared his belief that thenceforth the ordinary processes of law would suffice to cope with wrongdoing.

Nevertheless, society in the middle Fifties was still far from having attained that settled state which the more optimistic would have liked to believe. Engendered in fury and chaos, the young community by the Golden Gate was still a center of turbulence, was still the battlefield of a thousand conflicting passions; and most of the influences that had given birth to the Vigilance Committee were still alive, and were even waxing in strength. The city, it is true, was growing; the rude tents and shanties of former days had almost disappeared, and long rows of substantial-looking buildings had taken their place; the calamitous fires of 1849-51 had not recurred; vice was just a little less brazen, virtue a little more in evidence; the reputable citizen would no longer parade the streets beside the harlot; respectable women were not so few and far between as of old; the gambling halls, while still doing a large business, had mostly taken to cover; and, all in all, San Francisco had come to look more like a city, and less like a mere camping place. Yet under the surface, not all was serene. Crime and corruption still bred in the slime and darkness—in many ways less boisterous than in 1849, yet still daring and ostentatious, still stalking in lordship through the streets, still intimidating the law-abiding citizen with slungshot, revolver, and bowie-knife.

Perhaps the most conspicuous triumph of the professional scoundrel was to be seen in the realm of politics. Here, in truth, is a domain that the accomplished rascal has always claimed for his own, but in San Francisco and throughout all California he seemed to thrive especially well, somewhat like the rank purple thistles of the western countryside. "There probably had never been in the United States," says T. H. Hittell in the third volume of his *History of California,* "a deeper depth of political degradation reached than in San Francisco in 1854 and 1855." This may strike one as an extreme statement, particularly when one recalls the record of Tammany Hall and other not-incorruptible organizations of the East; but a brief examination of the facts will convince one that it would be difficult to find terms too severe to stigmatize the politics of San Francisco. The quotation from the *Annals,* regarding the public officers of the city, will serve only as a general introduction to conditions; one must glance at the details in order to form some idea of the full reeking foulness of municipal affairs. By the very nature of the circumstances, there is much that may remain forever unknown, since it has never been the way of political fraud to come out deliberately into the sun; but enough has been uncovered to throw a sad light indeed upon the politics of the day.

I have already made passing reference ·to the device of ballot-stuffing, whereby false sides and bottoms were fitted into the ballot-boxes, which contained scores of pre-deposited votes for the gang politicians; and I have also referred to the vote-repeaters, and the thugs hired to keep legitimate electors away from the polls. Let me now add that it was in the middle Fifties that these laudable methods reached their full bloom; and that various other plans, of equal efficacy, were resorted to whenever occasion required. "Carts loaded with voters drummed up from among the boarding houses and drinking saloons came galloping up to increase the crowd," we read as a minor commentary upon election methods, in the *Alta California* of June 1, 1855. Fighting now became common at the polls, the crackling of revolvers was heard from time to time, and the howls of rioting, half-intoxicated mobs; men who were not shot or pummeled were intimidated by the bullets; while in the notorious twelfth ward—which rarely reported its votes until those from all the other precincts were in—enough ballots could usually be supplied for the ballot-stuffing candidate to meet any deficiency encountered elsewhere.

There were, of course, occasional irregularities that must have looked somewhat glaring even by the hectic light of those times, as when, according to the *Alta California* for May 18, 1856, nineteen hundred votes were returned from certain San Mateo precincts that contained but five hundred residents! However, the manipulators of elections were waxing so strong and so bold that they apparently did not pause in their head-long course to read the handwriting on the wall. Yet that there was not only corruption, but a spirit of fierce resentment against the corruptionists, is indicated by the following from the *Herald* of September 8th, 1854:

"The men who have control of the ballot-box in the first ward have defied law and precedent in refusing to allow any witnesses of their midnight count. They have carried things with a high hand, even if the affiants who swear on the holy evangelists that they saw them destroying the ballots and put-ting others in their stead are guilty of perjury. . . . We say to the ruffians who have endeavored to take this election out of the hands of the people, who have been striving with bludgeon, dagger and pistol to ride rough-shod over the people, that there is a feeling abroad that bodes danger to them. They are stand-ing upon a volcano that may burst at any moment."

Not a great deal of respect for the State politicians is implied in the words of the *Alta* for December 26, 1853, when it de-clares that "The city is full of the Honorable, the members-elect of the legislature, and politicians and political gamblers are to be met with at every corner, ready to pounce on the State Treasury so soon as the wires can be arranged." And the high moral plane of politics in the State could hardly be more point-edly suggested than by a remark of a contemporary, José Fer-nandez, who, in a manuscript translated in Bari's *The Course of Empire,* speaks thus of the location of the State Capital:

"There is no doubt that San Jose is the most favorable place, but it remains to be seen if the inhabitants are disposed to buy the number of votes necessary to induce the legislature to prefer it to other petitioners."

It is obvious that, when elections are in the hands of unscrupulous men, who put their candidates into office regardless of the popular will, we can look for no honesty among the judges and executives that fill the usurped positions; we must expect the administration of justice to be on a plane not much higher than the morals of the "bosses." Hence we must not be surprised to find the years just preceding 1856 marked by a judicial callousness, a crassness, an inefficiency which bring to mind the worst days before the formation of the first Vigilance Committee, and which made it possible for the wholesale thief and the murderer almost invariably to escape scot-free, while the petty offender was severely chastised.

Not only the judges but the juries were seriously to blame. At a time when a hundred and one excuses for homicide were recognized in the popular code; at a time when it was considered legitimate to take life in defense of one's "honor," the assassin could usually convince some members of a jury of the propriety of even the most cold-blooded murder. "It is a high privilege which the laws afford to criminals, that of in a great measure selecting their own juries," laments the *Alta* of April 13, 1855. "But this privilege has become so subjected to abuse, through the instrumentality of brow-beating attorneys, that it seems now as though it were in some measure necessary to curtail these privileges. It is a humiliating fact, but nevertheless a fact it is, that it does seem to detract from the character of a man . . . to be allowed to sit as a juror in a criminal trial."

Encouraged by the laxity of courts and juries, the man-killers plied their deadly trade almost unchecked. There is no way of knowing how many men lost their lives at the hands

of their fellows in those crimson middle Fifties; but all esti-
mates agree in putting the figures high. The "fearful magni-
tude" of the toll is noted in the *Alta* of March 30, 1855, in which
it is stated that the number of homicides has defied all attempts
to keep an accurate account; while the death-rate from accident
and murder is supposed to be as high as five per cent of the
population. In addition, incendiarism was lifting its brute
head: to quote once more from the *Alta* (Steamer Edition,
June 16, 1855):

"There can be little doubt that a regularly organized band
of incendiaries exists in this city—their object to set fire to in-
flammable districts of the town and make what they can by
pillage. In the last few weeks we have recorded some five attempts to set fire to houses. . . ."

As if to make the tenure of property even more precarious,
the uncertainties of the law and of deliberate usurpation were
added to the peril from fire-bugs, so that many an owner was
fraudulently or violently deprived of his land. The suits and
counter-suits over titles to real estate were so numerous and
expensive that they may very well have cost more, on the whole,
than the land was worth; while the evil of "squatterism," at
which we have already glanced casually, had grown to such
alarming proportions that few pieces of land outside the heart
of town could be said to be safe unless strongly policed by the
owner. Practically from the moment of the Gold Rush, the
troubles with squatters had been serious; the uncertainty over
Mexican land-grants had closed the public domain to settlers;
and parties of adventurers, following the good old individual-
istic principle that whatever they were strong enough to take
was rightfully theirs, had helped themselves to any city or
country land that had suited their fancy. Hence bloody riots,

in which the sheriff and others were killed, had occurred at
Sacramento as early as 1850. In San Francisco—which at all
times endured its full share of this pestilence—the quarrels over
sand-lots, water-lots, and all other variety of lots was incessant,
and the almost invariable arbiter was gunpowder. We even
read of one daring appropriator who fenced in Union Square
and attempted to hold it at the point of the pistol, until finally
disarmed and dispossessed by the city authorities. So audacious
did the land-jumpers become that at last the realty owners felt
obliged to rise and organize in self-defense, and in 1854 formed
an "Association for the Protection of the Rights of Property,
and the Maintenance of Order," which numbered about a
thousand men, who asserted that their object was to uphold
the law. Although little if anything was accomplished by this
organization, and although all connection with the old Vigilance Committee was denied, the formation of this group is
significant of the temper of the times, and is indicative of the
existence of subterranean forces that might at any moment
bring a new Vigilance movement into life.

Various other influences of the day should also be noted: the
fact that a period of deflation had set in as the inevitable reaction from the wild flush times of '49; that prices toppled, that
mercantile and banking firms collapsed, and that multitudes of
destitute miners were forced into the cities. Added to this, there
was the specter of deliberate and wholesale fraud—fraud
among the great banking institutions, which dissipated or stole
the people's money; and fraud in the case of one of San Francisco's most notable and trusted citizens, "Honest Harry" Meiggs,
a man of great popularity and unblemished reputation, who
quietly disappeared one day on a richly provisioned bark, leaving behind him scores of thousands of dollars in forged lumber
stocks and forged notes, while carrying away enough sound
currency to form the basis of the huge fortune which he sub-

sequently established in Chile and Peru. Delinquent by more than two million dollars, he had cheated rich and poor alike; and in his depredations he had been aided, if we are to accept the word of Bancroft, by the street contractors and by members of the board of aldermen, among whom he had been numbered not long before.

All these forces are worthy of mention as factors that gradually goaded the masses to fever pitch, until the public mind was ready for the formation and acceptance of a new Vigilance Committee. But not until November, 1855, when United States Marshal William H. Richardson was murdered by the gambler Charles Cora, did an incident arise that might very well have filled the streets once more with companies of marching Vigilantes.

The source of the altercation appears to have been trivial enough: a quarrel at a theatre between Richardson's wife and the prostitute who, in token of her relationship to the gambler, called herself Belle Cora. To all appearances, the resulting dispute between Cora and the Marshal had been settled—so much so that had one been present on the evening of November 17th, one might have seen Cora and Richardson step together from the Blue Wing saloon on Montgomery Street, and proceed arm in arm around the corner into Clay Street.

Then all at once they pause; one of the men draws a pistol and points it at the other's breast, while grasping his adversary's coat collar with his left hand. "You would not shoot me, would you? I am not armed!" cries the threatened party. But almost instantly the report of the pistol rings out; the victim staggers, is supported for a few seconds by his assailant, then collapses and falls. And the murderer nonchalantly pockets his weapon, and turns away.

Immediately a wave of excitement sweeps the town. The citizens, learning who it is that has been killed, begin to gather in muttering, agitated groups; the streets near the scene of the crime are packed with a dense crowd; the ominous cries, "Lynch him! Hang him! Run him up a lamp-post!", once more fill the air. Speakers arise and harangue the mob with inflammatory words; they express regret that the old Vigilance Committee is no more; they echo the yell of the rabble, "Hang him! Hang him! Hang him!" At length a vote is taken on the lynching proposals; a thunder of "Ayes!" roars forth, but also a chorus of "Noes!", since the criminal has many friends among the gamblers and politicians. And so nothing is done— but after a time one hears the old portentous tap, tap . . . tap, tap . . . tap, tap of the Monumental bell.

Meanwhile, among those urging instant execution, is none other than that old Vigilante, Sam Brannan. As the reward of his efforts, he is arrested by the sheriff on the charge of inciting a riot, and is taken to the station house, followed by a crowd that every now and then breaks out in blaspheming threats against Brannan's apprehenders. Perhaps because of this menacing multitude, he is released immediately upon reaching the station house; but until early morning the aroused groups of citizens excitedly range the streets.

It may have calmed the feeling of the masses somewhat to know that Cora was being held for trial. Yet little confidence was felt in the outcome of proceedings; nor was much satisfaction expressed over the fact that the murderer, while in jail, was placed in the tender charge of his old bosom crony, Billy Mulligan. And when, after about a month and a half, the day of the trial arrived, outraged public feeling was not greatly soothed by the knowledge that the power of wealth was on the side of Cora: his fellow gamblers had rallied to his defense with liberal subscriptions, while the gold of Belle Cora had been poured forth without stint in order to secure the ablest lawyers.

This, however, was the least discouraging fact. If one can

afford to hire good lawyers, cannot one also spare something for the right sort of witnesses? It was but the old, old story—throw dust in the eyes of the jury! discredit even the most credible charges of the prosecution! Although a number of witnesses testified unequivocally that Richardson had made no attempt to defend himself, others could be found to swear that he had tried to slash Cora with a knife, and that the latter had struck in self-defense only. Little matter that some of the defense witnesses were caught in self-contradictions amounting to perjury! Little matter that there was obvious truth in the words of Mr. Byrne, attorney for the State:

"The witnesses for the prosecution could have no reason for speaking otherwise than truly; while those for the defense, there is every reason to believe, are influenced by friendship for the prisoner, or, what is worse, are perjurers for personal gain. . . . Upon the one side, we have witnesses unimpeached . . . while upon the other, we find them, by their own acknowledgement, to be gamblers and agents for cock-pits."

But the eloquence of the prosecution was of no avail. Regardless of the fact that the defense could not produce the knife which Richardson was alleged to have wielded, nor the boy who was said to have picked it up, nor substantiate the rest of its testimony; regardless of the fact that one juryman admitted having been offered a bribe by the defense, Cora and his friends were not cheated of the fruits for which they had paid. The jury disagreed! And the defendant calmly remained in the care of Billy Mulligan, awaiting another trial.

The nature of the popular reaction to the verdict may be judged from an editorial in the *Alta* of January 17th, 1856—an article that could only have acted as a thorn in the side of the already seriously mortified public feelings:

"It has been understood for some time past that criminals

having money or friends, could not be punished in this community. It has been a subject of common remarks that witnesses could be procured to testify to almost anything; that juries could be made away with at pleasure. The feeling was expressed very generally, as soon as it was understood that Cora's friends had money, that he would never be punished. . . . Indeed, so confident were persons in this respect, that they even pointed out men on the jury who would never consent to a conviction; and bets were offered that such and such men would go for acquittal. We believed these statements at the time, notwithstanding the outcries of the counsel for the defense in relation to prejudices created by the press; and they have turned out precisely as stated. The truth is, the public has been grossly abused. . . . Men were placed upon that jury who should never have been there. They went upon it in order to defeat the ends of justice—in other words, to 'tie' the jury. . . .

"It is not very agreeable to state that the conviction is almost universal, that crime cannot be punished in San Francisco. But it is, nevertheless, a duty which we owe . . . to put the people upon their guard. It is well for every man to understand that life is here to be protected at the muzzle of the pistol. The best man in San Francisco may be shot down tomorrow, by some ruffian who does not like what he has said or done; yet the chances are a hundred to one that the ruffian will escape punishment."

The words of the *Alta* were to be prophetic, curiously prophetic; at least, as regards the shooting of the best man in San Francisco—or one of the best men in San Francisco—by a ruffian who did not like what he had done and said. It was to be about four months later—while Cora was still in jail awaiting re-trial—that the community was to be convulsed by the assassination of James King of William, and was thereby to be stirred to the formation of a public tribunal even more powerful than the Vigilance Committee of 1851, and more spectacular in the methods by which it defied the lawful authorities and scattered terror among the criminals.

But before we turn to the activities of the Committee of 1856, let us go back a little and follow the career of James King, and observe how, by the consecration of his life and of his martyrdom, this remarkable man made possible the eventual repulse of those forces of evil which he had combated with all the energy of a dauntless determination and indomitable courage.

CHAPTER VIII

JAMES KING OF WILLIAM

In a world where fortitude and moral strength were as common as weakness and moral frailty; in a world where most men had the courage of their convictions and preferred death to dishonor; in a world where intrepidity was valued more than gold, and ideals were customarily translated into action, a man such as James King of William would have attracted little if any attention, since he would have represented but the average citizen. But precisely because of our human imperfections, precisely because few of us possess the inner hardihood that balks at no obstacles, precisely because so many of us repudiate by our example that which we advocate in thought and speech, the career of James King stands forth in brilliant and even heroic outlines, dazzling us, shaming us and inspiring us by its attainment of what is so often regarded as the quixotic, the chimerical, the impossibly chivalrous and noble.

In order to introduce ourselves to this character, let us go back a few years in our narrative; and let us wander south and east along the Pacific Coast as far as Panama. It is the summer of 1848; and among the travelers hailing from the United States, and making the difficult journey across the Isthmus, is a bushy-faced man of twenty-six, slightly under middle height, but nevertheless of an imposing appearance. Glance at him closely—dark of complexion, with big piercing eyes, aquiline nose, and black full-beard and side-whiskers, he boasts a large well-formed head with a wide, moderately high forehead, but walks with a slight stoop and is less robust-looking than many of the adventurers that push their way through these outlandish regions. Yet is there not in his aspect the suggestion of a strength that is more than merely physical? His lips, beneath the mustache, are firm and broad; his jaws are resolutely set; his eyes are straightforward and determined under the beetling brows; his whole manner bespeaks a decisiveness, a flinty, uncompromising quality of will that would make him a formidable foe.

This man is James King of William; he was born in Georgetown, in the District of Columbia; and he owes his unusual appellation to the fact that there were several other James Kings in Washington, with the result that his letters often went astray and he decided, out of self-defense, to add his father's given name as a trailer after his own name. He is now bound for Oregon, having been drawn there by the alluring accounts of his elder brother Henry, who had joined two of Fremont's expeditions; and he leaves a wife and small children in the East while he seeks his fortune in the remote unknown West.

None the less, he is not one of the gold-seekers. Although the yellow metal has just been discovered in the Sierra Nevadas, the information has not yet reached James King in these days of slow-traveling news; and he can still have no conception of the tumultuous life into which he is to thrust himself. More than likely—despite all the enticement of adventure—he looks forward to a peaceful, pleasant existence, in which he will gradually make his way in commercial pursuits amid the tranquillity of a simple environment, and will build a home in which his loved ones and himself shall live happily and comfortably.

So different, so very different, the expectation and the reality! Little can he anticipate the part for which fate has reserved him; little can he read in his past any clue to the turbulence ahead. For his life thus far has been relatively quiet and uneventful, and in no way extraordinary.

That there was nothing spectacular-looking about the man himself is indicated by a statement of his former employer, who, asked what he thought of King at the time of the latter's departure, remarked, "He is a very clever, steady sort of man, but I don't believe he will ever set the Pacific on fire"—a prediction that time was to prove just about as mistaken as could be. Like many another distinguished man, King kept the flame and iron of his disposition concealed beneath a mask-like exterior—a secret from many who thought they knew him best, and perhaps not wholly revealed even to himself. Yet that he early showed the stamp of his individuality is indicated by the fact that his father, according to a statement of the Rev. William Taylor, often said that James "was a drove by himself"; even in youth he stood out from his brothers by his capacity for thinking independently and acting in accordance with his views.

In illustration of King's power of critical detachment, Taylor cites an instance in which the young man, having applied for membership in the Methodist Protestant Church, was asked by the minister to state what he thought of proceedings, and replied in part as follows:

"Brethren and sisters, I have been listening attentively to all that was said during the progress of this meeting, and I cannot say, upon the whole, that I am pleased with it. Brother —— there says that 'he is a great sinner, one of the vilest of the vile.' Now, I don't believe that, nor do I believe that he thinks so himself; and if a man were to come in here from the street, and say of him what he had asserted, he would hit him. . . ."

Thanks to such forthright remarks, considerable opposition arose against the young church member, and eventually he was compelled to withdraw his membership.

These facts, along with many reminiscences irrecoverably lost to us today, may have been often in the traveler's mind during the slow, tedious days of his pilgrimage. Having crossed the Isthmus, he waited in vain for a ship to bear him up the coast to the Promised Land, and finally decided to sail south for Valparaiso, whence he hoped to be able to embark for Oregon. And as his vessel made its leisurely way over the calm, lake-like waters of the Bay of Panama and southward through the mild blue Pacific, he had abundant time to review the episodes of his past. Standing by the rail on the tossing deck and watching the spindrift and the flying-fish, while the great sails above him expanded in the breeze, he may have reflected that thus far he had been fairly fortunate in his career even if never outstandingly successful. Born in January, 1822, of Scotch-Irish parentage, he had received most of the advantages that the time afforded in the way of an education; had acquired a fair acquaintance with the Latin classics; was well read in the authors of his own country and of England; and was instilled with a thirst for knowledge that was never to leave him until the moment of his death. Nevertheless, his life had not been primarily that of a student. At the age of fifteen, he had left home to seek his fortune; and after spending a year in Pittsburgh, had pressed on into the wilderness of Berrien County, Michigan. But the rigors of that backwoods environment had been too much for his not over-sturdy constitution; in the latter part of 1839 he had become sick, and had returned to Pittsburgh.

There for a few months he acted as a post office clerk, but eventually left the employ of Uncle Sam in order to enter that field in which, years later, he was to achieve a success that would scorch its way across the history of the West. When he enlisted in the service of the campaign paper, Kendall's *Expositor,* he could hardly have known that it was journalism that was to make his name memorable; nor could he have had any foreglimmer of the future when, after six months,

he transferred his activities to the Washington *Globe*. So far
was King from realizing the path of his destiny that, in 1841,
at the age of nineteen, he deserted journalism for banking, becoming a bookkeeper in the house of Corcoran and Riggs,
with which he remained until his departure for the Pacific
Coast. Meanwhile his marriage in 1843 had served to establish him in a domestic life not greatly different from that of
thousands.

Let us now follow him from Panama to Valparaiso. At the
latter point, astonishing news burst upon him—news that is to
alter his plans and his life. Gold has just been found in California! And something of the fever of the new discovery possesses the traveler as he stands there in that southern city beneath the shadow of the Andes. Excitedly he gives up the idea
of going to Oregon—at least, for the present! He will join in
the quest of Eldorado! In order to carry out this project, he
engages nine Chileans to go with him to California and work
in the mines. With these men he sets sail; and for many weeks,
during the slow, arduous voyage up the coast, he has time to
reflect on the golden prospects awaiting him in the unknown
universe to the northward. But he will have to be a most extraordinary prophet to anticipate what vicissitudes lie behind the
unlatched gate of the future.

It is November, 1848, when he reaches San Francisco. Although six months have passed since the discovery of gold, the
full fury of the Gold Rush has not yet been felt; for the main
tide of immigrants from the East will not arrive until the following year. The city, although bustling with activitiy and
excitement, is still but a small, scraggly place, with rude wood-
en and canvas shacks irregularly dotting the bases of the hills
and the semi-circular eastern cove. But James King does not
remain long at this town, of which he is to become one of the
most celebrated citizens—all haste, and away for the mines!

But upon disembarking at San Francisco, he has met with his first reverse. Six of his nine Chileans, infested with the catch-and-grab attitude of the new metropolis, have decided to go gold-seeking on their own behalf; and without even a polite "By your leave, sir," they have broken their contract and deserted their employer.

But three of the men remain faithful, and with these King hastens away to the mountains. Their rendezvous is the point later known as Placerville (but originally called Dry Diggings, and subsequently Hangtown, in memory of three men put to death by the miners on a charge of robbery). Now for a time the life that King leads is a rude one; with pick and shovel and pan he attacks the brute earth, while stooping low into a stream to sift out its freight of precious dust. One wonders whether, at this period of his existence, he does not acquire some of that distaste for drinking, gambling and rioting which he is later to express with such force; for the shuffling of cards, the rattling of dice, and the sounds of brawling and of ribald and drunken merriment are all too conspicuous during the hours when the men are not working their claims.

But, fortunately, he does not have to remain long in a mining environment. These are the days when rich strikes are still frequent—and James King is to have his share of good luck. Within three weeks, he has taken out gold enough to pay not only for the goods he has bought, but for the expenses of the Chileans and himself from Valparaiso. And then farewell to mining! The gold-bearing veins of the Sierras may hold out irresistible lures to others, but never again will James King seek his fortune by means of the pick and shovel!

Returning from the mines, King entered business at Sacramento, then known as "Sacramento City," a town second only to San Francisco in its mushroom growth. But apparently he did not greatly care for life in this rough, raw city sprawled beneath the oaks on the flat lands by the river bank; or else he believed that his prospects were greater elsewhere. At all events, he conceived the idea of opening a bank in San Francisco, and, in pursuance of this project, undertook the long, onerous voyage back to the East in order to secure capital. Following his return, he established the contemplated bank on December 5th, in a small frame building, later to be supplanted by a substantial brick structure. And from that time forth, and for several years to come, James King of William was to be one of the most prominent and successful bankers of the Far West.

So well did he lay his foundations that he was able to withstand a panic in 1850, and by the following year was prosperous enough to send for his wife and four small children, who hitherto had remained in the East awaiting the outcome of his western venture. Month by month and year by year his profits mounted; by the middle of 1853, his fortune was estimated at half a million; he kept a carriage, and had a fine home, as homes went in those days—and his prospects looked more than rosy. But fortune was to play him some strange tricks. James King of William, the successful banker, was not the James King of William that was to enact a spectacular rôle in history. Before he should be ready for the new part, he should have to trip and stumble, as did so many men in those uncertain times; he should have to be pitched down from his perch of prosperity, stripped naked, and brought face to face once more with the grim, bare realities of existence.

During the years preceding the downfall, there occurred certain events indicative of the inclinations and character of the man. In 1851, as we noted in a previous chapter, he was a member of the Committee of Vigilance, having been enrolled as number 186; and while we do not know just how prominent a part he played in the proceedings, we do know that some of the Committee funds were entrusted to the keeping of his bank,

and that he was one of the group of forty-five that controlled
the affairs of the Committee on its reorganization in September,
1851. An interesting story, regarding one of King's exploits as
a Vigilante, is hinted at in the *Bulletin* for May 21, 1856:

"Many members of the old Committee will remember how
manfully he interceded for a suspected prisoner, before that
body, and actually armed himself to defend him—believing
that none but the vicious should be accused and none but the
guilty punished."

Even though this report be not absolutely authenticated, it
is altogether plausible, since it accords thoroughly with King's
attitude on other occasions.

Equally characteristic were his actions when summoned to
serve as a member of the Grand Jury in November, 1853. At
that time corruption was flourishing, and, in the attempt to
check the wave of blatant plunder, indictments were brought
against several citizens, including Hamilton Bowie, a city official. Some of the results are described by King in an article
in the *Alta California* for December 2, 1853:

"From the very commencement of proceedings against one
of the parties accused, threats were uttered to the effect, that if
we found a true bill against that gentleman, at least five or six
of us would most certainly be shot, and that a certain newspaper
in the city would be 'down upon us.' "

These threats did not, however, deter James King from what
he considered his duty. Subsequently, therefore, the defendants resorted to other wiles; and King was offered personal im-
munity from harm provided that he would forsake Mr. Young,
another of the grand jurors, who had been menaced with personal attack by the accused. Or, as King himself relates it:

"I was afterward importuned by a friend of Mr. Bowie (who claimed also to be my friend) to sign some papers or write a note stating my belief in Mr. Bowie's innocence; stating that the moment I did so, I should escape any injury, and 'Mr. Bowie would immediately attack old Young and those other fellows, don't you know.' I am prepared, when necessary, to make oath as to that quotation. I was also told that Mr. Bowie would not publish my note. To this I replied, that I would not sign a paper in secret which I should be ashamed of in public; and to desert Mr. Young and his companions in such circumstances would, in my opinion, cover any man guilty of it with a load of infamy from which he would never recover, either in the opinion of the community, or what was of more consequence, in his own conscience."

Undoubtedly, had King been of a weaker calibre, Bowie's threat would have achieved its purpose, as similar threats have done before and since. So real, in fact, was the danger that King was warned by his friends to arm himself; but with that disregard for his personal safety which he was subsequently to show under more trying circumstances, he refused to take any precautions. "I shall have no fears for anything that may occur," he proceeds, "and in conclusion will add, that though I shall feel bound to defend myself as best I can if assaulted, yet I know my position *too well* to allow any threats or editorial remarks from a certain quarter to tempt me from my present position."

He continues by stating that he had gone on the Grand Jury with reluctance, and at the cost of great neglect to his business, for which $2,000 would not compensate him. "I have endeavored to do my duty faithfully," he declares. "I trust the public, even if it does not think as I do, will give me credit for my intention; but whether it does or not, I cannot cater to the public's taste to the violation of my oath. . . . Whether they approve or dissent, I can meet the eye of any man living, and what is sweeter still, am at peace with my own conscience, and can look around in my family and know that mother and six little ones need not blush for me."

But apparently the public did approve; and that James King of William was a man of honor seems to have been recognized by the community. "San Francisco does not boast a more quiet, courteous, dignified and honorable gentleman than Mr. King," states the *Alta* of the date above mentioned. And the same paper, for March 2, 1855, remarks that "he has sustained a reputation for uprightness, fair dealing and superior business qualifications." This reputation was to serve him well during the days of adversity and financial stringency that were to come.

It was at about the time of the Grand Jury episode that, owing to the treachery of one of his agents, King was pitched down from the seemingly secure financial pedestal he had occupied for several years. A representative at Sonora, who had been his cashier during 1850 and 1851, betrayed his confidence by misusing a large sum of money sent him for the purchase of gold dust. Diverted without King's authorization or knowledge to the uses of the Tuolumne Hydraulic Association, these funds became hopelessly tied up; while for months King vainly awaited the badly needed receipts. "During all this time," he reports in a letter to the *Alta California* for July 26, 1855, "I was a prey to the most agonizing doubts and fears. For the first time in my life I was unexpectedly placed in a position where, in the event of a run, I could not possibly meet my engagements. No one that has not been similarly situated can imagine the agony I endured from day to day, and week to week, as I saw persons walk into my office and deposit money which, in the event of a panic before I could turn my property into cash, I knew I could not return!"

Although assured by his friends that his bank remained one of the strongest in the city, the distracted financier set about to sell whatever he could, in order to place himself in a position to meet his liabilities. Finally the matter was settled through the offer of a Mr. Woods, of the great banking firm of Adams and Company: that company would assume King's indebtedness in return for his assets—an offer which the latter was glad to be able to accept. This meant, however, that King was to be divested of his all: the surrendered property included not only a business building, vacant lots, and valuable stock, but personal possessions such as his home with all its furniture, a buggy, a pair of horses, harness, and the like.

During this period of emergency, when the world was crashing in ruins about him, the quality of the man once more stood forth: he refused assistance from the many friends who stood ready to help; he declined to avail himself of the protection of the bankruptcy act, through which—had he desired—he might have saved his house. And he took care that, if he erred, his mistakes should harm only himself. "After receiving the details of my assets," declares King, in the letter quoted from above, "Mr. Woods expressed himself highly pleased at the result, and said to a mutual friend, 'King is entirely too honest, he underrated everything he had. . . . I am satisfied I shall make from $100,000 to $150,000.' "

Upon the dissolution of his own banking house, King was still sufficiently esteemed to be, able to secure a position with Adams and Company, where he was employed at a salary of about a thousand dollars a month. Unfortunately, however, this new employment was not to last long—although this was in no way the fault of James King. He was not responsible for the fact that the huge concern was improperly conducted, and was actually insolvent; indeed, had the management paid more heed to him, there might have been some hope of averting the

impending crash; for King very early discovered that not all
was in order in the machinery of the great organization, and
did not hesitate to report his findings—with the result that, like
many another prophet of disaster, he was merely ridiculed.
Hence Adams and Company went its predestined way, and in
February, 1855, the city was stunned by the news of its failure.

While multitudes of investors were bewailing their loss, innumerable charges and recriminations were hurled back and
forth; and James King himself was not immune from attack,
for it was contended by some of his foes that he had reaped a
profit from the collapse of the great concern. But, as ever, he
was ready to defend himself from unjust accusations; and he
did so with such vigor and finality as not only to dispose utterly of the charges but to earn the approbation of the public.

Following the failure of Adams and Company, James King
of William was once more set adrift; and this time he sought
to solve his troubles by establishing a new banking business
with Henry Reed, a former associate in Adams and Company.
But the arrangement did not work out advantageously, and in
a little less than four months the partnership was dissolved.

King's next adventure was to be as editor of the *Bulletin*—
the vehicle of his fame and his tragedy. But before he was to
set out on his rôle as crusading editor and startle the city by
his sledgehammer blows, he was to be involved in one or two
other episodes in which his unique character was to assert itself.
And not the least of these was to be the affair of Alfred A.
Cohen—a prominent citizen who was to honor King by inviting him to fight a duel.

The trouble was an indirect fruit of the transactions of Adams and Company, and resulted from a card which King published in the San Francisco papers for July 14, 1855, defending
himself from the charges of complicity in the rather dubious
dealings of that concern. Something in King's remarks aroused

the animosity of Cohen, and when the two men chanced to meet on Montgomery Street, heated words passed between them, followed by blows, with the result that Cohen was struck several times about the head and shoulders—although, fortunately, neither man was hurt.

But Cohen, according to the ethics of the day, could not let the matter rest at this point. His honor—that sacred appendage which the lowest rascal was always ready to defend at the point of a revolver—had been jeopardized. He could redeem it only by a fight to the death! Hence, acting through one John K. Hackett, he sent King the challenge to a duel.

Here was a situation in which, according to the code of the times, King had no honorable choice but to accept. It is true that duelling was against the law; it is true that it was regarded as so objectionable—in theory—that no duellist was legally entitled to hold public office; it is true that a duel usually decided no question except which of the two fighters was the luckier, the more remorseless, or the better shot. But did all this affect the actual practice? Not in the least! It might almost be said that duels were bootlegged as abundantly as were certain spirituous liquors in our own century. They had risen to the status of a popular recreation, a sport; they were indulged in by business men, by editors, by judges, by politicians, none of whom suffered in social prestige or position if they survived; they were attended by interested crowds, who would convene at the appointed place, as eagerly as though attending a horse-race or a cock-fight; they were fought on all pretexts, great and trivial, but more often trivial, one instance being recorded in which a man was killed for having put his foot on a chair desired by another; and they were reported by the papers as if they were perfectly normal, legal proceedings, to which no one could possibly object. For example, turning the pages

JAMES KING OF WILLIAM IN EARLY MANHOOD

of the *Alta California* for the first part of 1855, one runs across many items such as the following:

"A duel was fought near the city on the morning of the thirteenth, by Colonel William Walker and Mr. Carter, formerly of Sacramento. They used pistols—distance eight paces."

And, similarly:

"Duels are becoming again fashionable. Two occurred on the twelfth, one in the vicinity of the Mission Dolores, between two French merchants, and another at Contra Costa, also between Frenchmen. The weapons were small swords in both instances."

Consider, then, the position in which King found himself. Duels were occurring continually; they were condoned by public opinion, and winked at by the officers of the law; they were fought not only by ruffians and gangsters but by many of the so-called "respectable" citizens, and were given publicity in the daily papers. Hence how could a man refuse when challenged? Would he not be deemed a weakling, a coward? Would he not be henceforth the laughing-stock of his associates? There is no question but that many reasoned thus; and that more than one, with these thoughts in mind, went forth needlessly to kill or be killed. But the power, the originality, the individuality of a man is to be measured precisely by the extent of his resistance to a tyrannical tradition; and King, in this case as in others, would not blindly obey a code that his reason disapproved. And so, instead of taking the easy course and accepting the challenge, he followed the difficult one and refused.

Here is the answer which he issued, through the San Francisco newspapers, under date of July 18, 1855:

"Mr. John K. Hackett

"Sir: I now proceed to give you my reply to the note you hand-ed me last night, and first, waiving other insuperable objections to the mode indicated of settling such difficulties, I could not consent to a hostile meeting with Mr. Cohen. The public have already been fully advised of my estimate of his character. The relative positions of Mr. Cohen and myself are entirely unequal in worldly fortune, and domestic relations. He is understood to be possessed of an abundant fortune. In the event of his fall, he would leave ample means for the support of his wife and child.

"Recent events have stripped me entirely of what I once possessed. Were I to fall, I should leave a large family without the means of support. My duties and obligations to my family have much more weight with me than any desire to please Mr. Cohen or his friends in the manner proposed. I have ever been opposed to duelling on moral grounds. . . .

"Whilst nothing could induce me to change my principles on the subject of duelling, my conscience is perfectly easy as to my right and the propriety of defending myself should I be as-saulted.

"Do not flatter yourself, sir, that this communication is made out of regard either to yourself or to Mr. Cohen. I write this for publication in the newspapers. I avow principles of which I am not ashamed, and shall abide the result."

As it happened, he did not have long to wait for the result. The community, which had seemingly been resigned to duel-ling and even indulgent of the bloody rites, was all at once awakened; the great majority of the newspapers endorsed King's stand and none openly opposed it; letters of sympathy and approval began to pour in upon him; and he was the re-cipient of a communication signed by seventy of the city's foremost citizens, who desired to express their "admiration of the moral courage and sound principle" manifested in the refusal to accept the challenge, and who tendered their thanks "for the bold, manly and uncompromising manner" in which the practice of duelling had been rebuked.

But the effect of King's forthright declaration was not merely to produce a shower of wordy approval; it had far more important results. There is no telling how many a man King's action saved from a cruel death, how many a man he spared the burden of taking a brother's blood, how many a family he rescued from bereavement. But this we do know: his pronouncement served as a powerful deterrent to a practice that had hitherto been on the increase, and definitely launched the movement that was to make duelling in California as obsolete as the dinosaur. While it is true that the custom did not terminate overnight (witness, for example, the celebrated case of the slaying of Senator Broderick by Judge Terry in 1859), yet it is also true that the practice became much less frequent from the moment when King attacked it.

It will therefore not be difficult to decide which was the more courageous course to pursue: to follow the path of conventional bravery and face an opponent's bullets on the duelling ground; or to refuse, as did James King, and to fling one's defiance not at the life-blood of a fellow man but at the heart of a pernicious institution.

CHAPTER IX

O n the eighth of October, 1855, a newcomer made its appearance in the already crowded field of San Francisco journalism. A modest little sheet of four pages, only ten by fifteen inches in size, it did not make an imposing entry; nor were the readers apt to be impressed by the fact that the editor was not a trained writer, but a fallen banker. The name of the paper was the *Daily Evening Bulletin*; its publisher was C. O. Gerberding; and the man at the editor's desk was James King of William, who had been encouraged to undertake the work by his success in publicly answering the charges arising out of the affairs of Adams and Company.

Perhaps the most important feature of the new journal was a certain agreement, which was at the very foundation of its existence, the agreement between King and the publisher providing that the former was to have complete editorial control; he was to be lord absolute of its policies, and from his word there was to be no appeal. Had it not been for this stipulation, it might have been possible to muffle the voice of the editor, as that of many another able reformer has been muffled; had it not been for this stipulation, the paper might never have launched itself skyward in such a glare of light as to amaze the entire State; had it not been for this stipulation, King might have been unable to set a new journalistic precedent, and to strike at evil and corruption with such devastating bolts as have seldom been witnessed in all newspaper history.

Yet how was it that this man, schooled primarily as a banker and with but little journalistic experience, had the temerity to launch himself into the newspaper field? Had he no doubt about his ability to write? his ability to match his pen against the quills of trained and tempered editors? Apparently he had the self-confidence that balked at no obstacles; he believed that if he had something to say, he would find the means of saying it. Yet even he was surprised at the talents he developed. An interesting light on this phase of his career is shed by an article which appeared in the *Bulletin* for May 26, 1856:

"A friend, shortly before Mr. King's death, said to him that he had never been more surprised than that one who had always been summing up figures at his desk should so suddenly develop a power of writing so tersely and powerfully. He replied that no one could be more astonished than he was himself; that he had previously had no idea of possessing any such power; that even then he had tried and found it impossible to sit down and write an article, take time to correct and polish it, and make it satisfactory to himself; that his only course was to write when his mind was full of a subject, and hand it immediately to the compositor."

Spectacular as the *Bulletin* was to become before it was out of its swaddling clothes, the opening issue gave little indication of the firebrands that were in preparation. The editor's "Salutatory" was, however, a plain and manly statement—and one that deserves to be read for an understanding of James King. After admitting "the apparent folly of starting a newspaper in this city where so many already exist," he goes on to declare:

"Necessity, not choice, has driven us to this experiment. No one can be more fully sensible than ourselves of the folly of newspaper enterprise as an investment of money. But we invest no money of our own (for we have none), and a few hundred dollars, generously advanced us by a few friends, is all that we have risked in the enterprise. If successful, we shall be able to feed, clothe and shelter our family in San Francisco.

"Whatever may be our political bias individually, as conductor of the *Evening Bulletin* we shall act independently of either of the political parties that now divide the State. By being independent of either party, however, we by no means intend a neutrality or indifference to public affairs; but in all matters of public interest we shall advocate such measures as may seem to us best for the public good."

It cannot be said that there is anything here that any other editor might not have said in substance. Yet, on the following day, King was to strike a more combative note. Already, it seems, an undercurrent of opposition was arising (for there were men in the city who knew that King's principles and their own could not agree); and accordingly the editor expressed himself, with more force than elegance, to those who had done him the honor of noticing his new venture:

"Well, gentlemen, some of you we thank; and some we don't. We will endeavor so to conduct our columns as to give no good grounds for complaint. It has been whispered to us that some parties are about pitching into us. We hope they will think better of it. We make it a rule to keep out of a scrape as long as possible; but if forced into one, we are 'thar.' *Entiende?*"

There could be no question of the effect of such a statement to make friend and foe alike sit up and take notice; nor could there be any doubt of the interest and sympathy awakened by the bit of self-revelation which King contributed to the paper on the third day of its existence. I quote from the middle of an editorial:

"It would require a higher power than any earthly tribunal to release us from that moral obligation imposed on us by the silent monitor within. We have ever endeavored to do right, regardless of consequences. We know we have made enemies by so doing, but that was to be expected. It has made us poor, but our health is as good, our slumbers as quiet, and we are prouder today than in our palmiest hours. It has kept us from church because we would not occupy the pew on which we could not afford to pay the rent, and has about forced us to first principles in domestic economy, but we enjoy our parlor and sitting room with patched carpets, and odds and ends of furniture, as much as we ever did the handsomer furnished rooms we once owned on Stockton Street."

It was on the following day—October 11th—that King really launched into the battle against corruption. Then it was that he fired his first salvo against Palmer, Cook and Company, the political banking house that was to quail beneath his assaults until his pen was stilled forever. The nature of this firm, which he branded as the "Uriah Heaps of America," is definitely indicated in King's opening charge:

"They are unlike other bankers, because forevermore they are at some scheme to elect, not good men to office but their own or such as can be so fashioned, and then, becoming bondsmen for them, get hold of public money with which to bribe and corrupt other public officers, both state and federal."

On October 12th King did a peculiar thing—a thing for which few editors, one fears, would have sufficient courage. In the previous day's issue, he had made a misstatement, to the effect that Palmer, Cook and Company were bondsmen of one Thomas J. Henley; but, finding this not to be the case, he publicly apologized, and admitted that he had been misinformed.

Nevertheless, he in no way relaxed his attack. Indeed, he returned to the assault in a way that must have caused much gnashing of teeth among members of the accused concern:

"We were favored yesterday with a visit from Mr. Edward Jones, the partner now representing the house of Palmer, Cook and Company, of this city. Mr. Jones assured us that he took no offense at, and his firm would not reply to, or take any notice of, our remarks in yesterday's *Bulletin*. His visit, he said, was not prompted so much by any wish to discuss the merits of our leader of yesterday, as to have defined to him certain personal relations between himself and us. . . .

"During the course of this interesting interview, Mr. Jones gratuitously informed us that no newspaper, that had ever attacked the firm of Palmer, Cook & Co., had made anything by so doing, but that his firm had always succeeded in silencing such journals. Mr. Jones did not intimate by what means his firm became so successful in these contests, but in a subsequent part of our interview in which the altered fortune of the editor of this paper was alluded to, Mr. Jones expressed much sympathy, and remarked that had he known it he would have aided us with pleasure, which aid we told him we would have felt bound to decline. A very remarkable man, that Mr. Jones!"

It is safe to say that, from this time forth, if any "friend" thought of offering a bribe to the editor of the *Bulletin,* he was careful to place a somewhat heavier veil over his proposal than Mr. Jones had taken the precaution to do.

On the same day that he thus silenced the representative of Palmer, Cook and Company, King effectively demonstrated his attitude toward other methods of money-making considered orthodox among the newspapers of the day. The following is also from the *Bulletin* of October 12th:

"We have been urged, lately, by different parties, to insert medical cards of a certain description that we do not think proper for the columns of any respectable public journal. We have declined acceding to the requests made, and are resolved so long as it may be our lot to conduct this paper, never, know-ingly, to admit anything of an obscene nature therein. What-ever is unfit to be read at our own fireside, is unfit to be sent into the parlors of our readers.

"One of these physicians called today, and on receiving a polite but firm refusal, he candidly approved of our principles, but remarked—'but I don't think you will succeed unless you change your views. Other papers take our cards, and are glad to get them; in fact, they could not get along without our sup-port.'

"Well, we are poor enough, in all conscience, but if we can-not get along without such aid, we will shut up our office and start for the mines. We have yet to learn that this community of San Francisco will not support us in our position."

The *Bulletin* was not yet a week old before its guns had been spouting fire at nearly every corner of the horizon; not only private individuals but public figures were to feel the fury of the editorial discharge. And among the especial objects of King's ire were the piratical politicians who had been looting the public purse, blocking the administration of justice, and converting both state and local governments into little more than "rackets" for the benefit of fraudulently elected officials and their henchmen. Whatever one may say of the editorial that appeared on October 13th, one will not contend that the writer was mincing words. Again I quote from the middle of the article:

"A man, unworthy to serve the humblest citizen in the land, has filled the highest office in the gift of the people. Judges have sat on the bench, whose more appropriate station would have been the prison house. Men, without one particle of claim to the position, have filled the posts of Mayor and Councilmen in this city, for the sole purpose of filling their pockets with the ill-gotten gains of their nefarious schemes, their pilfering and dishonesty. City and County Treasurers, and Recorders, have sought to obtain offices of trust and honor, who, had they met their deserts, would in other countries have formed part of the chain-gang years ago. And all the while the *press,* THE PRESS, either silent through base fear of personal injury, or yet more shameful, is basely bought to uphold this iniquity!"

The writer goes on to state that, whereas the public offices are occupied by corrupt men, "some as unknown to fame as others are notorious for their crimes," citizens "of acknowledged ability and tested honesty" do not so much as dream that they have "the remotest chance of election." Why is this? he inquires. And he mentions, among other causes, the ballot-stuffing, the lavish expenditure of money for corrupt ends, the employment of paid bullies and political tools by both parties alike.

"When," he challenges, "will the people rise in the majesty of their strength, and shake off the yoke that now oppresses them? When? We answer, when a fearless and independent press, by boldly stating the truth, shall expose these things. . . . We have taken up these matters of public interest, and intend to leave nothing undone that can be done, to rid our city and State of the pests that infest them. One by one we shall fall upon them when least they expect it. Nor shall threats, nor position, nor wealth, nor power, nor friends, nor the fear of things present or to come swerve us from the course we have marked out for ourselves."

Obviously, it is no ordinary journalist that is speaking here; it is a missionary, a crusader, the self-appointed protagonist of a consecrated cause. And how could words such as these fail of their effect? How could they be otherwise than as coals of fire to kindle public sentiment? Consider the fact that not all the citizens of San Francisco, nor even any great percentage of them, were actually vicious or corrupt; consider that there were thousands of good honest men who, in helplessness and despair, had seen the reins of government fall into the hands of the cutthroats and rowdies; consider that the attitude of many was not so much one of acquiescence in wrongdoing, as of sheer inability to combat the organized forces of political brigandage. The plunderers had had leaders in plenty; their foes, though more numerous, had been without effective command since the days of the first Committee of Vigilance. And now suddenly arises a prophet in the wilderness! Now comes a man with the courage to state publicly that which other men have merely thought! now comes a man who flaunts from the pages of the press that which formerly has been whispered behind closed doors! Now appears the knight who tilts single-handed at the dragon that has been devouring the body politic! who strikes resounding blows at the monster that most men have abhorred but none has dared to attack! Must not a spontaneous wave of applause arise? Must not men who had held back before, either out of timidity or from sheer hopelessness, now all at once enlist in the campaign? And must not popular feeling be whipped and goaded into fury, until the wave of resentment has mounted like a stormy tide and swept the usurpers out of office?

"A fearless and independent press!" had been the demand of James King—and both fearless and independent the *Bulletin* was, even to the point of taking off its gloves and striking repeatedly with unbared fists. It was not enough to refer to the pillaging politicians as a class, or by innuendo; they must be boldly mentioned by name, though they sat in the highest offices of the land. Let us begin with a United States Senator! Let us take that outstanding figure in the political life of the day, David C. Broderick! and let us call him to account! Had King been a duelling man, he might have been challenged to a life-or-death encounter for saying less than he did in the following sentence:

"Of all the names that grace the roll of political wire-working in this city, the most conspicuous of all. . . as high over all his compeers as was Satan among the fallen angels, and as unblushing and determined as the dark fiend, stands the name of David C. Broderick."

As if this indictment were not sufficient, King returned to the attack in subsequent issues, referring to his victim as "David Cataline Broderick," charging that he got himself elected Senator to serve selfish ends, accusing him of participating in the Jenny Lind Theatre swindle (wherein the city was fleeced of a large sum in the purchase of an almost worthless building), and laying various other gross offenses at the doors of the Senator. Broderick, according to King, had robbed not only the city but the State, had been instrumental in spreading crime and immorality, had been a corrupter of elections, and had sold offices to the highest bidders—an example being cited of an office for which $5000 had been offered, although its legitimate returns were but $1000 in excess of that amount.

Even the *Bulletin's* fellow newspapers, as we have seen, were not spared by the excoriating pen of the editor. Moreover, they were assailed not only as a group, but individually and by name. The following is an example of a frontal attack:

"The San Francisco *Herald,* head over heels in debt to them (Palmer, Cook & Company), is tied hand and feet; and the editor dare not open his lips except at the bidding of these moneyed tyrants."

Methods so direct and uncompromising, manifestly, would earn any editor a host of enemies no less than a multitude of friends and admirers. It was impossible to be neutral—one had to take sides either for James King or against him. And one could not ignore the *Bulletin,* even though one feared or loathed it; for one never knew what the next day's editorial was to bring forth, or who the next object of the editor's wrath was to be. Whatever it said was a fit subject for discussion on street corners and before the counters of saloons and gambling halls no less than in offices, stores and private homes; whatever it said was a matter of community concern, since it had become the mouthpiece of a large element that had hitherto been voiceless. Hence the paper grew at a surprising rate, in physical dimensions, in circulation, and in power: within a month, it printed nearly 2,500 copies; within two months, nearly, 3,500— more than any other journal in the city!—and thenceforth it continued its steady growth, until it had overwhelmingly surpassed all rivals in the influence it wielded.

What was the motive that sustained James King in his unflinching, violent attacks? is the question that has been asked more than once. Was it sheerly a disinterested, Messianic zeal? or was there a mingling of diverse forces? It is, of course, impossible to answer these questions with finality, since a thousand contradictory influences enter into every man's psychology, many of them concealed from the individual himself. Yet King's own words and actions offer clues that seem unequivocal enough. It may be, as is contended by Josiah Royce, that he was not altogether "free from selfishness in the conduct of his mission" and "not infrequently felt a good deal of personal spite against the sinners he assailed"; it may be that he had been spurred to fury in part by the sense of his own defeat as a banker, and that he was given to not unnatural human aversions and animosities; it may be that he was guilty of prejudices, that he exaggerated, that he perpetrated injustices, that he committed the common fault of the reformer in tending toward an intolerant extreme. The possibility of all this must be admitted, even in the absence of conclusive proof; for if James King had been above this possibility, he would have been above humanity. Yet, no matter what concessions one may make in these respects, the fact remains that the causes espoused by King were basically just, that he was but expressing the views of outraged thousands who had hitherto been voiceless, that he was battling on the side of the gods and the angels, and that he proceeded with apparent disregard of all personal interests and in contemptuous defiance of the peril that was daily deepening about him.

His own position—the feeling of one who has assumed a sacred responsibility, the feeling of one who is above the lures of mere worldly emoluments—was enunciated time after time, and always in terms vibrant with sincerity. "Were we to resign the post as Editor of this paper," he writes, little more than a month before his assassination (*Bulletin,* Steamer Edition, April 5, 1856), "we should be ashamed to walk the streets of San Francisco. There is not a man, woman or child, from Shasta to San Diego, who would not say that we had been bought off. 'There!' would be the exclamation, 'we did think we had at least got *one* honest editor in San Francisco, but he has been bought also!' Gentlemen, you have not gold enough in your vaults, nor is there enough in the hills and gulches of the State to buy us! We *have* been wealthy, and know the uses of money; but in our poverty we have learned practically that there can be *more* real happiness in the poorly furnished cottage than in the most magnificently furnished apartments. We would not exchange the hearty welcome of the mechanic and the laborer and the honest merchant for all you can offer."

It may be remarked that there is here just a little of the triumphant and self-conscious flaunting of the editor's own incorruptibility. Yet he, if any man, was entitled to such speech, since his actions had vindicated his words in advance, and he had steadfastly resisted all attempts of his adversaries to silence him by buying him out or otherwise securing a controlling interest in the paper.

Before turning to the tragic culmination of his career, let us glance at a few other features of the campaign he waged. He was determined to sweep with nothing if not with a thorough-going broom; and not only crime but vice in all its manifestations was assailed by his trenchant pen. Thus, he dealt resounding blows at the houses of prostitution, which then existed not only with an abundance but with an openness that offered, as it were, a continual stench in the nostrils of the more respectable citizens. It was not only that the institution, in an organized form, blatantly existed; it was that it was impossible to avoid proximity with it: that it had invaded every quarter of the city, nudged the shoulders of decency at every corner, and left not a single large clean neighborhood to which it was possible for a good citizen to retire with his wife and children. How long this situation would have continued, had it not been for King, there is no way of knowing; but tooth and nail he plunged into the attack—and with methods that were certain to bring results. Charging City Marshal North with neglect of duty, he challenged (in the issue of November 7, 1855):

"If the city council find that they have not power or lack the will to remove Mr. North or make him do his duty, we will have the records searched and learn who own the houses rented to these people; and we will publish their names, that the respectable portion of the community will know who to admit and who to reject from their firesides. It's no use trying to dodge the *Bulletin,* gentlemen!"

As a result of King's method of direct exposure, the aldermen were forced into action; they appointed a committee, which conducted an investigation demonstrating that conditions were fully as bad as King had claimed; and they recommended the remedy of a complete reorganization of the police. Hence the people of San Francisco could thank the editor of the *Bulletin* for the fact that vice, if not extirpated, was thenceforth to be forced to take in its horns a bit.

Another object of the *Bulletin's* attack was an institution which had been one of the features of San Francisco life ever since the days of the Gold Rush,—the institution of gambling. Of late years, the gamblers had not been quite as gaudily open or ostentatious as in 1849, but they still throve in large numbers, and exercised a pronounced influence on the city's moral, social and political life. Consequently, King plunged in to the assault with his usual incisiveness. He maintained that public opinion in California had never actually favored gambling, but had merely tolerated it, at first because of the absence of any restraining law, and subsequently through mere habit. The professional gamblers, he argued, were criminals; nor were they to be condoned even when they acted in accordance with the letter of the law, since a good citizen does not consult the enactments of the State for his guidance in ethics. Only of late had the popular sentiment against gambling begun to find a chance to assert itself; for the State, founded amid the flow and counterflow of a thousand chaotic currents, was now barely arriving at a condition that could be regarded as normal.

In ringing terms he flung a challenge both at the gamblers and at the prostitutes following the disagreement of the jury which tried Cora for the murder of Richardson. "Hung be the heavens with black!" he lamented. "The money of the gambler and the prostitute has succeeded, and Cora has another respite. . . . Rejoice, ye gamblers and harlots! rejoice with exceeding gladness! . . . Your triumph is great—oh, how you have triumphed! Triumphed over everything that is holy and virtuous and good; and triumphed legally—yes, legally!"

There were those among the gambling fraternity who sought to answer King's strictures. Was it fair, they asked, to denounce men who only gambled as the law permitted, in order to relieve the monotony of narrow lives? men who did not make gambling a profession, but merely a means of recreation? One of these assailed individuals went so far as to remonstrate patiently with the editor, urging him to "rest from the thankless and unprofitable task which you have imposed upon yourself. You are pursuing a course that will certainly drive you to despair if persisted in." But for King there was to be no rest—not so long as he breathed the air of this troubled planet. The issue of battle had been joined, and there could be no end except victory or death.

And so the determined contest went on, day by day, and day by day—and with each new issue of the paper he delivered fresh blows. He was not altogether destructive in his work, for he demanded not only the eradication of innumerable evils, but much constructive activity, such as the furtherance of public education and the establishment of means for the employment of the industrious poor. Yet it must be acknowledged that his arm was more powerful to uproot iniquity than to erect new social structures. He continued to be the bane and the terror of Palmer, Cook and Company, whom he characterized as "the greatest enemies to the public weal," and whom he pounded with such persistent and relentless strokes as to drive the firm to eventual ruin. And he was as the avenging fury to all corrupt judges, dishonest officials, bought jurymen and political hirelings, and thundered forward in his crusade until many a man, who previously had felt secure in corruption, began to read in the words of the *Bulletin* the fateful "handwriting on the wall."

It is hardly an exaggeration to state that each issue planted fresh seeds for the formation of the second Vigilance Committee,—that great Committee which was to spring into being only after the fighting editor had been silenced forever. King himself probably did not fully realize the tendency of his own words, for (as already mentioned) he had announced himself to be opposed to a revival of Vigilance, and had declared on January 17, after the trial of Cora: "We want no Vigilance Committee, if it can be avoided; but we do want to see the murderer punished for his crimes."

Yet his own statements sometimes hold a none-too-deeply veiled threat of the re-appearance of the Vigilantes, as when he writes, on December 12th:

"The people of this city are not in favor of taking the law into their own hands if justice can be done in the courts; and no class of men can be found in this community more in favor of law and order than the members of the old Vigilance Committee. But if the courts were to relapse into the former farcical apologies we had, it would require but a few hours to again call into action the same body of men."

Much more inflammatory, as we have already seen, were some of King's remarks in the Cora affair; but his indignation was particularly aroused at the knowledge that the criminal was calmly lodged in the care of his jailor-friend, Billy Mulligan. Whatever virtues the following words may possess, they are not those of moderation; nor do they indicate the author's belief that justice is to be attained most easily through orthodox legal channels:

"Hang Billy Mulligan! That's the word! If Mr. Sheriff Scannell does not remove Billy Mulligan from his present post as keeper of the county jail, and Mulligan lets Cora escape, hang Billy Mulligan, and if necessary to get rid of the sheriff, hang him—hang the sheriff! Strong measures are now required to have justice done in this case of Cora. Citizens of San Francisco! what means this feeling so prevalent in our city that this dastardly assassin will escape the vengeance of the law? . . . Merchants of San Francisco, mechanics, bankers, honest men of every calling, hang your heads in very shame for the disgrace now resting on the city you have built!"

It was all very well for King to say that he did not favor a reorganization of the old Vigilance Committee; his words were as a rallying call to the Committee members, and were not to be forgotten during the stormy days to come; while, even at the time, there was talk of a return to the rule of Vigilance.

It was, however, not so much by his life as by his death that James King of William was to ignite the conflagration. Only a moment was reserved for him—a moment of glorious battling in the sunlight—and then it would be for others to continue the combat which he had so valorously begun. But there had been premonitions a-plenty, and fore-rumblings of the end; and it is not the least remarkable feature of the man that he continued on his way unswervingly, contemptuous of all perils, scornful of all threats.

In the following chapter, accordingly, we shall consider briefly his attitude in the face of increasing warnings; and then shall turn to witness the speeding of that bolt which, paradoxically, was to terminate his activities and at the same time to consummate his mission on earth.

CHAPTER X

MURDER STALKS ABROAD

W HATEVER may be said as to the martyrdom of James King of William, one cannot regard him as one of those heroes who plunge to their doom because they have not been warned, or because they have not the imagination to visualize the dangers. Reckless he assuredly was; yet, if he tiptoed at the brink of a precipice, he did it deliberately and consciously, and not because he could not see the threatening abyss. This fact is made evident by several circumstances. For one thing, we have the direct testimony of his son, Charles J. King, who, in an article on "Early Days in San Francisco" (*Overland Monthly,* March, 1888), declares:

"My father . . . went armed and practiced with his pistol in our backyard. I had seen him many a time hit the mark he was aiming at repeatedly in succession. His idea was, if he should ever be attacked, to throw up his left arm as a defense, while he drew his weapon with his right hand and fired. He never dreamed of being attacked in the streets of the city, where some inoffensive passerby would be imperiled."

But it is unnecessary to turn to the words of mere onlookers for our evidence. King's own statements on numerous occasions make it evident that he realized his peril, but that, being constituted as he was, he could not be diverted from his course by the thought of personal risk.

"Bets are now offered, we have been told," he announced in his issue of November 22nd, "that the editor of the *Bulletin* will not be in existence twenty days longer, and the case of Dr. Hogan of the Vicksburg paper, who was murdered by the gamblers of that place, is cited as a warning. Pah! We passed unscathed through worse scenes than the present at Sutter Fort in '48. War, then, is the cry, is it? War between the prostitutes and gamblers on one side, and the virtuous and respectable on the other! War to the knife, and the knife to the hilt! Be it so, then! Gamblers of San Francisco, you have made your election, and we are ready on our side for the issue!"

Even more outspoken, even more defiant was King in the case of a gambler named Selover, who made threats against the editor's life following the latter's refusal to meet him in a duel. "Mr. Selover, it is said, carries a knife," wrote King on the 6th of December. "We carry a pistol. We hope neither will be required, but if this rencontre cannot be avoided, why will Mr. Selover persist in perilling the lives of others? We pass every afternoon about half past four to five o'clock, along Market Street from Fourth to Fifth Street. The road is wide and not so much frequented as those streets farther in town. If we are to be shot or cut to pieces, for heaven's sake let it be done there."

It is not recorded that King ever felt the actual steel of Selover's knife; but there can be no question that he lived in constant jeopardy of assassination—and that no one was more aware of this fact than he. Again and again, during the brief term of his editorship, we find references to threats upon his life. Consider, for example, the following (from the *Bulletin,* Steamer Edition, of April 5th):

"A highly respectable gentleman of this city has called this morning to say that he has just been accosted in the street by a Frenchman, who, drawing a revolver, asked him if he was James King of Wm.? Our friend declined the compliment (!) implied, and the man put back his pistol and walked on. Who the man is, what could be the motive, or whether he was in his right mind or not, we have not the most distant idea. We cannot at this moment recall any act of ours against any Frenchman that would justify such hostility. May the Lord have mercy on the soul of that Frenchman if ever he draws a pistol on us—and may our after life not be embittered by the slightest remorse for any hasty action under such circumstances."

Again, in the Steamer *Bulletin* for March 26, the editor speculates on a project for slaying him:

"We have lately been watching the maneuvers of Colonel Baker and his friends, who have been seeking some pretext to attack us. The latest report, we hear, is that Mr. Baker . . . will offer an indignity to Park, with the hope of exciting us to an act of aggression against Baker, when the latter will have an excuse (?) for shooting us. To lying and slandering, Colonel Baker desires to add assassination. . . . There are enough hounds who would gladly seize some pretext to get us out of the way."

So menacing had King's enemies become that it would have been evident even to the most casual observer that the editor was daily gambling with his life. "I well remember," writes W. O. Ayers in an article in the *Overland Monthly* for August, 1886, "meeting him but two days before the curtain rose on the terrible tragedy that was to follow, and looking at him with a sort of reverent wonder, as of a man who carried his life in his hand."

What were King's own sentiments on this subject we do not know, except from his journalistic utterances; but there is every reason to accept the summary given in the *Bulletin* on May 21, 1856, after the pen of the editor had been forever laid to rest:

"There was no blanching in his features, no backing in his heart. He well knew the dangers that surrounded him, but he was inspired by the justice of his cause, and despised them all. He often gazed at that wife, now a widow, those children, now orphans, and almost faltered when he remembered how soon they might hear the signal of his death."

It is easy, of course, to be positive after the event, and to assert that what happened was inevitable, and that if King had not been killed by one man he would have been slain by another. Yet it is difficult to see how, in those days of tempestuous emotions and reckless disregard for life, he could have had other than a violent ending; for he had made himself obnoxious to a large and growing class of citizens, and had steadfastly refused to let himself be removed by any of the gentler conventional methods, such as bribery, direct purchase, and intimidation. It must have been painfully obvious to hundreds of his enemies that, unless he were swept away in an abrupt and bloody fashion, no power on earth could interfere with the deadly daily bolts he was hurling at vice and corruption.

The particular agent of the eventual tragedy was an ex-convict and prominent politician known as James P. Casey. This individual, who appears to have been popular with his election-fixing associates, was one of the many who throve upon the perversion of democratic institutions; it was as a ballot-stuffer that he had attained especial eminence. Recently he had achieved the feat of being elected Supervisor from a district of which he was not a resident, and in which his name had not even appeared as a candidate; while, in his capacity of inspector of elections for the sixth ward, he had decided more than one election in omnipotent disregard of the popular will. It was stated in some quarters, although denied in others, that he had accumulated a fortune owing to various skilled transactions; but, in any case, it is certain that he had acquired sufficient to start a newspaper, the *Sunday Times,* regardless of the fact that he was incapable of writing a word for publication. Altogether, he was quite a dashing character, was James P. Casey, and thoroughly typical of his times; but it was not to be expected that he was the man to appeal to the scrupulousness of a James King of William.

On the fateful fourteenth of May, 1856, the *Bulletin* contained an editorial in which reference was made to a certain Mr. Bagley, and incidentally to his quarrel with Casey. "Our impression at the time," writes King, "was, that in the Casey fight Bagley was the aggressor. It does not matter how bad a man Casey had been, nor how much benefit it might be to the public to have him out of the way, we cannot accord to any one citizen the right to kill him, or even beat him, without justifiable personal provocation.

"The fact that Casey has been an inmate of Sing Sing prison in New York, is no offense against the laws of this State; nor is the fact of his having stuffed himself through the ballot-box as elected to the Board of Supervisors . . . any justification for Mr. Bagley to shoot Casey, however richly the latter may deserve to have his neck stretched for such fraud on the people. . . However much we may detest Casey's former character, or be convinced of the shallowness of his promised reformation, we cannot justify the assumption of Mr. Bagley to take upon himself the redressing of these wrongs."

Severe words, no doubt—but no severer than the *Bulletin* had used on numerous occasions. Nor can it be said that there was anything particularly striking about the reference to Casey's prison record, even though it may have been a cruel thrust, and one not strictly demanded by the circumstances. Casey was by no means unique in this respect, since more than one of California's gallant political fraternity had come under the shadow of eastern penitentiaries; moreover, Casey's past had been aired before: on the preceding November 2nd, he had testified in court as to his prison term, and an editorial calling attention to his Sing Sing career had appeared on the following day in the California *Chronicle* and had been re-published in the *Bulletin* of November 5th.

But for some reason it appears that Casey, although thick-skinned as a wart-hog about such a matter as "managing" an election for his own aggrandizement, had peculiarly soft and delicate susceptibilities when it came to the Sing Sing episode. His feelings were offended; in fact, they were deeply and violently offended, and his fury broke out in a perfect gale. The story has it that certain of his friends, and in particular the sagacious Ned McGowan (whom we last saw exercising his capacities as judge) took care that Casey should be stimulated to the proper degree of indignation; McGowan, it is said, lost no time about rushing to Casey with the offending paper and goading on his irascible friend by every method that his fertile brain could devise. The truth is that there are indications of a plot, in which McGowan was one of the principal actors; but the facts, if there was a plot, have never been fully brought to light—although the evidence is clear that several persons, including McGowan and a certain Peter Wightman, knew in advance of Casey's impending attack on King.

It was at about three o'clock on the afternoon of the 14th that the papers containing King's reference to Casey appeared on the streets; and it was at about four that King received an uninvited caller at his office. No less a character than James P. Casey excitedly burst in upon him. We can picture the man as he came storming into the sanctuary of his rival—a short and slender figure, with thin delicate features and bright blue eyes burning with emotion; the florid face, now more flushed than usual, lined with side-whiskers; the dark hair scantily sprinkled above a high, wide forehead.

The ensuing conversation—as reported in the *Bulletin* for the 15th—was brief and to the point; and every word of it was overheard by two persons in an adjoining room, which connected with King's office by an open doorway.

"What do you mean by that article?" began Casey, his breath coming short and fast.

"What article?" asked the editor.

"That which says I was a former inmate of Sing Sing prison."

"Is that not true?" shot back James King.

"That is not the question," retorted Casey. "I don't wish my past acts raked up; on that point I am sensitive."

"Are you done?" demanded King, pointing. "There's the door—go! Never show your face again."

Casey started toward the open door; but paused there long enough to fling out, "I'll say in my paper what I please."

"You have a perfect right to do as you please. I'll never notice your paper."

As far as King was concerned, the matter was now closed; but Casey, slipping his hand to his breast, uttered the warning, "If necessary, I shall defend myself!"

At these words, the editor of the *Bulletin* arose from his seat. "Go!" he repeated, with such force that Casey immediately disappeared. "Never show your face here again!"

And with those words—although he little guessed it—he had sealed his doom.

It is unfortunate that he was not equipped with powers such as certain clairvoyant souls are said to possess; for then he might have known what foul designs were afoot, and might have read an imperious "Beware!" As it was, he seems to have had no suspicion that the present occasion was different from any other; and when, shortly after five o'clock, he left his office as usual for dinner, he apparently had no premonition that he was departing never to return. Absorbed in his own thoughts, he walked northward in front of Montgomery Block, then crossed the street diagonally toward the Pacific Express office. He was wearing, according to the custom of the day, a short cloak or "talma," which was buttoned or held together in front and covered his arms; but his fingers were not reaching toward any concealed weapon, nor was his aspect or manner that of a man who dreads assault.

A short while before, Casey had been observed skulking on the opposite side of Montgomery Block, as if watching for King's appearance. And now all at once, with murderous haste, he launched himself upon his victim.

There was some slight disagreement among eye-witnesses as to what actually ensued. Some maintained that Casey issued a warning note, "Arm yourself!"; but others declared that they heard nothing of the kind; and, at all events, even if the warning was spoken, Casey's action followed so swiftly upon his words that the victim had no chance to defend himself. King, according to his own testimony, was taken utterly by surprise; he heard a sound as of a person crying "Come on!"; and, looking up, he saw Casey, only a few paces away, throwing off his short cloak and aiming a revolver. Instantly there came a puff of smoke and the report of the weapon; King staggered beneath the impact of the bullet, as it drove its way through his chest. "Oh God!" he exclaimed. "I am shot!" And with the blood flowing profusely from a wound in his left side, he groped his way toward the office of the Express Company, which he might not have been able to reach had not several passers-by rushed to his rescue and supported him.

Gaining the office, he was assisted into a chair; and, a little while later, was provided with a bed; while his wound, which was exceedingly painful, continued to bleed abundantly. But medical aid was quickly secured, and after a time his condition, although critical in the extreme, appeared to be improved somewhat.

Meanwhile Casey, the confident assassin, had unloosed pandemonium in the streets of San Francisco. It is certain that he had never reckoned with the furies that he was to set free; certain that he had had not the remotest prevision of the fruits of his crime. So audaciously entrenched had lawlessness become, so safe did thieves and murderers feel in the protection of the authorities, that Casey had not realized that he was taking any great risk by shooting his victim in broad daylight; while, in order to shield himself after the crime, where should he place himself but in the keeping of his gentle friends, the sheriff and the jailor? Surrounded by men of his own ilk, he was hastened to the station house in order to avoid the rapidly assembling crowds—but no station house, he was to find, was to be strong enough to contain him.

In less than five minutes, a dense throng had packed the streets; in less than ten minutes, it had reached as far as the eye could see. Surging back and forth with impatient mutterings, it had an angry, ominous look; it burst toward the station house with cries of "Hang him! Run him up a lamp post! Hang him! Hang him!"; it shouted imprecations at the officers, and seemed ready to burst open the doors of the station house itself. Meanwhile the Monumental bell, sounding its portentous tap . . . tap, tap . . . tap, tap . . . tap, was like a call to arms.

Apparently if Casey were to remain in the station house, it would be but a question of minutes before the mob would batter its way through the doors—and a rabbit in the jaws of grayhounds would have as good a chance as would the assassin in the hands of the infuriated rabble.

Hence he was rushed into a carriage, to be taken to the county jail, some blocks away. But this act was only to add to the popular frenzy.

An excellent account of this episode is provided by W. O. Ayers ("Personal Recollections of the Vigilance Committee," *Overland Monthly*, August, 1886):

"A carriage was standing at the entrance to Dunbar Alley,

the rear of the police office; it was evidently about to start. I sprang on the step, and as I did so Dave Scannell's pistol was thrust directly into my face. I looked in, and saw Casey on the seat with Scannell, and his pistol pointed out of the opposite window. The driver started his horses and I was thrown to the ground but was on my feet in an instant, and away with the crowd who were pursuing the carriage at full speed, yelling with every breath, 'Kill him! Kill him!' "

Upon reaching the jail, Ayers was astonished to see, perched on a bank eight or ten feet high across from the building, "every one of the most noted of the gamblers and shoulder-strikers of the city." All stood heavily armed, looking down upon the crowd. "How," demands the writer, "came these men to be at that place, at that time? They certainly never could have met there by chance, and they as certainly did not come with the crowd, for they were standing calmly on the bank when I, among the first of the rush, ran around the corner of Dupont Street. The only possible inference is that they were there by previous appointment."

It was not long before the street in front of the jail was packed by a solid mass of threshing, shouting, muttering men. Stationed on the steps leading up the bluff to the prison, was Marshal North, surrounded by a strong force of deputies and policemen, while the mob was making constant threats of assault upon the building. Some of the more boisterous spirits would raise their voices and demand that the jail be instantly taken; others would shout back, "Good!", "That's it!", "Let's take the jail!"; and from moment to moment their fury and excitement seemed to increase.

The emotions of the rabble were fast approaching the bursting point when Thomas King, brother of the stricken man, appeared upon the scene. Eager to address the crowd, he attempted to climb the bluff where the officers were standing, but was forced back; then, crossing the street, he mounted the balcony of a two-story building, and broke into speech:

"Gentlemen and fellow citizens, I have but little to say about this matter. My opinion of it is, that it is a cool, premeditated murder; perpetrated by the hand of a damned Sing Sing convict, and by a plan of the gamblers of San Francisco ... About an hour ago I was at the old Natch's pistol gallery, and he told me that my brother was to be shot. If he knew it did not the gamblers know it? and was it not a premeditated plan; and that by the gamblers of this city? Why did not the officers know it and interfere? Gentlemen, we have got to take that jail, and to do so we must kill those officers, if they do not give way to us; and we must hang that fellow up."

Tremendous cheering greeted these words; and meanwhile Officer Nugent descended from the bluff and approached the speaker as if to arrest him. However, the crowd blocked the policeman's passageway, and hisses and execrations rained in his ears. At about this time, Thomas King came down from his balcony, and, after strenuous urging, heeded the advice of friends, entered a carriage, and allowed himself to be driven away.

Shortly afterwards the mob was thrown into a new furore by the sight of a row of bayonets turning the corner of Dupont Street. Vehement cheers resounded at the appearance of the glittering weapons ... but gave place to hisses and groans when it was found that the armed men were not friends, as had been at first supposed, but members of military companies arriving to reinforce the authorities at the jail. The newcomers numbered about twenty in all, and did nothing to relieve the tension as they mounted the bluff in front of the prison, some of them ascending to the roof, and all of them drawing themselves up in battle array.

By this time the streets, as far as the eye could reach, were filled with people. The roofs, windows and balconies of all buildings in the neighborhood were packed with solid masses of humanity; while here and there some particularly enthusiastic individual, lifting his hands in declamation, was rallying a body of followers, whose shouts, cheers and cries only served to add to the growing commotion and confusion.

So serious had the disturbance become that Van Ness, Mayor of the city, thought it his duty to interfere. After arriving at the jail and conferring briefly with the Marshal and the Sheriff, he removed his hat, motioned to bring order to the turbulent multitude, and launched into speech:

"Gentlemen, I desire to say to you that you are creating an excitement which may lead to some occurrences this night which will require years to wipe out. You are now laboring under great excitement, and I advise you to quietly disperse, and I can assure you that the prisoner is in safe custody. Let the law have its course, and justice will be done."

"Look at the case of poor Richardson! How was it in his case? Where is Cora now?" came furious voices, in interruption. "Down with such justice! Let us hang him! Let us hang him!"

Such a storm of shouts and ejaculations filled the air, such howls, hoots and execrations, that His Honor was glad to be able to withdraw.

Regardless of the menacing attitude of the mob, the police now rushed forth and seized and arrested two or three of the ringleaders; but, in the ensuing mêleé, Officer Nugent had his skull fractured by a brick-bat.

A new source of excitement appeared upon the arrival of a second military company—and now for an instant the situation trembled on the borderline of disaster. Some one had the temerity to hurl a lump of dirt at the soldiers, as a result of which their guns were leveled at the crowd; but, fortunately, they were checked before taking the bloody revenge that would have been all too easy.

All evening new troops kept arriving; all evening the restless, surging, vociferous mob jammed the streets before the jail. Why was it that they did not attempt an attack upon the building, as it was in the minds of thousands to do? Was it merely that they feared the troops? No! for mass emotions rarely reckon with obstacles; besides, there was some question as to just how far the soldiers would go in firing upon their fellow citizens. The simple fact was that the throng lacked a leader. As the *Bulletin* expressed it in its issue of the 15th, "The people were ready and willing to act, and only needed a determined master-spirit to lead them on." But since such a master-spirit did not make his appearance (and, surely, it is fortunate that he did not!), the crowd loitered in the vicinity of the jail until toward midnight, when it gradually dispersed without having attempted any action.

Meanwhile, however, exciting rumors were traveling through the air—rumors of the revival of popular justice, rumors of the re-establishment of the Vigilance Committee. Little knots of citizens gathered in numerous places throughout the city, agreeing that "something must be done!"; groups of the old Vigilantes assembled, and spoke of once more resorting to summary methods. Early in the evening, William T. Coleman had been approached on the Plaza by several fellow members of the Committee of 1851, and had been asked to establish a new Vigilance Committee; and, while admitting the necessity for such an organization and promising his aid, had refused to accept the tendered leadership. Somewhat later that night, however, we find him in company with one G. W. Frink, discussing the advisability of securing a hall for a popular meeting on the following day; and we see how, having decided to make use of a building on Sacramento Street, near Montgomery, they issue the call for an assemblage that is to prove historic:

"THE VIGILANCE COMMITTEE

"The members of the Vigilance Committee, in good standing, will please meet at No. 105 1/2 Sacramento Street, this day, Thursday, 15th instant, at nine o'clock A. M.

"By order of the   Committee of Thirteen."

There may be some doubt as to the justification of the use of the term, "Committee of Thirteen"—but the members of the old Committee had disbanded under the name of "The Thirteen," and that, seemingly, provided sufficient excuse. At all events, Coleman and Frink were not to be deterred by any such triviality. Making five copies of the notices, they went to the various newspaper offices, where publication of the announcements was promised, free of charge—and thus, with swiftness and certainty, the foundation was laid for the second Committee of Vigilance.

Meanwhile what of him who had been the innocent cause of all these preparations? What of him, the people's champion, who had been felled by the representative of fraud and corruption? So great had been the concern felt for King's life, so vast the crowds that pressed around for news of his condition, that ropes had to be placed about the building where he lay, in order to keep off the too-eager populace. The victim— attended by some of the most reputable physicians of the city, but served, it appears, by too many doctors, since they disagreed violently among themselves—dragged out the feverish hours painfully, with occasional intervals of sleep. At his bedside, from seven in the evening until dawn, sat his grief-stricken wife; while King, perfectly lucid in his mind despite the agony he was suffering, was tormented not only by the wound in his left side but by the thought that his work, so vigorously begun, might now be terminated forever. More than once, during that night of misery, he turned to Dr. Beverly Cole and inquired if there were no hope for him; for even then he was haunted by the phantoms of the approaching end. Not easy is it for a man such as James King of William to bid farewell to life; not easy is it for one who, in the robustness of his thirty-four years, has launched himself into a resounding battle for right-eousness and truth; not easy is it to take leave of the field with the engagement still but half fought, to close one's eyes upon the warming, welcome sunlight, to look no more into the faces of friends, to pass beyond sight of cherished little ones, to feel the clasp of love grow faint and feeble and the inundating oceans of blackness swallowing all familiar sights and sounds.

But perhaps it would have been some comfort for King to know that not all was lost; that the cause for which he was fighting would not founder with his death; that, instead, it would gain new power, and that many ends for which he battled would be consummated more quickly and more com-pletely than if he had lived. Little as he realized it, he was to be the martyr who gave his life-blood to bring about a city's redemption; and all during the tumultuous days that followed, when the breath had passed from his body but the spirit of his words still sounded like a trumpet-call, we may imagine the soul of James King of William as leading the drive against the scourge of corruption, and we may picture his shade, like an ascendant god, rising triumphant above the ashes of that vice which was to be forever dissipated by the heroism of his life and the tragedy of his death.

CHAPTER XI

LONG before the specified hour of nine, on the morning of the fifteenth, a crowd had gathered before the premises at 105 1/2 Sacramento Street, where the meeting of the Vigilantes was to occur. And throughout the day the throng kept growing in size; while would-be members of the new Vigilance Committee formed themselves into a line, which reached far down the block and around the corner as the applicants awaited their turn for hours.

Meantime within the hall, on the third story of the building, momentous events were taking place. Numbers of the old Vigilantes had convened, and had chosen as their leader William T. Coleman, who had accepted after being promised those two things which every head of a dictatorial party must demand: absolute secrecy, and implicit obedience. As secretary, they picked the man who had filled the same position in 1851: Isaac Bluxome, Junior, who was henceforth to sign himself with those dread words, "33 Secretary"—a signature as greatly feared among certain classes as though it had been the symbol of a bloody autocrat. And having made these appointments, the Vigilantes busied themselves with enrolling new members, who came in by the hundreds and the thousands during that day and the succeeding days. Great care was taken in the selection of the men, who had to be certified as to character, and who were received only after passing three guards, one of them stationed at the foot of the stairs, one at the head, and one at the entrance of the Committee rooms. Despite these precautions, however, and despite the fact that many applicants were rejected, the number accepted was so great that by noon about fifteen hundred had been enrolled,—men of many races and professions, Frenchmen and Irishmen, Scotch and Italians, Jews and Gentiles, merchants and stevedores, physicians and bootblacks, butchers and bankers,—although one must admit a singular limitation on the democracy of the selection when one recalls that Negroes and Chinamen were not admitted.

Owing to the extraordinarily rapid growth of the new Committee, it was found necessary to remove to larger quarters for the second meeting, which was held on the evening of the fifteenth; and the place selected was the Turn-Verein Hall, on Bush Street near Stockton. At these headquarters the organization was completed, and the Committee began to assume that markedly military character which was to distinguish it throughout its career, and which was to give it quite as much the aspect of a rebel government as of a mere tribunal. Following the old Roman plan, the men were organized into centuries—in other words, into companies of a hundred men each, all of the companies being permitted to elect their own officers. And in order that they should have something more than the shadow of power, they were all provided with muskets, several thousand of which were hired from one George Law, who had purchased them from the government at a fraction of their original cost. Expenses were defrayed by means of voluntary contributions—and thus, within one day, the Committee developed the nucleus of a formidable military organization.

Was it, then, that the Vigilantes expected war—civil war? Was it that they thought that justice could be established only by force of arms? that they were prepared to go even to the length of violent rebellion in order to overcome the forces in control of the courts and the government? Apparently so—for on no other grounds can one explain the immediate and wholesale martial demonstrations.

It is apparent, moreover, that having undertaken the task,

they intended to execute it with nothing if not with thoroughness. It was not sufficient to organize and equip the men; it was necessary that they be whipped into a state of fighting efficiency. Here, surely, was a task that might have daunted Coleman and his associates; for it is one thing to give a man a gun, and another to teach him to use it. How develop this miscellaneous group of merchants, clerks, and mechanics into an effective army corps? and how accomplish this Gargantuan labor within the very few days at the Committee's disposal? Commentators have always marveled that the Vigilantes did produce a capable fighting machine, and did produce it almost overnight, but the explanation is not really far to seek: first, that the members of the Committee drilled willingly, regularly, and with their entire hearts and souls, and not with the listlessness and mere mechanical monotony of the ordinary recruit; secondly, that many among them were military men, and applied military methods, and that several regular companies of the militia were organized as companies of Vigilantes. Beyond this, they had the assistance of numbers of the city police, who resigned their positions with the municipality; while a continuous supply of arms was assured by the fact that Edward H. Parker, the agent of Eastern manufacturers, was so moved by business zeal that he agreed to loan all muskets and ball cartridges the Committee might require.

While the daily military drill proceeded, the Committee endorsed the Constitution of 1851, subject to later modification; adopted the symbol of the Watchful Eye, which had been used by their predecessors five years before; continued to register new applicants, until the membership amounted to more than eight thousand, about three fourths of the adult white male population of the city; and established permanent headquarters in a building on Sacramento Street, prosaically known as number 41, but familiar to history by the more colorful appellation of Fort Gunnybags. Truly, this name is a just one! for the front of the building did come to resemble a fort of gunnybags. Along the entire frontage of the premises, and from the walls to the middle of the street, sacks filled with sand were piled to the height of eight or ten feet—these breastworks having been erected following rumors of an impending attack by a band of Texans, who planned to rescue one of their number from the hands of the Committee, and were frustrated by the unexpected barricade.

Since the gunnybags were hardly sufficient in the way of military defense, several cannon were placed on the roofs of Fort Gunnybags and adjoining buildings, so as to command all approaches; while, from every port-hole, a field-piece bristled. Sentinels with muskets, pacing on the roof and in front of the building, added to the military appearance; stables, containing cavalry and artillery horses, contributed their mite to the preparations; four-pounders, loaned by vessels in port and mounted on improvised carriages made from the fore-wheels of wagons, lent no inconsiderable increase of power to the defenders; and a huge steel triangle and a bell, placed on the roof and waiting to be sounded at any hour of the twenty-four, were held in readiness to summon the thousands of Committeemen to the defense of the Cause.

While the Vigilantes were making their preparations, the waves of sentiment and counter-sentiment ran high throughout the city. The storm of popular emotion, manifested on the evening of the shooting of James King, gave no sign of subsiding throughout the following days; indeed, in many respects it appeared to be aggravated with the passing of time. The city was divided, as it were, into two hostile camps; the majority being on the side of Coleman and his band of cleansers and purifiers; but a powerful minority being aligned against them.

Some idea of the strength of the prevalent passions will be

JAMES KING OF WILLIAM AS EDITOR OF THE BULLETIN

gained from the fact that, of the numerous papers in the city, only one dared flatly to oppose the Vigilance movement—and that one thereby signed its own death-warrant. This paper, the *Herald,* had been among the best established and most popular in the city; its editor, John Nugent, had won a place as one of the outstanding journalists of the State, and was known as a supporter of the Vigilance organization of 1851. What, then, was the astonishment—not to say the dismay of his readers—to find him unreservedly opposed to the new uprising! It is possible that he was actuated, in part at least, by enmity to James King, who, as we have seen, had condemned him in no uncertain terms, and had gone so far as to denounce him as "recreant to every principle of honesty and care of the public good"; but, in any case, he was surely exercising no more than an editor's right to free speech when he wrote, in the edition of May 15th:

"An intense excitement was caused in this city last evening by the affray between Mr. James P. Casey and Mr. James King of William. Motives of delicacy needless to explain force us to abstain from commenting on this affair; but we could not justify ourselves in refraining from the most earnest condemnation of the mob spirit last night. The editor of this paper sustained the Vigilance Committee in past times to the peril of his life and fortune; but at a time when justice is regularly administered, and there exists no necessity for such an organization, he cannot help condemning any organized infraction of the law. . . . We wish to be understood as most unqualifiedly condemning the movement."

The writer was doubtless ill-advised in terming the murder of James King a mere "affray"; he was also, to say the least, on questionable ground when he stated that justice was "regularly administered"; but, after all, he had the right to his own opinion, and it is therefore astonishing to find that, as Bancroft states, "For a time feeling seemed to run higher against the *Herald* than against Casey." In one day, the paper lost hundreds of subscribers, and the valuable advertisements of the auctioneers; copies were burned in a great pile by indignant merchants on Front Street; the Vigilance Committee passed, in the face of Coleman's opposition, a resolution pledging its members to withdraw their advertisements and subscriptions and to urge others to do likewise—and, as a result of all this, the *Herald* appeared on the following day in a reduced format; and, never able to regain its lost ascendancy, was eventually compelled to suspend.

Much more in accordance with the predominant sentiment of the day was a handbill posted throughout the city under the signature of "Brutus":

"Emergency of the moment! To the people! Friends and fellow-citizens, lend me your ears! The time was when in San Francisco many of us, law-abiding citizens, regretted the acts of the Vigilance Committee, and were willing to hope that if the law of the day had been duly supported the guilty would have met with their deserts. Since then experience has convinced us that the law is here a mere mockery; that the weak, the poor, the stranger may pay his misdeeds by the forfeiture of his liberty or his life; but the rich villain, the powerful gambler, supported by his rich confederates, laughs at the impotence of the law. . . . Patience is a virtue, but there is a point beyond which it degenerates into cowardice. . . . When law is effete, or its protection becomes tyrannical, resistance becomes the duty of every freeman. Such is the present emergency to our view."

In order further to stir up the troubled waters, challenging articles appeared in some of the papers, and particularly in the

Bulletin, to which one William H. Rhodes contributed under the pseudonym of "Caxton".

"The emigration to this State from the first discovery of gold," he writes in the issue of May 19th, "has consisted principally of two classes of men: those who came to work, and those who came to steal."

After a commendation of the first class, he proceeds to describe the opposing fraternity:

"The second class stand all day at the street corners, flourishing whale bone canes and twirling greasy mustachios. At night they flock to the gambling halls, abounding in all our thoroughfares, where they feast and carouse, bet and blackguard, damn their owns souls and take the name of God in vain. Or else, flushed with the pillage of some poor miner, or despairing clerk, elated with wine and lust, they throng the houses of prostitution, and there, in the presence of male and female comrades in crime, rehearse the downfall of their last victims, plot the ruin of others, and gloat in hellish triumph over the desolation they have made. . . .

"These two classes have hitherto been battling against each other in secret. Now an open war has broken out in relentless fury. One or the other must succumb."

After characterizing James King of William as "the representative of the first class" and James P. Casey as the representative "of the second," "Caxton" proceeds to an analysis of the political corruption of the day, and declares that the consequences of the "dreadful scourge" were felt in all the business relations of life:

"Public confidence was shaken, public honor suspected. Many of our best and worthiest citizens sacrificed their property and sent their families to the East. No man felt secure for a moment in the possession of life, property, or reputation. At this juncture Mr. King started the *Bulletin*. At first he was scoffed at as a madman, then pitied as an enthusiast, then respected for his courage, then applauded for his independence, then beloved for his purity, his self-sacrifice, and his noble magnanimity. Finally, by a revulsion of public sentiment in his favor, which is without parallel in our history, he stood forth the acknowledged champion of public and private morality, the scourge of villainy, the vindicator of the freedom of the press, the friend of every social reform, and the benefactor of his country."

Nowhere had the case been more clearly stated: the issue was not merely that of the conflict of two men, a James King on the one hand and a James Casey on the other: it was a question of the clash of two irreconcilable classes, the one typifying all those forces of social constructiveness and morality for which civilization has been battling for thousands of years; the other typifying the rapacity of the brigand, the ruthlessness of the plunderer and the destroyer, the fury of the wrenching claw and the grinding hoof. And this fact the people realized; this fact they recognized less with the pondering mind than with the fury of vehement unleashed emotions: hence their enthusiasm to rally in support of the Vigilance Committee; hence the almost hysterical frenzy with which they repelled opposition, as manifested in the pages of the *Herald;* hence their savage determination to persevere in the face of threats, guns, and even the peril of armed revolution.

Not merely the City of San Francisco, but scores of towns and villages throughout the State, were swept by the common furore. From the Santa Clara Valley, on the 16th of May, came the message: "The Vigilance Committee of San Francisco can have a thousand men from San Jose, if they are needed." And at numerous points—at Sacramento, Stockton, Vallejo, Marysville and Sonora—public meetings were held, and resolutions expressing sympathy with the vigilance movement were passed. It must have been painfully evident to the authorities that the eruption of public sentiment was not only city-wide but state-wide.

But despite the unexpected force of the opposition, the so-called defenders of "law and order" spared no effort to resist the Vigilantes. They kept a large armed contingent at the jail; they provided the building with numerous guns; they put their armories in readiness for war-like maneuvers; they ordered out sheriff's *posses,* and supplied them with firearms; they called a meeting, presided over by the sheriff, at which about sixty judges, lawyers and election officers promised their support to the anti-Vigilantes; and, as a result of this gathering, numbers of men were sworn in by the sheriff as special officers, and about one hundred were placed at the jail as guards to see that the prisoner was held safely and that any lawless movement should be suppressed. Certainly, the building looked more like a military encampment than like an ordinary prison, with the armed sentinels pacing on the walls, and the musket-bearing guards gravely commanding the entrances!

Yet these measures had been taken only after the defenders of the law had faced difficulties of the most serious nature. That the condition of the city was well-nigh revolutionary is indicated by the fact that not only the ordinary citizens but even the militia had grown refractory. "The citizen soldiers that have been called out by the Mayor," writes a contemporary observer (Frank F. Fargo), "acted, if at all, with great reluctance, and if called upon to fire upon good citizens would probably have fired into the air rather than at persons with whom they sympathized." Worse still! on the sixteenth of May, only two days after the shooting of King, both companies of militia had refused further to guard the jail, and had disbanded and returned to civilian clothes.

As an indication of the strength of the popular feeling, the story is told of a Mrs. Hutchinson, the keeper of a boarding house near the jail. Asked by the officers to provide for some of the troops, she refused the opportunity of profit, but stated that her establishment was at the disposal of those who wished to re-take Casey. Thus did pro-Vigilance sentiment permeate the population!

But offsetting to a certain degree the force of the prevalent emotion, there was the fact that James King, by the unrestrained directness of his attacks, had aroused numerous personal enemies; and that these in many instances made common cause with the criminals and corruptionists. "It thus became apparent," states William T. Coleman, in the article already referred to, "that the committee had to prepare for more serious work than was anticipated, or by rights should have been forced upon them. James King of William was honest, brave, and terribly in earnest, but often rash. Unhappily, he had arrayed against him several classes of people. He had severely, though in the main justly, castigated that portion of the press that upheld or apologized for excess or irregularities in political affairs. He had aroused a Roman Catholic influence hostile to himself by ill-advised strictures on one of their clergy. He had invited the bitter animosity of a large portion of the Southern element by his denunciation of them as the unworthy chivalry who had captured and held or virtually controlled, for their own benefit, the offices of city and state. All of these elements, separately and combined, were inimical to King, who by his impetuous methods and reckless personalities had unfortunately and needlessly made himself many bitter personal enemies. Thus, the Committee was assailed as his champion by all these parties, when in fact it was not such, but merely the champion of justice and of right—the child of the stern necessities of the hour."

It was just when the winds and counter-winds were blowing the most threateningly that William T. Sherman, of later Civil War fame, was made major-general of militia by the Governor, and assumed command of the forces of "law and order." It was at about this time also that the Governor, finding matters drawing toward a climax, felt that the moment was ripe for his personal intervention, and so made possible an episode which, to express it mildly, was not the least curious among the many strange happenings that checkered the career of the Committee.

On the evening of Friday, the sixteenth, word was brought to Coleman that J. Neely Johnson, the chief executive of the State, was at the Continental Hotel and desired to see him at any place that might be designated.

Coleman thereupon at once repaired to the hotel, where he engaged in an interesting colloquy with the Governor. Asked what the Vigilance Committee wanted, he stated, "Peace— and, if possible, without a struggle. But, if need be, we will seek it even at the cost of war."

The Governor's next question was as to what the Vigilantes hoped to accomplish, and to this Coleman replied:

"Just what the Committee of 1851 accomplished: to see that the laws are executed and a few prominent criminals do not go unpunished; to drive some notoriously bad characters out of the state; to purify the moral and political atmosphere, and then disband."

"Now, Governor," declared Coleman, (according to his own subsequent statement), "you are called upon by the mayor and a class of people here to bring out the militia and try to put down this movement. I assure you it cannot be done, and if you attempt it, it will give you and us a great deal of trouble."

Nevertheless, Coleman was quite willing that the Governor

issue his proclamations and manifestos, in order to save his face and maintain the dignity of his office; but he demanded that the actual work be left to the Vigilance Committee. What they were attempting was, after all, a mere local reform! "We shall get through with it in a short time and quit, and quit gladly!" he promised.

At these words the Governor, coming over to Coleman, slapped him on the shoulder in a friendly fashion, and exclaimed, "Go to it, old boy! But get through as quickly as you can. Don't prolong it, because there is a terrible opposition and a terrible pressure."

Here we have a truly singular situation! J. Neely Johnson is the head of the State Government, the man pledged by his oath of office to uphold the laws and resist any assault upon them; yet he not only personally recognizes a private group acting in defiance of public authority, not only attempts to treat with the leader of that group, but pledges his passive support and even his encouragement to the insurrectionary movement!

This, however, was not to be the last of the Governor's vagaries. Perhaps it was that, being a politician, he had come to scorn such mere bourgeois virtues as consistency and respect for the sanctity of a promise; at all events, he was to accomplish a complete about-face with even more celerity than is usual with gentlemen of the political fraternity. Later that same evening, he was to seek another interview with Coleman; and, on this occasion, he was to assume a much more militant attitude.

Like a small boy emboldened by the presence of his big brother, the Governor seems to have taken courage from the fact that, during the second interview, he enjoyed the support of General Sherman, Mr. Garrison, and others. From the beginning, declares Coleman, the Governor's manner was much changed: he flung a number of questions at the President of the Vigilantes, as to his intentions, etc., just "as though he had not asked the same questions a few hours before."

Hence we find a scene of farce intruding in an act of serious drama! Coleman repeated his former assurances, as though he had not already made them sufficiently plain; repeated his statement that the Vigilance Committee was not organized as a mob, but as "government within a government," intended to combat certain abuses in the administration of justice. To all this the Governor listened, precisely as if he had not heard it already; but this time he did not respond by slapping Coleman on the shoulder and ejaculating, "Go to it, old boy!" Quite the contrary! His attitude now was that of the stern executive, whose prerogatives have been invaded, and who means to assert his authority.

"Let the regular officers handle this affair!" he said, in effect. "Cora and Casey will be tried by the courts, and I pledge myself to see that the trials are conducted swiftly, and that justice will be executed!"

It is not surprising if Coleman was reluctant to accept the pledge of a Governor who had already broken one promise that evening.

"The people," he replied, "no longer have any confidence in the officers, many of whom have been known to associate with the prisoners. No! the Committee shall go through with its work! and no power on earth shall stop it!"

In order to avoid all misunderstanding, Coleman called several members of the executive committee into the conference, and these heartily endorsed his position. The proposals of the Governor stood unanimously rejected!

One agreement, however, was reached—an agreement whose very possibility casts a queer but revealing light on the tangled relationships of the day. One would not expect the captain of a ship to treat with a mutinous crew, unless under the compulsion of an irresistible force; nor would one expect him, unless overpowered, to arrange to give his rebellious subordinates access to an essential part of the vessel. Yet Governor Johnson, although still not overwhelmed by the force of the Vigilantes, made a compact granting Coleman an important concession: ten or more Committeemen should be permitted to enter the jail as a guard, to supplement the state and county officers in insuring the safety of the prisoners. True, the Committee, in its turn, pledged itself not to take the jail or make any attack upon it without first withdrawing the guard and giving the Governor formal notice—but, even so, is it not extraordinary to find the Governor of a State entering thus into an arrangement with a private group acting *outside the law* in defiance of his own authority?

The agreement, as it happened, was to remain in force for less than two days. Before the sun had set the following Sunday, the Vigilantes were to emulate the example of the Committee of 1851, which, as we have seen, planned an attack upon the jail in order to regain possession of Whittaker and McKenzie. Well might Casey and Cora tremble in their cells! Well might they scrutinize the steel bars, and wish that they were a hundred times as strong! Well might they gaze at the dozens of guards designed to protect them, and pray that these be multiplied by a thousand! For, despite all the measures taken to shield them, they would be like beetles caught in an avalanche beneath the pressure of the armed multitudes of Vigilantes. The principal question, it appeared, was whether they would be taken without resistance, or only after a bloody combat.

Despite the fact that the Committee had been in existence for less than forty-eight hours, it now had most of the characteristics of a well established insurgent government. It had a complete and adequate internal organization; it was controlled by a well defined executive group; it commanded an imposing armed force, which it did not scruple to use; it was supported by the active services and the good-will of a majority of citizens; and it had as yet not encountered its match in the authority of the State. Moreover, it possessed that will, that determination and that initiative which elected politicians so frequently lack; it not only had power, but was not afraid to apply it; and once having chosen its course, it did not vacillate. Whatever one may think of the Vigilance Committee—of the desirability or the propriety of its conduct—one can at least compare the directness of its course most favorably with the worm-like convolutions of the typical political group.

Never was the uncompromising vigor of its methods better illustrated than in the case of the drive upon the jail, which was to make Sunday the eighteenth one of the most exciting days in the history of San Francisco. Upon the Saturday preceding, the plans had been laid with detailed thoroughness; the entire Vigilant soldiery, numbering about twenty-six hundred men, were ordered to be reviewed, so as to have them in readiness for Sunday's action; the movement of the troops was carefully pre-arranged, the route of each division toward the prison was precisely established, and the time of departure of each company determined exactly, so that all might converge simultaneously at their destination. Yet no commander of any division was to have any knowledge of the orders given his fellow commanders.

At nine thirty on Sunday morning, the Committee withdrew their guard from the jail, and sent a message to the Governor:

"To His Excellency J. Neely Johnson:—

"Dear Sir: We beg to advise you that we have withdrawn our guard from the county jail.

"By order of the Committee.   No. 33, Secretary."

This simple-sounding communication, of course, really implied far more than it said. Its meaning was as plain as though it had expressly stated:

"Dear Sir: We beg to advise you that we are planning an immediate attack upon the jail."

Now would have been the time for the Governor to call out the State forces to put down the impending assault. He had between two and three hours in which to act—and what did he do? Precisely what one would have expected—nothing!

It was at the noon hour that the Vigilance companies began their march. The main body, proceeding from the Committee headquarters westward along Sacramento Street toward Montgomery, made a glittering display, and the hundreds of steely blue bayonets stood out menacingly from amid the dark-clad, uniformed men. The day was a serene, sunlit one, when nature was at her loveliest, and when the gentle breezes blowing in from the bay and ocean seemed to breathe of peace and tranquillity; but there was something solemn and portentous beyond words in those armed, marching companies that moved forward with the grimness of some unspoken determination. As the troops advanced, dense bodies of spectators kept pace with them, not noisily, but with the awed manner of men who anticipate dread events; while the doors and windows along the way were packed with thick masses of the curious.

If one had stood among the thousands that watched from the heights of Telegraph and Russian Hills, one would have witnessed an astonishing and impressive sight. From many directions—along Montgomery Street, as well as along Kearny, Stockton and Dupont—one would have seen the marching companies, each moving as the part of a well coordinated plan, until all converged before the jail and took up their pre-as-signed stations with almost clock-like regularity. One would have observed contingents not only of infantry, but of artillery, and would have noted how the latter, establishing itself directly before the prison, planted a gun with its muzzle pointed at the front door of the building, loaded it with powder and ball, and lighted a match as if for instant action.

Within a few minutes, the jail had been completely surrounded by the armed detachments. And then it was that Marshal Doane, of the Vigilance forces, rode up to the prison door and presented the following message for the sheriff:

"David Scannell, Esq.:—

"Sir: You are hereby required to surrender forthwith the possession of the county jail now under your charge to the citizens who present this demand, and prevent the effusion of blood by instant compliance.

"By order of the   Committee of Vigilance."

Here was, truly, a hard situation for the sheriff! To submit would be, to say the least, ignominious and inconsistent with the duties of his office; to submit would be to deliver certain of the prisoners, including his friend Casey, to almost inevitable death at the hands of the Committee. Yet not to submit would be to face an attack in which he and his deputies, not to speak of the prisoners, might be blown from the face of the earth.

It was with a grave face, accordingly, that Sheriff Scannell approached Casey with the dread document from the Vigilantes. And Casey, struck by the concern in the officer's demeanor, was suddenly filled with terror.

"What!" he cried. "Are you going to give me up?"

The sheriff's grimness did not relax. "James," he said, "there are three thousand armed men coming for you, and I have not thirty supporters about the jail."

"Not thirty!" groaned Casey, all at once disillusioned in his visions of the brave friends who were to see him through safely. "Then do not peril life for me! I will go!"

But the next instant, drawing out a long knife which he had hitherto kept concealed, he swore, "I will never be taken from here alive!"

Nevertheless, in spite of his wild threats and flourishing blade, he was not the man to drive the cold steel into his own heart. After being assured by Committee members that he should be treated as a gentleman, and not be dragged through the streets in irons; after being promised a fair trial, in which he could summon witnesses, Casey laid aside his knife and permitted himself to be escorted away by members of the Committee.

When Coleman and his fellow Vigilantes appeared at the prison door with Casey in their midst, a cheer rose to the lips of the waiting multitude, and gradually grew in volume, until the hills would have echoed with the sound—had not Coleman, removing his hat and raising his hand, motioned for silence. And the applause, still but half-born, died on the lips of the watching thousands.

With eyes downcast, the prisoner was escorted to a carriage; and, entering, was driven away in company with Coleman and others. And meanwhile the strange silence of the city continued; a silence broken only by the crunch of wheels starting to roll away; a silence which, as one spectator (W. O. Ayers) declares, seemed as "something frightful, something unnatural, a silence that could be felt, like the darkness that fell upon the land of Egypt."

Accompanied by the main body of the Vigilance force, Casey was taken to the Committee rooms, and placed in a small cell, where he was relieved of his papers and a second knife.

Meanwhile a peremptory notice had been sent to the sheriff

that, within one hour, he must deliver the person of Charles Cora, the murderer of Richardson; and a large body of Vigilantes had remained behind to guard the jail. Upon the expiration of the hour, Scannell asked another thirty minutes, which were granted—and finally, after being assured that none of the other prisoners were desired, the sheriff yielded to the unavoidable, and Cora also was removed to the Committee rooms.

Now let both Cora and Casey pray for the recovery of James King, who was still hovering between life and death. For, unless the editor of the *Bulletin* survived, the two prisoners of the Vigilance Committee would follow him very swiftly into the Great Unknown.

CHAPTER XII

EXIT A HERO AND TWO VILLAINS

W HILE the Vigilance Committee was organizing, making its plans and launching its attacks, the unhappy cause of the whole movement still lingered on the borderline between two worlds.

From the beginning, grave fears had been expressed as to the chances of James King of William for recovery; yet at first hope had not been altogether abandoned, and certain reports issuing from the sick-bed had seemed to justify a degree of optimism. Never did a city hang more attentively on the bulletins regarding one of its citizens; every new announcement was awaited by eager crowds, and each indication of an improvement in the sufferer's condition was met with manifestations of delight. Thus, the anxious throngs showed every sign of relief when, on the sixteenth, it began to be thought that there was no serious danger and King, apparently improving throughout the morning, conversed freely and expressed an interest in all that was occurring. But by noon on that day his condition appeared less favorable, and from that time forth the tendency was downward, although it is said that on the following Sunday he was still well enough to be aware of the tramp of the Vigilant troops as they marched to the jail for Cora and Casey, and alert enough to inquire as to the meaning of the demonstration.

Disheartening words have been whispered as to those few days during which some hope was still entertained for King's life. It has been contended that he was the victim of improper medical methods; that the room where he lay was greatly overcrowded with his too-eager friends; that the multiplicity of physicians produced some unfortunate disagreements as to means of treatment; that the strain to which King was subjected when he should have had rest, and the tense and solemn atmosphere of the sick-room, and the change in medical attendants, were all contributory factors in producing a result that might have been avoided. Indeed, Dr. Beverly Cole, King's own physician, who withdrew from the case before its termination, went so far as to charge "gross malpractice," and to claim that a sponge inadvisedly left in the wound for several days was one cause of the fatal issue.

But at this late date it is useless to indulge in speculation or comment. It is sufficient to note that the physicians were in all probability stunned by the gravity of their responsibility; sufficient to remark that, had present-day medical methods been applied, James King of William might have continued to stir the City of San Francisco for many years more with his hammering editorials, and the subsequent history of California might have been considerably altered.

But fate was not to decide thus. Perhaps, in the eternal book of fortune, it was written that King must complete his life-work by suffering martyrdom. Perhaps, as Royce puts it, "It was expedient just then that one man should die for the people. . . . King's services had been so excellent that the gods seem to have held him worthy of an unspeakable honor; and they chose him as the man." At all events, it was his passing that gave the final and decisive impetus to the forces organized in opposition to the evils which he had combated so courageously.

Yet that he himself would have desired extreme measures is questionable, both in view of some of his previous published statements, and in the light of a remark which, according to the Reverend William Taylor, he made while on his deathbed. "If I die," he said, "I don't want them to kill Casey." Considering the grievous suffering which he had undergone at Casey's hands, this was indeed to manifest a spirit of Christ-like benevolence!

"Calm, patient, and self-possessed," says Taylor, was King until the morning of his departure. For almost a week he had lingered, sometimes with the hope of surviving, but gradually sinking toward the inescapable brink; while the prayers and entreaties of his friends, the agonies of his suffering family, the grief of an entire community and his own intense desire to live, were all unavailing to prevent Casey's bullet from fulfilling its original intention.

Yet, until the last, his death was not believed inevitable. Such was the uncertainty among his physicians that, although he had passed a most unsatisfactory night on the nineteenth and his condition was declared to be critical, at a little after noon on Tuesday the doctors maintained that he still had a chance to live. But at a quarter past one, James King of William breathed his last.

Immediately, as the sorrowful tidings were made public, the city went into mourning. The doleful tolling of the Monumental bell signalized the passing of a beloved soul; the stores of merchants and the offices of lawyers were instantly closed; festoons of crêpe appeared at the doors of many private residences, and badges of mourning were placed at the entrances and windows of offices; members of the Vigilance Committee and other citizens paced the streets with strips of black on their left arms; and, during the whole afternoon the suspension of business continued, and one could hardly have found even a restaurant or a saloon which was not closed to the public and did not display the insignia of grief. "Friends met, but spoke not," reports the contemporary journalist, Frank F. Fargo, "and the sober, downcast look at once expressed the feelings of a sorrowing heart. Truly the people went mourning about the streets, and sadness rested upon the countenances of a whole community."

Even the ships in the harbor wore their flags at half-mast; while the members of the Howard Engine Company hung the following inscription between the *Bulletin* office and the Montgomery Block, where King had died:

"The great, the good one is dead. Who will not mourn?"

Among those who, many years later, recalled that sad day, was Joseph L. King, one of the six children of the slain man. Writing in old age on the events of his childhood, he tells us (in the *Overland Monthly* for December, 1916) that during the illness of the father, "We children were left at home in charge of a servant, my mother being able to pay her home only a hurried visit each day. It was deemed best that we should attend school as usual. . . . On Tuesday, the twentieth of May, I, a boy of ten, was studying in my seat at school. . . . Suddenly, at half past one, a bell tolled, and soon numerous bells were tolling throughout the city."

Young Joseph was then called to the desk and excused from school; but the teacher would not positively answer his questions. "I was told that my father was very low, but the continual tolling of the bells . . . soon forced the knowledge upon me that I was fatherless."

Later that afternoon, a melancholy file of thousands of citizens trooped slowly past the spot where lay the remains of the man who had died for them, to gaze their last upon the immobile, unresponsive face. It is safe to say that never in life had James King been such a center of interest as now when only his empty shell was left.

And when, two days later, he was escorted to his last resting place in the fog-swept, barren environs of Lone Mountain, half the city paid him honor. "No demonstration," reports the *Bulletin* of May 23, "was ever made in California as a tribute of respect and esteem to a private individual more general and imposing than was that which took place yesterday in honor of James King of William." During the morning, cloths of black appeared even on many business houses and private dwellings which had not previously displayed crêpe; the flags of the city were at half mast, as were those of the ships in the harbor; and numerous meetings of various groups and societies took place, with a view to participating in the ceremonies of the afternoon. At the overcrowded Unitarian Church, where the bier was placed before the altar, the audience was reduced to tears; and the Reverend Mr. Cutler delivered an address calculated deeply to stir the already overwrought emotions of his hearers:

"We are assembled, friends and fellow citizens, to pay our last honors to the dead. All around us we behold an unaccustomed spectacle. On all sides are hung the tokens of grief— everywhere do we see some memento of mortality. These streets, with their signs and emblems of woe—the vast throng of citizens who pour along the sidewalks to see and join in the solemn procession; this dense crowd which now fills this place of God's worship, and the sadness upon every countenance, all testify that a public calamity has come. Such an unusual demonstration of mourning shows that the sorrow is deep and universal. . . . And what is it, fellow citizens, that has produced this warm and widespread sympathy and respect thus manifested toward the deceased? It was, I reply, undoubtedly in the first place, the character of the man; in the second place, the circumstances of his death; and in the third place, the brief but efficient work he accomplished as a fearless conductor of a public journal. A man has fallen among us—a man, in the best sense of that great word."

After proceeding to state that "manliness and integrity of character were his distinguishing traits," the speaker declared that King had "died a martyr to the cause of public virtue and reform," a martyr to the "progress of society". "The prophets of humanity," he remarked, "are first stoned by those to whom they are sent, and their monuments are reared over their ashes and their sepulchers are garnished. Over the bones of the prophets, heroes, saints and martyrs, the world's progress has ever gone."

Following the sermon, in which the preacher eloquently called attention to the "vacant pew, draped in black," the services dragged on to their solemn end, and then the funeral procession started on its way to Lone Mountain. Despite the request of King's family that all unnecessary display be avoided, the spectacle was such as San Francisco had not previously witnessed; the demonstrations of mourning and respect were as great as though a President or an Emperor rather than a mere private citizen had been felled by the assassin's bullet. The number of persons in the procession has been estimated at five or six thousand; all along the line of march, the streets were crowded with solid ranks of spectators, and women and children stood watching from the balconies of every house.

The procession is thus described in the *Bulletin* of the twenty-third:

"As it defiled solemnly along Washington and Montgomery streets, its ranks were rapidly augmented by horsemen, footmen, and carriages, until there seemed to be no end to the mournful cortege. . . . Certainly not less than twenty-five thousand persons witnessed the scene and participated in the honors paid to the dead. It is impossible to say with any certainty how long the procession really was. It must have extended greatly over a mile, and possibly . . . reached a mile and a half. Nor was it composed of any one class of our fellow citizens, or of any one nation. Every trade, avocation and profession was represented, and natives of almost every clime were marching in its ranks. Silently, thoughtfully, mournfully, they walked behind the corpse—strangers, most of them to his person while living, but friends of the principles he advocated, and mourners now at his funeral. Even the lowly African was there, trudging along with tearful eyes and saddened heart, for he remembered that Mr. King when alive pleaded most eloquently for all who were oppressed, poverty-stricken and unfortunate."

But let us leave the procession as it follows the plumed hearse westward toward the base of Lone Mountain. Let us bid farewell to James King as his mortal remains are deposited within the shadow of that tall, round, dismal hill of sand, with its scraggly desert-like vegetation beaten by continual winds from the sea. Let us leave him there to the eternal solitude; let us leave him, knowing that no more than the memory of him is there, but that his restless spirit is still abroad, and is powerfully to move the life of that San Francisco for which he fought and died.

While the solemn procession wound on its way, other momentous events were occurring. With a curious and ironic timeliness, the slayer of King was reaping the grim penalty of his crime at the very hour when the body of his victim was being conveyed to rest. The trials of both Casey and Cora—by a strange coincidence—had been in progress when the tolling of the bells had announced the passing· of the soul of King; and Casey, upon learning how well he had accomplished his purpose, had trembled violently, and his face had gone suddenly white. Could he have brought King back to life at the cost of his right arm, would he not have done so, and gladly?

For was it only the death-knell of the editor of the *Bulletin* that Casey heard in the long-repeated, dismal pealing of the bells?

Yet both he and Cora were allowed the benefit of a trial— a trial stripped, it is true, of the protection of legal formalities, but one in which witnesses could be called and evidence given, and in which each defendant might enjoy the services of an attorney of his own selection. But despite all the evident efforts of the Committee at justice, the prisoners were denied the advantages of outside counsel; their advocates must be chosen from among the members of the Vigilance Committee —in other words, must be selected from among those who, by their very enrollment with the Vigilantes, had indicated a hostile attitude of mind. One may admit that the Committee members were filled with a great and not wholly unjustified loathing of lawyers, whose methods of chicanery and indirection had been responsible for many a miscarriage of justice; and one may acknowledge that they had sincerely pledged themselves to give a fair and honest verdict; nevertheless, it is impossible to see how men can be fair simply because they vow to be so, or how justice can be administered by a self-constituted body of men that refuse to entertain the pleas of any outside power.

But whatever may be said on these points, it is certain that the crime of Casey had been such that no unbiased court of law could have hesitated about its decision; while Cora, despite some disagreements in the testimony (presumably due to hired witnesses) does not seem to have had any legitimate excuse of self-defense in his slaying of Richardson. The trial, in any event, was conducted in an orderly and business-like fashion, and not in the passionate manner of the mob; the evidence on most points was explicit, the testimony was taken down in writing, and from the beginning, the termination in both cases seemed unavoidable: the verdict GUILTY; the penalty, DEATH by hanging.

At first it had been the Committee's intention to defer the executions until Friday, the twenty-third; but, partly owing to reports that an attempt would be made to rescue the prisoners during King's obsequies, it was decided to bring Cora and Casey to their fate at the very time when the funeral was in progress. Despite the large crowd taking its way toward Lone Mountain, the streets in the vicinity of the Committee rooms, on the afternoon of the twenty-second, were jammed with people, and had to be cleared by the Vigilance soldiers, whose gleaming bayonets gave the scene a grim and war-like aspect. Outside of the two-story granite building where the Committee made its headquarters, workmen were seen to busy themselves at about one o'clock, and it was not long before platforms had been extended from the windows of the upper floor —platforms sustained by cords and equipped with a rope of an ominous, telltale nature.

Now the prisoners, dressed in their ordinary clothes but with pinioned arms, appeared at the windows, looking down upon the crowd that had come to witness their last struggles. Of the two, Cora was the more composed; little sign of emotion was detected in this gambler who was so soon to make his last play. A short while before—such are the freaks and whimsies of human conduct—he had been united in marriage to Belle Cora, the prostitute who remained devoted to him until the end; for, without the sanctification of an earthly ceremony, the priest had refused absolution to his soul.

As for Casey—he presented a truly pitiable figure. Despite his vicious behavior, one cannot help feeling concern for this poor wretch, buffeted by torrents of emotion and cursed by his own evil spirit. Restlessly he had paced the floor on the last night of his life. "Oh, my God!" he had exclaimed. "Has it come to this? Must I be hung like a dog?" And now, when the ultimate moment had arrived, he appeared on the platform white-faced and with bloodshot eyes, and was permitted to say a few last words before taking leave of this world. His speech, made up of wild and redundant exclamations, was in part as follows:

"Gentlemen: I hope this will be forever engraved on your minds and on your hearts. I am no murderer. Let no man call me a murderer, or an assassin. Let not the community pronounce me a murderer. My faults are the result of my early education. When I was reared, I was taught to fight, and to resent wrong was my province. . . . I have an aged mother, and let her not hear me called a murderer or an assassin. I have always resented wrong, and I have done it now. Oh! my poor mother, my poor mother! How her heart will bleed at this news! It is her pain I feel now. This will wring her heart; but she will not believe me a murderer. . . . Oh! my mother, God bless you. Gentlemen, I pardon you, as I hope God will forgive me, amen."

*   *   *

But let us draw a veil across this painful scene. Without a word, Cora went to meet his fate—and who knows whether his secret sufferings were not greater than those of the more voluble Casey? And simultaneously the slayer of King was swung to his doom—and thereby the feelings of an outraged community were soothed, and the idea was spread abroad that the practice of murder was no longer so safe as of yore.

While Casey's body was being borne to its grave, with an escort of eighty-four carriages, eighty horsemen, and four hundred followers on foot, a mere six hacks made up the funeral procession of his less notorious fellow criminal, Cora. Meantime, newspapers were still filled with comments on the stirring events of the twenty-second and the preceding days, and orators still made them the theme of their discourses; and, amid the eulogies of King, the execution of his assassin by the Vigilance Committee was relegated to a position of secondary importance.

Not only in San Francisco, but throughout the State, the passing of King had been the signal for general mourning. In scores of scattered towns, the bells tolled a dismal dirge when the news arrived that the editor of the *Bulletin* was no more; in scores of scattered towns, business had been suspended, homes and offices were decked with crêpe, and melancholy assemblages met in token of respect for the departed. Funeral rites were performed in Oakland, in Sacramento, in Stockton, in Marysville, in Sonora, and in numerous other towns; a message was sent by the citizens of Coloma to the San Francisco Vigilance Committee, "If you need help, let the sea speak to the mountains"; and meanwhile one-dollar subscriptions were taken at many points for the benefit of the family of the slain editor.

Page after page might be filled with quotations from the speeches and sermons made in memory of James King; but, as typical of the best of them, in their tendency to arouse public opinion against the evils of society, I shall confine myself to an excerpt from the address delivered by the Reverend Walter Frear of Iowa Hill on May 25, 1856:

"What means this wave of deep emotion that moves through our land with ocean force . . . calm and still and powerful as the rising tide?

"It has come to light that our editors are in jeopardy, that they cannot attack knavery and vice without the risk of being shot down in the streets like dogs. . . . A spell has been cast upon the spirit of freedom. An incubus, a hideous nightmare, has been resting upon the sentinels of public virtue. It is *this* that gives the death of James King of Wm. its significance.

"If James King of Wm., by his life, has slain his thousands, we may say, as it was said long ago of Saul and David, that by his death he has slain his tens of thousands."

Many of the tributes paid to King were of a more personal nature, and not a few were embodied in letters and poems sent to the newspapers. Even those papers which had opposed King during his life were compelled, by the force of public opinion, to eulogize him in their editorials; while his own paper, the *Bulletin*, was but echoing the general view when it proclaimed, on May twenty-first:

"In him, the Press has lost its noblest ornament, society its greatest benefactor, education its wisest guide, the people their firmest friend. Farewell, thou soul of honor!"

By no means all of the tributes to King were of a conventional nature; here and there, as one glances over the newspaper files of that remote date, one will find something of a singularly revealing nature. To my mind, the following letter, which appeared in the *Bulletin* for May 24, and which had been left at the office the day before "by a pretty and modest young lady of about fifteen years of age," is more eloquent than many a more formal testimonial, as indicating the human qualities of the man, and his interest in children:

"Mr. Editor:—Ever since Mr. King first started the *Bulletin*, which my Father takes, I have considered it one of my greatest luxuries, on returning from school, to read it and to think over its contents. I never heard Mr. King speak, but I have seen him, and his countenance did not belie his noble character.

"I hope you will receive this 'voice from the children' in whom, while living, he took such an interest. Even they can appreciate the integrity of the character of James King of Wm."

One might go on to describe numerous other tributes—such as, for example, the resolution passed by representatives of the press, to the effect "That in the assassination and death of James King of Wm., a blow has been struck at society, the virtue of the citizen, and all good government." But it would be as futile as it would be repetitious to enumerate all the tokens of esteem and honor that were laid at the feet of the fallen hero. Enough has already been said to show that the death of princes might be greeted with far less of a popular demonstration, and certainly with a much less sincere manifestation of grief, than attended the passing of this private citizen who in a few short months had won his way into the hearts of his fellow men. Truly, "the pen is mightier than the sword"! For it was with the pen alone that James King had conquered; it was with the pen alone that he had driven his rivals to the wall, pummeled and routed the forces of organized iniquity, and lit such a flame of righteous indignation that when he fell it was as a warrior in a triumphant cause, as a commander who by the example of his death has rallied his troops to more noble and more devoted effort.

CHAPTER XIII

A WEB OF NEW TROUBLES

I<small>T</small> might have been expected that, with the dispatching of the two most notorious villains, the Vigilance organization would disband and leave the treatment of crime to the local and State authorities.

Such, however, was not to be the case. It was not considered desirable by Coleman and his followers to dissolve, in view of the fact that they had merely scraped the surface of the vast mound of evil and corruption; and it did not prove practicable or even possible, such was the unexpected opposition they met from the officers of the law—opposition that at times threatened to produce nothing less than civil warfare.

That Casey and Cora were out of the way meant that there were two criminals less to be dealt with—but it did not mean that others as bad were not left. As a matter of fact, a whole nest of rowdies, thieves and ballot-stuffers remained, not to speak of one or two offenders of an even more odious stripe; and it is seriously to be questioned whether the two executed men were quite the lowest or the worst of the scoundrels that infested the city. They merely happened to be apprehended in particularly aggravating crimes at a particularly crucial mo, ment—and for that reason they suffered the penalty which some of their less unlucky confreres escaped.

There was, for example, the case of Rodman M. Backus, a man who, upon a word from his lover of the demi-monde, pursued and shot to death a defenseless stranger. This crime was, if anything, more cowardly and reprehensible than that of Cora—yet Backus had been sentenced to a mere two and a half years for *manslaughter,* and had appealed the case to the Supreme Court, with an excellent chance of being set at liberty.

But suddenly the Vigilance Committee appeared upon the scene, and the appeal to the Supreme Court ceased to have any practical importance—for it was all too likely that, while the slayer's hearing was pending, the Committee would settle the matter once and for all by means of a rope. So Backus was glad, exceedingly glad, to be able to compromise by withdrawing his appeal, and to hasten across the bay to the shelter of the firm walls of San Quentin.

There were, likewise, the cases of Peter Wightman and of Edward McGowan, who were suspected of having plotted the death of James King of William, and who were wanted by the Committee on a charge of murder. Both of them fled, and were hunted remorselessly; while McGowan, coming down from the dignity of the bench, hid himself for months among distant thickets and in the chaparral of wild and lonely canyons . . . until, after the better part of a year, he deemed it safe to make his reappearance. Then, securing a change of venue so that his case might be heard at Napa City, which made a specialty of granting acquittals, somewhat as Reno now does of issuing divorces, he went through the travesty of a trial, and was vindicated to his own satisfaction—although he subsequently sought further vindication by means of a book, the nature of which may be judged from its title: *Narrative of Edward McGowan, including a full account of the Author's Adventures and Perils, while persecuted by the San Francisco Vigilance Committee of 1856.*

Unlike McGowan, Wightman and Backus, most of the rascals sought by the Vigilance Committee were not wanted on a charge of murder. And, acting with more leniency than the Committee of 1851, which, as we will recall, executed several men not proved to be murderers, the Vigilantes refused to exact the death-penalty except for the deliberate taking of human life. But what other penalty could it demand? It could not sentence the offenders to prison, where many of them doubtless deserved to be; for there was no permanent prison at its disposal; nor could it remain perpetually at guard over the culprits. Again, it did not desire to invoke such a brutal and obsolescent penalty as flogging—a penalty which, moreover, would not have solved the problem of clearing San Francisco of its human refuse. The course that it followed, therefore, was to deport the undesirables. It was willing to pay for their passage—often with first-class accommodations, and to destinations of their own choice—but it wished to be certain that they would no longer haunt the environs of San Francisco. Moreover, it had daguerrotypes taken of the rogues, so that their likenesses might be distributed among police departments in various parts of the world. As to the actual policy of deportation—this may have been a little like emptying one's refuse in one's neighbor's back yard; but doubtless the members of the Committee felt that, since the ruffians had all come from elsewhere, it was not unjust that they be sent back whence they came.

And so some of the most corrupt among the corrupt politicians, the most vicious among the shufflers of elections, the most arrogant among the bullies who had hitherto managed public affairs as a private "racket," were seen on the decks of outward bound steamers. They who had seemed beyond the law, they who had appeared secure in careers of unblushing fraud, were now all at once hurled into exile from the city they had intimidated and plundered. Billy Carr, Woolly Kearny, Charles P. Doane, Martin Gallagher, Alexander Purple—why go through the whole list, except to say that it included drunkards, blackmailers, browbeating politicians and manipulators of elections—all those who, by the power of organized ruffianry, corruption and terrorism, had polluted the life of the city at its very source? Within one month after the death of King, seventeen of the gang he had most bitterly opposed had been shipped to various points, including Panama and the Hawaiian Islands. And were the sentences in any case unjust? Not if we can accept the word of Billy Mulligan, the one-time friend of Casey, and guardian of the county jail. Bancroft tells us that, before his departure on the *Golden Age,* on which he had been given passage without having any choice in the matter, Mulligan spoke as follows to one of the guard:

"I know that my punishment is just. I deserve it, and more. I find no fault with the Committee. They are all respectable gentlemen, and are acting rightly, and they ought not to stop with what they have done. There are a hundred others as bad as I, that deserve the same treatment. There is not an officer in the city or county of San Francisco who is legally elected. They are all thieves from the mayor down, and should be driven from office. I shall hope to hear that they have all been made to resign."

But perhaps these words should be taken with just a grain of salt; or it may have been that Mulligan's resentment was to grow with time and distance. For the fact remains that he did not act as though he considered his punishment to be just; after reaching New York, he made a specialty of loitering about hotel entrances, assaulting Californians whom he recognized as being of Vigilance persuasion.

While Mulligan and all his guild of grafting politicians were being swept out of California, the Committee followed the precedent of its predecessor of 1851 in refusing to assume jurisdiction in the case of crimes of passion. Thus when two friends, sitting in the reading room of the Rassette House, fell into a dispute over the doctrine of hell, and ended with a practical demonstration by means of knives, the Executive Committee decided that the case was one for the regular courts, and not for the Vigilantes. Thus, also, the Committee paid no heed to

THE SURRENDER OF CASEY AND CORA

the thousands of letters that were received, charging Bill Jones or Ted Smith or Pete Brown with any one of a large variety of misdemeanors; for, even if the accusations were justified, it was not within the Committee's province to pass upon matters mainly affecting private individuals.

In the course of rounding up the political ruffians, the Committee ran face to face with a tragedy it had not intended, and which for a time caused considerable consternation. Among the rogues under arrest and presumably awaiting deportation, was one Yankee Sullivan, an ex-pugilist and a man of no little value to the ballot-stuffers, since, by his own confession, he had played an active part in selling elections for the benefit of the Caseys and the Mulligans. Sullivan, it appears, was a man with whom alcoholic abstinence did not agree; he normally lived in a state not far from drunkenness, and from fifty to eighty drinks a day was declared to be his usual ration. Hence, when arrested by the Committee and reduced to slaking his thirst with water, he fell into a morose and depressed condition. It is hard to say how much the denial of his ordinary indulgence had to do with his unhappy end; but, at all events, we know that his mind was filled with morbid imaginings, and that, on awakening on the morning of May thirty-first, he told the guard of a ghastly dream which he had just undergone, a nightmare in which he saw himself condemned to die, his arms pinioned, his person seized and borne to the Committee window, where the fatal noose was adjusted about his neck, and, to the accompaniment of the hoots and derision of the mob, the trap was sprung and he was launched into the agonies of strangulation. This dream must have been singularly vivid; for Sullivan was in an intense state of excitement, and was not pacified by the guard's assurance that he stood in no danger of hanging. So disturbed was he, indeed, that an hour or two later, when the attendant came in with breakfast, the prisoner was lying in his own blood—the victim of a suicidal impulse.

The members of the Vigilance Committee were naturally not a little distressed by this event, and resolved thenceforth to allow all prisoners their usual alcoholic ration. And meanwhile the enemies of Vigilance attempted to make capital of the tragedy by proclaiming—without adducing any evidence—that Sullivan was not a suicide at all, but had been murdered.

At about this time, troubles with far more serious potentialities began to confront the Committee. J. Neely Johnson, the Governor of the State, had suddenly decided upon a course of action—and one that contrasted strangely with the vacillation and uncertainty of his earlier attitude. All at once he seems to have made the discovery that it was his duty, as Chief Executive, to rid the State of the lawless group that had flouted his authority. And he was prepared to take any measures—even steps that would incur civil warfare, and that might make a bonfire of the most populous city in the State. So, at least, one may judge from the order which he issued on June 2 to William T. Sherman, then major-general in command of the second division of California militia:

"Sir: Information having been received by me that an armed body of men is now organized in the city and county of San Francisco, in this state, in violation of the law, especially by preventing the service of a writ of *habeas corpus* duly issued, and is threatening other acts of violence and rebellion against the constitution and laws of this state. You are therefore commanded to call upon such number as you may deem necessary of the enrolled militia, or those subject to military duty; also, upon all of the volunteer or independent companies of the militia. . . ."

The writ of *habeas corpus,* referred to above, had been issued shortly before, for the person of William (alias "Billy") Mulli-

gan; but the Committee, following the methods of the organization of 1851, had paid no heed to the writ, merely taking the
precaution of removing the prisoner from the building before
permitting the authorities to conduct a search.

At the time that the Governor issued his order, Sherman was
by no means reluctant to act. Just what his motives were, it is
difficult to say, either from a reading of his *Memoirs* or from a
survey of his actions; doubtless he did sincerely oppose the
Vigilance Committee, as an illegal organization; but the extreme measures he was willing to take, in initiating actual warfare against an entire city, indicate that his was the attitude of
the typical military mind: to fight without questioning why;
to strike out regardless of consequences to the enemy; to prevail by superior force, and leave fine questions of right and
wrong to the dialectitians. Otherwise, how explain his statement (*Memoirs,* Volume I) that "Some of the best men of
the 'Vigilantes' came to me and remonstrated, saying that collision would surely result; that it would be terrible, etc. All I
could say in reply was, that it was for them to get out of the
way." And how account for his plan to secure arms from
John E. Wool, commander of the military department of California? and to borrow a vessel from Captain D. G. Farragut,
head of the Mare Island Navy Yard? and, having enrolled
volunteers, to proceed to San Francisco, take charge of the
thirty-two-pound gun battery at the marine hospital at Rincon
Point, order the Vigilance Committee to disband, and, if refused obedience, to open fire upon the city? Undoubtedly,
from the sheerly military point of view, this scheme looked
attractive enough; and if it should result in the spilling of some
innocent blood, and even in the wreckage of a city, what true
warrior could give time or thought to such minor considerations?

And so the plans of the military party proceeded. Sherman

saw General Wool, and claimed to have received a promise of the requested arms (a promise afterwards vigorously denied by Wool); and measures were taken that, if endorsed by any considerable proportion of the citizenry, could only have resulted in aligning one half of the State against the other. In keeping with the Governor's message, Sherman issued a general order, in the course of which he said:

"All citizens of San Francisco county, between the ages of eighteen and forty-five years, not members of regularly enrolled volunteer or fire companies of the city, or not otherwise exempt from military duty, are hereby commanded to enroll themselves into companies of from fifty to one hundred men."

And on the following day the Governor, as if to drive a further wedge between the two opposing factions, published a proclamation, of which the essence follows:

"Now therefore I, Neely Johnson, Governor of the State of California . . . do hereby declare the county of San Francisco in a state of insurrection, also all persons subject to military duty within said county, to report themselves for duty immediately to Major-general Wm. T. Sherman. . . . I furthermore order and direct that all associations, combinations or organizations whatsoever, existing in said county of San Francisco or elsewhere in this state, in opposition to or in violation of the laws thereof, more particularly the association known as the Vigilance Committee of San Francisco, do disband, and each and every individual thereof yield obedience to the constitution and laws of the state, the writs and processes of the courts, and all legal orders, of the offices of this state, and of the county of San Francisco."

Whatever else this proclamation may have done, it drew the line sharply. On one side it placed the Governor, the law-courts, and the officers of county and state; and on the other side, as rebels, outlaws, and violators of the peace, it placed the members of the Vigilance Committee. Moreover, it called for a test that could not but be decisive, a test that, far more thoroughly than any election, would register the views of the people. For if a majority sympathized with the Governor and the established authorities, then there would be such a response to his call that the Vigilance Committee would be overwhelmed by the sheer weight of numbers; but if, on the other hand, the opinions of the Committee represented the sentiments of the masses, then the Governor would be merely as one who shouts on a lonely eminence to command the winds. It is, accordingly, of the utmost interest to note the results of his proclamation and General Sherman's orders.

One indication of the response to the appeals of Johnson and Sherman is to be seen in the action of the National Guard, which, at a meeting held at their armory on the evening of June tenth, passed the following resolutions:

"That in consequence of our arms having been taken from us by the Adjutant-General of the State, this corps do now disband; preferring this course to that of becoming the slaughterers of our fellow citizens.

"That this corps do now re-organize, under the name of Independent National Guard, holding ourselves subject only to such rules and regulations, in sustaining the cardinal interests of the community, as our best judgments may dictate—hereby repudiating all connection with the present state authorities."

The Governor's edict, owing to the late day at which it came, was the source of considerable laughter among citizens throughout the State; while General Sherman's order was taken so far from seriously that, on the first day, only about seventy-five men enlisted. And these, according to the *Alta California,* which gives their names and records, were mostly the rogues and ruffians of the city—which leads the editor of that paper to severe censure:

"What does Major-General Sherman wish to do? Is it his wish to bring the army of ballot box stuffers and rowdies which he may raise, in collision with the decent, respectable citizens of San Francisco? Is the military glory which he might attain, by leading a horde of villains against the citizens, sufficient to compensate for the execution which he will justly receive?"

The opposition of the Governor seems, if anything, to have strengthened the Vigilantes, who received much sympathy and numbers of fresh recruits. So many were the new enlistments, in fact, that by Friday June the sixth the Vigilant forces contained about six thousand fighting men. Meanwhile their opponents continued to enroll new sympathizers, and on the sixth (if we are to accept their own statement) they had about three thousand supporters. But apparently we cannot accept their statement; for we are told by Bancroft that, "on searching the facts in the case," he has been unable to find more than about six hundred men. This is not widely at variance with the assertions of Sherman, who claimed only eight hundred— and therefore we cannot but conclude that the Governor and his party were vastly outnumbered.

Nevertheless, this must not be taken to mean that the danger was not acute. A party of six or eight hundred men, equipped with arms and ammunition, would provide formidable opposition to the Vigilantes; indeed, any conflict with such a band might prove disastrous, staining the streets of the city red and perhaps laying waste a large part of the town.

This peril was clearly recognized by Coleman and his associates; but, having reached a point at which they could not retreat without surrendering the citadel to the forces of corruption, they had no choice except to go on in the face of all risks. Hence their organization, which from the beginning had assumed a military aspect, began to bristle with an even more pronounced martial air; and preparations commenced to be made as if for a siege.

Fort Vigilance, the Fort Gunnybags already mentioned, was accordingly strengthened in every way possible. New guns, including a thirty-two pounder, were secured to defend the premises; two cases of muskets, discovered in the cellar of a saloon, were appropriated for the Committee's use; the numerous cannon were planted behind ramparts of sand-bags, in readiness to guard all approaches; sentinels were posted for unintermittent duty; while, in order to avert utter disaster even in the event of the capture of their headquarters, the Committee ordered a great part of their arms to be removed from the premises and placed in the hands of members and in private depositories.

But not only by means of arms did the Committee seek to defend itself. It was able to fight with the pen as well; its manifesto "To the People of California," issued on June ninth, is an eloquent exposition of its aims. Although this pronouncement is much too long to quote in its entirety, one or two brief excerpts will give an idea of its nature. It begins by stating that,

"The Committee of Vigilance, placed in the position they now occupy by the voice and countenance of the vast majority of their fellow-citizens, as executors of their will, desire to define the necessity which has forced this people into their present organization."

After declaring that "Great public emergencies demand

prompt and vigorous remedies," it enumerates some of the evils against which it has been fighting: the pollution of government at its source, the fraudulent ballots deposited at midnight, the ballots nullified "by false counts of judges and inspectors at noon-day," the "organized gangs of bad men, of all political parties," who parceled out offices among themselves, the "bullies and professional fighters" who destroyed tally-lists by force, the stuffed ballot-boxes, the felons from other lands and states that controlled public funds and property, and "often amassed sudden fortunes without having done an honest day's work with head or hands." The tampering with jury-boxes, the shielding of murderers in manipulated trials, and the shooting down of unoffending citizens on the streets, are all mentioned, leading to the enunciation of the Committee's central position:

"Embodied in the principles of republican government are the truths that the majority should rule, and that when corrupt officials, who have fraudulently seized the reins of authority, designedly thwart the execution of the law and avert punishment from the notoriously guilty, the power they usurp reverts back to the people from whom it was wrested."

The document goes on to state that, "We have no friends to reward, no enemies to punish, no private ends to accomplish. Our single heartfelt aim is the public good; the purging, from our community, of those abandoned characters whose actions have been evil continually."

There follows a passage in which the Committee asserts the right of the public to "withdraw from corrupt and unfaithful servants the authority they have used to thwart the ends of justice." And the message closes on a vigorous note:

"We have spared and shall spare no effort to avoid bloodshed or civil war; but undeterred by threats or opposing or.-ganizations, shall continue peaceably if we can, forcibly if we must, this work of reform, to which we have pledged our lives, our fortunes, and our sacred honor. Our labors have been arduous, our deliberations have been cautious, our determinations firm, our counsels prudent, our motives pure; and while regretting the imperious necessity which called us into action, we are anxious that this necessity should exist no longer; and when our labors shall have been accomplished, when the community shall have been freed from the evils it has so long endured; when we have insured to our citizens an honest and vigorous protection of their rights, then the Committee of Vigilance will find great pleasure in resigning their power into the hands of the people, from whom it was received."

Well might the spirit of James King of William, as it looked down from the heights of some less troubled domain, rejoice to hear these words! Well might it find consolation for its sufferings! since the warmth and the animation and the determined purpose of the martyred editor were still alive, were still speaking to the people of the State, and still promised to exercise a potent influence for good.

CHAPTER XIV

FURTHER SNARLS AND ENTANGLEMENTS

Rocky and tempestuous was to be the road followed both by the Vigilantes and by their opponents of the "law and order" party. Innumerable unforeseen obstacles were to be confronted, innumerable unexpected paths to be taken; and if, amid the imbroglio, the Committee seemed to be emerging victorious, their very triumph was to involve them in a new and unpredictable difficulty, which was to prove embarrassing if not perilous, and was to prolong their deliberations far beyond the date originally contemplated.

At the time of the Governor's proclamation there were still some good citizens who, not having taken sides with either faction, believed in the possibility of an amicable settlement. A group of such men, all of them respectable and responsible individuals, arranged for a conference with the Governor at Benicia on the evening of Saturday, June seventh; and the results were such as not to speak well for the chief executive's tact, nor for his independence of judgment. The delegation of citizens was antagonized, in the first place, by being compelled to present their application for an interview formally in writing; they were further antagonized by being obliged to stand during the conference, when the Governor sat puffing at a cigar, with his feet slanted above his head; while his adviser, Judge Terry, reposed with his feet on an even higher plane, and with his hat perched nonchalantly on his head and half covering his eyes. But, most of all, the Committee was antagonized by the Governor's reply, which, according to General Sherman (also a witness at the meeting) "was scratched, altered and amended, to suit the notions of his counselors," and which stated the pious hope that the "unhappy difficulties" would soon be over, but went on to assert that "if unhappily a collision occurs, and injury to life or property result, the responsibility must rest on those who disregard the authority of the State."

Incensed at their treatment by the Governor, and at the failure of their efforts at conciliation, the citizens returned to San Francisco, where they called a mass meeting, to be held on the following Saturday, June fourteenth. This, although not under the official charge of the Vigilance Committee, turned out to be a pro-Vigilance rally, and went far toward enlisting many still-hesitant citizens on the side of the Vigilantes. The affair was made into a gala occasion; little if any business was conducted on the appointed day; a crowd, including many women and estimated to number about fifteen thousand, gathered in front of the Oriental Hotel, and jammed the open spaces and the windows and balconies of all buildings in the vicinity.

Promptly at twelve o'clock, Colonel Bailie Peyton assumed the chair, and made a Vigilance speech, in which he reviewed some of the evils of the day; reminded his hearers that "people are afraid to go to the polls, for their lives are in danger"; and stated that "Every man in the community read his fate in that of Mr. King. If he could be shot down with impunity, who among us was safe?" Maintaining that the Committee would not have arisen "without good and sufficient cause," he attacked the Governor's proclamation; declared that the chief executive was "amiable and kind-hearted," but had "unfortunately listened to bad advice;" and suggested that "were he now to consult his own feelings, he would withdraw the proclamation."

Prolonged ovations greeted Peyton's speech; and when the cheering had died down, a resolution was passed wherein the meeting proclaimed "the fullest confidence" in "the people's organization known as the Committee of Vigilance of San Francisco and in their ability and determination to maintain the common safety." A further resolution called for contributions to a "Safety Fund" to be held subject to the orders of the Chairman of the Vigilance Committee; and after the unanimous passage of this and the other recommendations, another pro-Vigilance speech was made; following which the chairman, Colonel Peyton, produced a sensation by holding up to view the double back-action ballot box, recently discovered by the Committee.

"I beg to introduce to you the harp of a thousand strings," he said. "I am sorry that I cannot present to you the harpist— Ned McGowan."

As soon as the applause at this sally had died down, the workings of the fraudulent ballot box were demonstrated; the slides were drawn, and the hidden ballots revealed.

"This is a powerful machine," continued Peyton. "It will elevate the meanest vagabond in the country to the highest office in the State."

Vast was the effect of this exhibition. The people were impressed—more powerfully impressed by the sight of the cheating ballot-box than they could have been by any words of the speaker. And the result was a wave of indignation that drew many new adherents to the Vigilance cause.

Meanwhile the "law and order" faction were persisting, even in the face of many setbacks. Shortly after the Benicia meeting, General Sherman had resigned his post, partly in disgust at the Governor's treatment of the committee of citizens, but principally, it seems, because his hands were tied and it appeared impossible for him to accomplish his ends. He had tried—and tried in vain—to procure Federal arms from General Wool, who maintained that he had no authority to issue the munitions, and would not permit himself to be bulldozed by the attitude of Governor Johnson and of Sherman. All in all, the task before Sherman was a hopeless one, for a general with few followers and no arms is in an unenviable position, —and he at least had the wisdom to recognize that fact.

Such, however, cannot be said of his successor, General Volney E. Howard, a man of less flinty disposition, but capable of a good deal of bluster. He does not seem to have done much for the "law and order" cause except to war by means of words—but in this respect his efforts were gallant, particularly in the case of the Sacramento mass meeting which he addressed, and in which he was so heckled by the audience that he was forced to withdraw amid a commotion that apparently did more damage than good to his party. Later he exercised his oratorical gifts at other points, but without results that are written large in the history of the State.

While General Howard was doing what he could to rally the anti-Vigilantes, his chief, Governor Johnson, was addressing an appeal to the highest authority in the land. None other than Franklin Pierce, President of the United States, was the recipient of his message, which spoke of "unlawful proceedings" that could not be arrested because of the lack of arms and ammunition. Asking for a requisition of the desired weapons, Johnson went so far as to state that the insurrectionists "doubtless will proceed with such acts of aggression and disobedience toward the government as will ultimately result in its entire destruction."

But was the Hon. Franklin Pierce alarmed at these gloomy forebodings? Apparently not! for, instead of arms and ammunition, all that he transmitted to the Governor was an example of diplomatic verbiage. Through Secretary Marcy, he conveyed his "serious doubts of lawful power to proceed in the manner indicated"; and through the attorney-general, to whom the matter was submitted "for advisement," he reported the finding that there was no evidence "that there has been committed or threatened any act of resistance or obstruction to the Constitution, laws or official authority of the United States."

In other words, Governor Johnson might whistle for his arms and ammunition! The President had no desire to stick his hands into the affair—a fact which was fortunate; for not only might ruin and bloodshed have resulted from the conflict of armed forces; but the people of California were at that time in such a dangerous temper of mind that any opposition would only have spurred them to further resistance, and the application of Federal power might have led to open rebellion—with results that may be surmised but had better not be contemplated.

But despite the succession of handicaps and rebuffs which they had suffered, the "law and order" party persisted in their militant attitude. On their side were aligned the companies of "the San Francisco Blues," the "Marion Rifles," the "Sarsfield Guards," the "Continentals" and the "National Lancers"; moreover, they were to enjoy the services of the United States vessel *John Adams,* which, under Captain E. B. Boutwell, was to be sent for "moral effect" to anchor near the foot of Sacramento Street, within easy striking distance of Committee headquarters. Again, they were expecting various important consignments of arms, including six cases of muskets, which General Wool, while refusing to grant other munitions, felt obliged to send as the quota due the State.

Truly, the arms and ammunition consigned to the anti-Vigilantes had explosive possibilities in more ways than one! They were to be the cause of some acts which, construed in the strictest sense of the term, can only be regarded as piratical; they were to be responsible for bringing the conflict between the two factions to a head; they were to lead to the complete dis-

comfiture of the "law and order" group, but at the same time
were to be indirectly to blame for placing the Committee in a
predicament that would require the sanest of good judgment
and the maximum of discretion before it could extricate itself.

In their efforts at the seizure of arms, the Vigilantes manifested the same practical, realistic spirit that actuated them
throughout their dealings. It might be unlawful to take weapons belonging to the State; it might be theft, brigandage or
insurrection—the Committee members did not care what
term was employed; all that they knew was that the arms were
intended to be used against them and their followers, and that
they could not stand idly by and permit themselves to be shot.
And so, when Captain Hutton of the schooner *Bianca* brought
word that a quantity of muskets was hidden in a vessel in the
bay, they did not hesitate to send men in search of the weapons,
nor to remove the twelve cases of rifles and the six cases of
ammunition which they found concealed in a brick-laden
ship. Likewise, when informed that a shipment of arms was
on its way from Corte Madera, in Marin county, they did not
delay about dispatching a corps of twenty-two armed men to
the spot designated; nor did these twenty-two scruple to leap
with cocked pistols aboard the munition-bearing schooner,
to lift the hatches while the crew was intimidated by the threat
of gunfire, and to carry away eleven boxes of muskets and
three of pistols.

Similar in its nature, but more momentous in its results,
was the raid conducted by John L. Durkee, a former member
of the San Francisco police force, who had resigned in order
to join the Vigilantes. Informed that somewhere at the north-
ern end of the bay there was a vessel containing arms for the
enemy, Durkee set sail with twelve men; and late at night,
amid the mists of San Pablo Bay, discovered a dark hulk lying

at anchor. Cautiously the scouts approached the apparently lifeless schonoer, which lay silent and still, without a light or any sign of an occupant. Noiselessly drawing up to the ghostly object, they made their own ship fast to it, then crept aboard. Never did a pirate on the Spanish Main glide forth more daringly for loot—who knew what sleepless eyes were watching amid the impenetrable darkness? who knew what blades were being slyly lifted, what gun-barrels were being stealthily aimed? But Durkee and his men, as it turned out, had little to fear; the captain and crew of the invaded ship, reclining in a drunken slumber, scarcely knew what was happening until large quantities of guns and sabers had been removed from the schooner. Nor were they able to make any resistance, even after coming to their senses, for it would have been far from wise to defy the cocked pistols of the intruders. Hence not only the arms were taken, but three prisoners: Rube Maloney, the charterer of the vessel, and his assistants, John G. Phillips and James McNabb.

This little adventure in piracy, if one wishes to use the term subsequently applied to it by the United States authorities, was to have results that no one could foresee, and least of all Durkee himself. And before all the indirect fruits were culled, the Committee would be severely shaken, and the life of a justice of the Supreme Court of the State of California would tremble in the balance.

Nevertheless, it is only fair to remark that the actions of the Vigilantes were not so piratical as they might have been; for the Committee promptly and fully paid for damages sustained by the *Julia,* the vessel boarded by Durkee. Moreover, the captured arms were not used, but were held for their legal owners until such time as peace should be restored, the only object of the raiders being to forestall the employment of the munitions against themselves.

This, however, did not prevent some serious after-effects, which we shall consider in due time. But first let us observe what happened immediately after buccaneer Durkee returned to San Francisco with his prisoners and booty. Unfortunately— most unfortunately, as it turned out—the Committee gave orders that both Maloney and Phillips be released, since neither was under accusation of crime. But instead of being grateful for their escape, the two discharged men made a round of the saloons, with boisterous threats against various members of the Committee; and these facts being brought to the ears of Coleman and his associates, the order was sent out for the immediate re-arrest of both men. Unwise, exceedingly unwise, had Maloney and Phillips been; but, though they could not have known it, they were acting as unconscious pawns in a greater drama.

As it happened, the commission for the seizure of the two men was given to Sterling A. Hopkins, one of the Committee handy men, an artesian well-borer by trade. Bancroft speaks of him as a person "of great pertinacity, good at obeying orders, and afraid or ashamed of nothing." But T. H. Hittell, less favorably disposed, tells us that "He appears to have been a man who by his officiousness had foisted himself upon the Committee, one of those undesirable characters of whom the organization had not yet purged itself." At all events, he had already earned unenviable notoriety by serving as the executioner of Cora and Casey; and he was now suddenly to win vastly more prominence, and to plunge the Committee into the most vexatious dilemma of its career.

Setting out with three or four followers in quest of Maloney, Hopkins discovered him in the apartment of the naval agent, Richard P. Ashe. Several of Maloney's friends, including Judge Terry of the Supreme Court, cocked their pistols and ordered Hopkins to leave, which he apparently had little hesitation about doing. But placing some of his men at the entrance of the building and directing them to keep a careful guard, he hastened off for reinforcements.

Meanwhile Maloney, Terry and their associates, feeling none too safe, decided to withdraw. Accordingly, they left the building, but, before they had gone very far, were observed and followed by Hopkins. An exciting chase ensued, during which Maloney and five companions every now and then wheeled around to point double-barreled shot-guns at their pursuers; while Hopkins and four assistants kept resolutely at the heels of the fugitives. At length, on Jackson Street near Dupont, they caught up with the retreating six; and thereupon Hopkins, in his eagerness to seize Maloney, attempted to dash past Ashe and Terry, who were in the rear.

Heated with passion as the men were, shaken with fury and with haste, they were precisely in the mood for any murderous act. Hence it is not surprising that, within a moment, a deed of bloody violence had occurred. To prevent the passage of the impetuous Hopkins, Terry stuck up his gun; and this Hopkins seized and wrested away, with the result that a general mêlée ensued, and those ahead of Hopkins rushed back and forced him to the ground. In the midst of the scuffle, the accidental discharge of a revolver acted like dynamite upon nerves already overwrought; Terry, thinking an assault intended upon his life, whipped a bowie-knife from its sheaf, and, with a vicious lunge, drove it four inches into Hopkins' neck.

His throat flowing with red, Hopkins staggered to his feet. "I am stabbed!" he groaned. At these words, Terry, Maloney and the others rose and took to their heels, closely pursued by two of the Vigilantes, but managed to find refuge in the armory of the Blues, whose iron doors slammed to a close be-

hind them, while the Vigilantes remained without to prevent
any person from passing. Meantime Hopkins had been taken
by friends to Engine House 12, where his wounds were examined by a physician, and pronounced to be serious, but
probably not fatal.

Almost instantly the city was shaken by excitement rivalling
that of that celebrated afternoon over a month before, when
James King of William had been felled by Casey. As soon as
the news of the stabbing reached Vigilance headquarters, an
order went out for the arrest of Terry; the tap, tap, tap of the
alarm bell sounded; the streets began to fill with people; Vigilantes, with muskets bristling and sabers glistening, rushed
out to take their places with their companies; common citizens hastened forth, with shouts and commotion, to witness
what was going on; whole squads of armed men were seen
running back and forth; draymen hurriedly unhitched their
horses, flung off the harness, and, climbing to the backs of their
steeds, clattered away to join the Vigilance cavalry. Within
a few minutes, the crowd around the Committee headquarters
was so dense that men had literally to fight their way through
it; within a quarter of an hour, the greater part of the Vigilance
force was not only assembled but was under march toward the
armory of the Blues.

It would be interesting to know what thoughts swarmed
through Judge Terry's mind as he glanced out of the armory
windows and saw the dense, surging mob below, which milled
and muttered like some great beast intent on his blood. In
subdued tones, broken by an occasional curse, he carried on
conversation with his comrades—and was not the fate of
Casey painfully fresh in his thoughts? Did he not realize
that, Supreme Court Justice though he was, not all the arms
in the State of California would be sufficient to save him from

the vengeance of the Vigilance Committee should his victim die? Let Judge Terry offer up prayers to whatever powers might be to spare the life of Sterling A. Hopkins!

The position of Terry and his associates was worse than precarious. Surrounded by a multitude thousands strong, what hope had they of escape? What choice was there other than to capitulate? "Gentlemen of the Vigilance Committee," wrote Captain Ashe, "if the executive committee will give us protection from violence we will agree to surrender." And to this message the reply was made that if the defenders would give up Terry, Maloney and Phillips, along with all the arms and ammunition in the building, they would be shielded from harm. Harsh terms, no doubt! but there was no need of dickering; upon the expiration of the time limit of fifteen minutes, Ashe and his companions bit their lips and accepted.

And so the doors of the armory were thrown open; and in marched a company of twenty Vigilantes; and three hundred muskets and other arms were removed, piled up in a dray, and carried off to Committee headquarters. Meanwhile two carriages were hurried up to the armory; and the prisoners of war, Terry and Maloney, were escorted out by a strong guard, conducted to the coaches, and driven away; then, attended by the flashing bayonets of the infantry and the stamping hooves of the cavalry, were taken in triumph to the Committee rooms, and were both lodged in cells.

One would have thought that the Committee would have considered this activity sufficient for one day. One would have thought that, having captured an armory and its contents along with a justice of the Supreme Court, the Vigilantes would have deemed it proper to rest from their exertions. On the contrary, however, they were only moved to increased efforts; like conquering warriors, they hastened to follow up their advantage.

When the news of Terry's arrest was brought to the Executive Committee, a motion was made and carried, "That the grand marshal be ordered to take possession of all arms and munitions of war that may be found in the hands of our opponents, or that may be likely to fall into their hands." And, in order to make this resolution effective, action was taken upon it immediately.

Forth once more marched the Vigilance forces, in battle array, and with sabers gleaming; and every armory of the "law and order" party was promptly surrounded and compelled to surrender. So quickly were the maneuvers executed that the enemy had no time to rally; some of their men managed to make their way into the armories before the arrival of the Vigilantes, but many were excluded, and, despite much warlike brandishing of weapons, were reduced to impotence by fear and by superior numbers. Meanwhile the Vigilantes pressed on relentlessly; and having gained entrance to all the armories, proceeded to strip them of rifles, pistols, swords and ammunition, which were carted off in drays; while close to two hundred prisoners were taken, and, led out two by two, many of them handcuffed together, were conducted to the Committee rooms amid an escort of more than a thousand infantry and cavalry.

Subsequently these men were discharged, with the warning of bitter penalties should they ever again arm themselves against the Committee. But the purpose of the aggressors had been accomplished. The "law and order" party, at one audacious stroke, had been stripped of its power; and while some occasional rumblings and mutterings were still to be heard from its direction, no serious attack was now to be anticipated.

Yet the troubles of the Committee were by no means over; indeed, in certain ways they were only beginning; and the horizon was still black with menace. In the following chapter, accordingly, we shall observe the nature of the predicament in which Vigilance found itself owing to the Hopkins-Terry affray.

CHAPTER XV

A LIVE TIGER IN A NET

LET it not be imagined that the Committee was pleased at the privilege of entertaining Judge Terry in a private cell. Its sensations, upon the arrest of this personage, were similar to those of a fowler who, hunting for small game, finds a live tiger entangled in his net. It was, veritably, caught between the horns of a dilemma! Could it let the Judge go? Obviously not! for he had been guilty not only of assault, but of assault upon one of the Vigilance police officers—and it was by no means certain that his victim would survive. Then should it hold him for trial, with the possibility that he should have to face the death penalty? Apparently this was the only course still open—but how fervently Coleman and his colleagues must have prayed for Hopkins to live! For the execution of a Supreme Court Justice, though the Committee would not flinch should it become necessary, was not to be taken lightly; and its repercussions, in arousing fresh and formidable opposition to the Vigilance cause, might be such as Terry's jailors would not care to face.

Had it not been for the Terry affair, the Committee might have terminated its activities much sooner; the harassed members of its executive board, weary with their continual sessions, might have been able to leave their labors with thankful sighs, and to return to the homes, the families, the business interests they had been neglecting. On June 18th, in fact, a Committee had been appointed to take steps leading toward adjournment; but three days later, with the occurrence of the Terry episode. all plans for disbanding had to be renounced; and, for many strenuous weeks, the leaders of Vigilance had to wrestle with new problems.

But in one respect, at least, there had been a gain. Previous to the assault upon Hopkins, there had still been a better element of public opinion which, while acknowledging the evils attacked by the Committee, had denied the necessity for the tactics employed, and believed that there might still be safety in the ordinary methods of law. But now that Terry—Terry, a leading representative of legality—had descended to the methods of the rowdies and slashed his man in a miserable street scuffle, the sympathies of many of the "law and order" group were alienated, and the Vigilance Committee gained their tacit if not their open approval.

Severe was the castigation that Terry received in many of the papers—particularly severe in view of the fact that his attack upon Hopkins was but the climax of a whole series of anti-Vigilance acts, which included the issuance of the *habeas corpus* writ for Billy Mulligan, and the open attempt to stir up sentiment against the Committee on the streets of San Francisco. It is true that the *Herald,* faithful to its "law and order" stand, took up the cudgels in his defense, and found him not guilty of any crime; but the *Alta California,* reflecting a more prevalent sentiment, listed a whole category of his offenses. The following is from the issue of June 25th:

"It is said that Terry is greatly affected by the position he now occupies, and deeply regrets the causes that led to his incarceration. The narrow compass of his dungeon, and the close proximity of a number of armed soldiers, are not calculated to give one of his proud, spirited feeling very agreeable sensations. His confinement will provide him an opportunity for mature reflection upon his unjustifiable course for the last month. . . . It should be remembered that his offense does not consist merely in the attack upon Mr. Hopkins, but he is justly censured and properly held responsible not only for the blood

of Hopkins, but his continued and uncalled for warfare upon
the Committee, the issuance of the worthless but mischief-
making proclamation, as well as the illegal writ of habeas corpus, and the collection of arms in our midst, to be used against
those who oppose his will. These acts, as well as his continual
presence in the city, ready to encourage and bring on a collision
between the parties, are chargeable to him."

It must be noted that we are here listening to a pro-Vigilance
organ, and one which, accordingly, cannot be expected to have
presented Terry's cause in too favorable a light; but, on the
other hand, the truth of its central assertions is undeniable.
Terry was assuredly within his rights in opposing the Vigilantes; but this does not mean that the methods he employed
were consistent with the dignity of a justice of the Supreme
Court, nor that he was advancing the cause of law and order
by encouraging armed conflict. The simple fact appears to
be that the man, although invested with the robes of judicial
impartiality, was of an unusually bellicose disposition: this
is indicated not only by the part he played in the present
affair, but by the charges against him of previous assaults upon
various citizens—on J. H. Purdy of San Francisco, on a Mr.
Evans of Stockton, on a Mr. King at the charter election at
Stockton, and on a Mr. Broadhurst in the Stockton court house.
But even more forcibly is the character of Judge Terry shown
by the manner in which, in the summer of 1859, he was deliberately to pick a quarrel with Senator Broderick because of
an imputation by the latter against his honesty, was to demand
the satisfaction of a duel, and was coolly to shoot his rival
dead.

One would therefore seem justified in concluding that the
Committee's new prisoner was indeed something of a tiger,
was indeed a man in whom temper ran high and passion surged

fiercely—a man who, despite the pride of his high office, was in more ways than one a blood brother to those ruffians whom the Committee had hunted and deported.

Nevertheless, he must have had some amiable and attractive qualities, for his friends were many, and fought for him with unyielding loyalty. The stubbornness of Terry's supporters was to be the source of much uneasiness, not to say peril, for the Committee; indeed, it was often impossible to say where the fight for Terry ended and that for "law and order" began. Some idea of the temper of the times may be gleaned from the story—whether true or not—that a marksman lay concealed for weeks some distance from the Committee headquarters, ready to sever with a bullet the rope with which the Vigilantes might attempt to hang Judge Terry. And an even clearer indication of the violence and passion of Terry's followers may be gained from the statement of Dr. Beverly Cole, the physician in attendance upon Hopkins:

"So great was the interest felt in Judge Terry's fate by his friends in every part of the State, that I was hourly in receipt of telegrams from medical men and laymen from every quarter, particularly from Stockton, inquiring as to Hopkins' condition . . . and I know that there was an organization brought into existence after the stabbing of Hopkins, composed of the friends of Judge Terry who were sworn in the event of Hopkins' death to take my life."

Fulminations in the anti-Vigilance newspapers, speaking tours throughout the interior of the State, personal importunities to Coleman, and warnings by the Governor that he would overwhelm the San Francisco area with Federal forces—these were but a few of the manifestations on behalf of the endangered judge. Worst still were the written threats against members of the Committee—threats inspired less by Terry than by enmity to Vigilance in general—threats against both life and property—threats indicating that it was the plan of the enemy to capture members of the Executive board, and hold them as hostages if they did not dispose of them in some more summary fashion. So seriously was this menace taken that some Committeemen did not dare go home at night, while others would not leave headquarters without cocked revolvers.

Even more serious was the peril from the United States vessel *John Adams,* which, as we have seen, was anchored for "moral effect" at the foot of Sacramento Street, within a stone's throw of the Committee rooms. The commander of this ship, Captain Boutwell, had been addressed on June 27th by the Governor, who had asked him to take steps protecting Terry from punishment by the Committee; and he had likewise received an appeal from the Judge himself, who referred to the Vigilantes as "traitors and assassins", spoke of his hourly danger of "suffering an ignominious death" at their hands, and invoked the protection of the flag of his country. On June 28th (which, incidentally, is the date of Terry's letter) Boutwell wrote to the Committee, asking the surrender of Terry, and referring to the necessity "to use all the power at my command to save the life of a native-born American citizen, whose only offense is believed to be in his effort to carry out the law."

In reply to this communication, Boutwell received a brief note, non-committally telling him that his message would "receive consideration"; and on the following day he wrote to the Governor stating the difficulty of his position, which was such that any interference might endanger the life of Terry, and any attempt to fire upon the city would certainly work havoc to friend as well as foe. However, he ended by promising that, were Terry to be condemned to die, he would make an effort to save his life.

Despite the fact that Boutwell had not the sympathy of his

superior Farragut and was acting largely on his own responsibility, the danger from the *John Adams* was too grave for the Vigilantes to ignore. Realizing that Fort Vigilance was far from impregnable, they made every effort to bolster its defenses, and, in particular, blocked all approaches through the sewers, by which, it was rumored, gun-powder would be transported to blow up the buildings. At the same time, they conceived a plan for a direct counter-attack upon Boutwell, should he open fire upon Vigilance headquarters: two hundred sharpshooters, concealed in an old hulk, were to be borne by tugs to the *John Adams*, which they were to board and capture. Since the tugs and the marksmen were in constant readiness, it was estimated that half an hour would suffice for the subjugation of the naval craft.

Another plan called for floats laden with combustibles, which were to bear down upon the *John Adams,* in the event of the failure of the first scheme of attack; while the Committee also entertained a project to occupy Alcatraz Island and other forts in the bay, and, with the aid of the naval men in the organization, to bring a destructive gunfire down upon Boutwell's vessel.

It will therefore be seen that the Committee was, literally, getting into deep water; into water so deep that no one could estimate where the bottom lay. Should the Vigilantes, even in self-defense, attack and destroy a United States naval vessel, was it to be supposed that the Government could remain indifferent? Would it not be compelled, like Governor Johnson, to recognize the existence of "a state of insurrection"? And would it not, consequently, be obliged to send troops to crush the rebellion and punish the rebels? But would this not mean that the Vigilantes, in order to shield their lives no less than to save their cause, would be forced to tighten their organization and make all possible resistance? In other words, civil warfare might ensue; and in view of the remoteness of California from the central Government, in view of popular sympathy with Vigilance principles, it is by no means certain that the conflict would not have turned into a War of Secession.

But whether such eventualities would become probabilities; whether the spark of Vigilance would ignite the blaze of revolution, depended in the main upon two factors: first, on the life of Sterling A. Hopkins, who for many days lay critically ill, and whose death would render it obligatory on the Committee to execute the murderer; and, secondly, on the arbitrary will of Captain Boutwell, who, in case Terry were to be sentenced to the gallows, would have the power to precipitate a major explosion by turning his guns on the walls of Fort Vigilance.

*　　*　　*

While the city and the whole State thus rested, as it were, on the rim of a smoldering volcano, plans went forward for the trial of the imprisoned judge. And meantime, excited rumors were circulating—rumors to the effect that Terry would resign from the Supreme Court. Many of his critics, including the *Alta California,* contended that he had "forfeited his moral right" to his office; and it would have occasioned little surprise had his resignation been announced. He himself, in his letter to Boutwell, charged that "All sorts of terrorism are resorted to to compel me to resign my office"; but since he was at that moment faced with either one of two penalties worse than resignation—banishment from the State, or execution—it is hard to see how the retention of his official position could have been uppermost in his mind. There is, in fact, reason to suppose that his resignation might actually have been tendered, had it not been for the attitude of his wife, who, supporting him stanchly and maintaining that he had been in no way to blame, declared that she would sooner see him hung from the Committee windows than released shorn of the robes of his office.

During the interval before the trial, Terry's position was in many ways less onerous than it was subsequently to become. For one thing, he was still permitted to see his wife and friends; and this must have served in some measure to compensate him for the overshadowing presence of the guards, the uplifted muskets and evilly shining bayonets. But after the trial had begun, the privilege of seeing his intimates was denied him, evidently out of fear of conspiracy; and neither the complaints and accusations of Mrs. Terry nor the grumblings of the anti-Vigilance papers served to influence the Committee to lift the harsh restriction.

The sensations of the prisoner, as he went to trial, must have been a little like those of some poor wretch confronting the solemn tribunal of the Spanish Inquisition. Cut adrift, as it were, from all familiar moorings of the law; faced with a body of men who cared nothing for technicalities and were resolved only on getting at facts regardless of rules or precedent, he must have felt as one who is heard before a strange judge in a strange land. Yet he could not but bow to the authority of the Committee; for in its hands, as he knew only too well, rested the power of life or death. Day after day, for twenty-five days consecutively, the trial dragged on; day after day, in what must have been an ordeal straining every nerve, a punishment scarcely gentler than months in prison; day after day, while in most cases two sessions were held in every twenty-four hours. Most seriously did the Committee take the case, and they were resolved to leave no stone unturned in their investigations.

The Executive board as a group constituted the court, and from thirty to forty as a rule were in attendance. Following their previous method, the Committee permitted Terry to

choose an attorney from among their number; it allowed him
to send for any witnesses he might desire throughout the State,
and in some instances paid their expenses; it granted him the
privilege of pleading his own case, and of making a written
statement. Yet all the while it realized that the issue of the
trial depended not only on proceedings before the tribunal,
but on the recovery of Hopkins, who by his life or death would
determine whether the maximum charge against Terry would
be murder or felonious assault. And since, for a long while,
Terry's victim remained on the border-line between this world
and the next, the tidings from the sick-bed seemed quite as important as the testimony before the court.

But the surgical efforts on behalf of Hopkins turned out to
be more successful than in the case of a much better man, James
King of William. Eventually the patient was announced to
have taken a turn for the better, and finally he had completely
recovered; indeed, he was seen on the streets before the trial
was over; and on the fifth of August, some six or seven weeks
after his injury, he had the audacity to appear before the Committee with the request that he be allowed to see Terry, in order to negotiate a cash settlement of the whole affair!

But so much for Hopkins. We will let him go on his way,
very far from being a corpse; and we will consider just how
his recovery affected the dilemma of the Committee. It made
the hanging of Terry out of the question, since, thanks to the
skill of a surgeon, the estimable judge was innocent of murder;
but it left the matter of his punishment as much in doubt as
ever. Assuming that he was found guilty—as the Committee
at length felt obliged to find him—what penalty could be
meted out? Had he been an ordinary vagabond, without
friends or position, he would doubtless have been promptly
sentenced to depart on the first vessel for Panama, or Callao, or
the Hawaiian Islands, with the warning not to return, under

penalty of hanging. But David S. Terry, justice of the California Supreme Court, could not be shipped away like any common ruffian. Even if the Committee were successful in getting him aboard ship—as they doubtless could have been—how control his subsequent movements? How prevent his return in defiance of their mandate? How carry out, without widespread strife and much spilling of blood, their threat of execution in case of disobedience of their orders? How ward off a devastating blow to the Committee's prestige and authority? And worst of all—if Terry successfully defied the Committee's orders and returned to the State after being deported, how restrain other banished criminals from following his example? Would not the greater part of the good accomplished by the Vigilance movement be neutralized? Would it not, moreover, be necessary to maintain a permanent Vigilance organization in order to cope with the new situation?

All these considerations, and others akin to them, weighed powerfully in one direction; but, on the other hand, there was the belief that Terry, having committed an offense, was deserving of punishment; there was the popular attitude to be considered, since for weeks thousands of persons had been impatiently awaiting the decision, and it was far from any one's mind that the Committee, having punished the weak and the friendless, would now hesitate to execute judgment simply because the offender was a man of position and influence.

It was on the twenty-second of July that the trial of Terry ended; but not until the seventh of August did the Committee complete its deliberations. There had been a deadlock among the Vigilance forces; the Executive Committee had found the prisoner guilty only of plain assault; while the board of delegates, acting in conjunction with the Executive division, declared him guilty of the more serious offense of assault with intent to kill. It was long before the latter group was made to

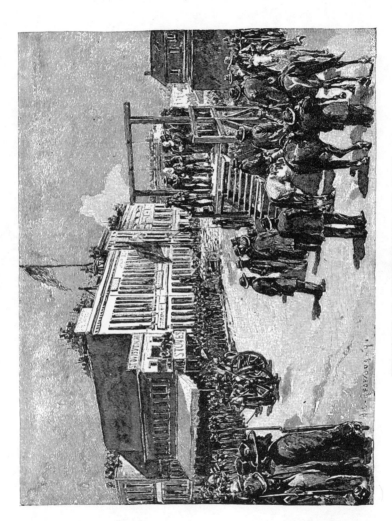

EXECUTION OF HETHERINGTON AND BRACE

concur in the judgment of the Executives; and there was much excited and even violent talk before the delegates accepted the view that Terry had already suffered sufficiently, and that there was nothing to be done except to release him—nothing to be done except to say, in effect, "Judge Terry, you have committed a base crime, and we condemn you; but that is all we are able to do. You will now find the door open. Good-day!"

It is true that a resolution was passed, declaring that the interests of the State imperatively demanded the resignation of Judge Terry from the supreme bench—but this, after all, was a mere breath of wind, without power and without effect, and served in no way to deter the one-time prisoner of the Vigilance Committee from resuming his place in the court and from handing down decisions with the same magisterial pomp and finality as of old.

But how was the news of the Committee's decision received by the public? Naturally, it fell with no welcome accent upon the ears of those thousands who had awaited eagerly and confidently the decision of the Vigilantes. It did not gratify the passions of the multitude, who are always ready for vengeance and for blood; but, more than that, it did not satisfy a certain inherent craving for impartiality—for, it might be argued, the offenses of some of the banished men had been no worse than that of Terry. Even if the Committee could not have made its sentence of exile permanently effective, was that any reason for not passing judgment as in the case of more humble men? Let it at least make the effort! then there could be no suspicion that justice was not even-handed! Thus many persons must have reasoned, not without some show of plausibility; indeed, no action of the Vigilance Committee was ever so widely criticized among its supporters as the release of Terry.

The manner in which the release was made is in itself indicative of the emotions of the times. President Coleman afterwards stated that it was his plan that "Terry should be formally discharged in broad daylight, in the presence of the whole Committee assembled for the occasion, and escorted by the military from his place of imprisonment." But quite otherwise was the actual delivery of the man. A group of the Executive Committee met at night, and decided that, since Terry was in danger of attack, it would be best to free him at once. But, being one short of the twelve required for a quorum, they roused another member of the Committee out of his bed before being able to vote the desired release. At a quarter of two in the morning, the necessary ballot having been taken, Terry was conducted out of the cell in which he had passed so many days, and brought to the home of a friend a few blocks away, where he proceeded to make merry with wine over his deliverance.

But his rejoicing was premature; it was not long before he realized that his life was still in danger. A mob of angry men, estimated to be a thousand strong, were ranging the streets in search of Terry; and several of his former captors, learning of this fact, rushed to him to notify him of his peril. Terry was even offered a haven in the home of Isaac Bluxome—the dreadful "33 Secretary" whose signature had appeared on so many a formidable document. Declining this honor, he accepted the alternative of stealing away to the wharf, whence a small boat could convey him to the safety of the sloop of war *John Adams*. Furtively, like a jail breaker anxious to avoid detection, the Supreme Court Justice, with but one companion, hastened away to the waterfront, where he found refuge in a boat secured for him by his friends.

But even now the storm was not over. The next day, when the news of Terry's release became generally known, a mob of three thousand excited men surged about the Committee headquarters, cursing and shouting and demanding explana-

tions; while Coleman tried as best he could to throw oil upon
the troubled waters. To the people, who had felt assured of a
verdict of guilty, it seemed as if they had been betrayed; nor
was it easy to reason with them, nor to convince them that it
had been more courageous to pursue the path of clemency.

Some of the papers expressed great dissatisfaction with the
verdict, the *Bulletin* going so far as to refer to it as "criminal
and weak"; but in the course of time, as passions were soothed
and it became possible to see with wider perspective, the con-
census of opinion gradually swung toward approval of the
Committee's attitude.

Yet even at our own remote date, when all the mists of emotion have been cleared away, who shall say which was the
wiser and more equitable course to pursue? "Better to err,"
says the law, "on the side of mercy than of harshness"; and
shall we condemn a popular tribunal for having chosen to act
upon this precept, rather than to let its feelings and prejudices
serve as judges, and to commit a harmful act and set a dangerous precedent merely in the interests of a fancied consistency?
After all, it was not for the persecution of men of Terry's type
that the Committee had been organized; it had set out to clear
the community of the Caseys, the Coras, and the Mulligans,
of the ballot-box stuffers and the deliberate murderers; and
this task it had largely accomplished when Terry, a blunder-
ing and passionate man, an affront to the judiciary but perhaps
not at heart a vicious character, had entangled his feet in the
web Vigilance had spun for other prey, and so had forced
upon the Committee a decision of a type it had never intended
to make, and for which it had not been established. Under such
circumstances, are we justified, from our distant vantage point,
in throwing stones? Are we justified in maintaining that, so
far as Terry was concerned, the Committee failed in its purpose and betrayed its principles and its supporters?

CHAPTER XVI

W HILE the Committee was still deliberating the case of Judge Terry, two men of vastly less prominence were faced with the extreme penalty. These were Philander Brace and Joseph Hetherington, whose names are generally associated, although their lives were not linked until both came under the dread scrutiny of the Vigilantes. Brace was accused of several crimes, including robbery and murder; while Hetherington was known to have killed Dr. Andrew Randall, under circumstances that pointed as much to an outburst of violent passion as to premeditated crime. It has been remarked, and may be remarked again, that no rational man, acting in cold blood, would have chosen to commit murder at the very hour when the Vigilance Committee was in session; yet it was on July 24th, during the heyday of the Committee's power, that Hetherington made his assault upon Randall.

The two men, it seems, had formerly been friends—but money, the curse of friendship, as of most human relations—had come between them, and Randall had borrowed from Hetherington in order to engage in some real estate transactions. Subsequently, it appears, he was unable to repay the sum; at all events, he did not repay it; and Hetherington, insulting him and threatening to shoot him on sight, proved anything but an obliging creditor. At length, on the fateful twenty-fourth, the two one-time friends chanced to meet at the St. Nicholas Hotel, where the physician had come to register. "Ah, I've got you now!" cried Hetherington, reaching out and seizing the doctor's ample beard. And Randall had the by-no-means agreeable sensation of feeling himself jerked by the whiskers and pulled four or five feet across the room.

Which of the men first drew his revolver, was the subject of disagreement among witnesses of the subsequent shooting. Some said it was Hetherington; others maintained that both combatants lashed out their guns simultaneously; but, in either case it was not an instant before the bullets were flying. And thereat the hotel underwent a lightning transformation. While the whizzing and banging of the shots mingled with the yells of excited humans, there was a dash for all accessible places of refuge—behind desks, tables and other shielding objects. Randall himself, still unhurt despite the reckless interchange of bullets, rushed around the room, then sought safety under the counter, where he crouched beside the terror-stricken clerk. But Hetherington, not to be cheated of his prey, followed in swift pursuit, reached down beneath the counter, pointed his gun at the doctor's head, and fired—inflicting a mortal wound.

Arrested by an officer of the law, Hetherington was transferred without a struggle to the custody of the Vigilance police; and on the morning of the twenty-sixth, two days after the commission of his crime, he was brought to trial by the Committee, which on the following day passed judgment of death. In common with Brace, who was simultaneously convicted of murder, he was sentenced to hang on the twenty-ninth— all of which represented a rapidity of trial and judgment quite unknown to the orthodox courts of law.

At the scheduled time, the event took place, and was observed by a multitude which crowded the streets and housetops for many blocks, and, with the usual sadism of the mob, appeared to find something enticing in the prospect of witnessing the death agonies of two fellow beings. Attended by companies of infantry and cavalry, and by the loaded brass cannon of the artillery, the grim drama was enacted—an element of the grotesque being added by the executioner's assistant, who appeared in a black cap and long black robe, which were intended to conceal his identity, but served only to add a touch of the ludicrous and sardonic. Hetherington, before meeting his doom, seemed perfectly composed, and proclaimed himself at utter peace with the world and with his maker; while Brace, white-faced, restless and profane, burst into continual execrations, his most striking sally being to the effect that he wished to die with Hetherington executed on one side of him and Judge Terry hanged on the other, like the Savior between two thieves. It is said that he was intoxicated at the time—but, intoxicated or not, it matters little, since he was so soon to throw off the vestments of mortality.

While Hetherington and Brace were undergoing sentence and punishment, two members of the Vigilance Committee were themselves under trial in a United States court, on a charge that might incur the death penalty. John L. Durkee and Charles E. Rand, two of the principals in the capture of the State-owned arms from the vessel *Julia,* were indicted on a charge of piracy—a charge doubtless justified technically, since they had overhauled and robbed a vessel. Yet since it was known that the intention of the men had not been that of pirates and that they had acted in response to the orders of the Vigilance Committee, the trial seems to have been merely one of the innumerable methods adopted of striking back at the Committee. If its purpose was to cause annoyance, it succeeded; for bail to the amount of $25,000 had to be provided for Durkee, and the accused men had to be defended through a dragging trial. But the consequences, fortunately, were not serious, since the verdict was acquittal. Yet the case throughout was fraught with explosive possibilities: if Durkee had been sentenced to hang, the Committee would undoubtedly have set out to rescue him, and the result would have been a clash with the authority of the Government, which might have taken retributive measures provocative of endless trouble.

Before the affair of Durkee and Rand had been settled, the Committee had formally renounced its control over law and justice in San Francisco. Nearly three months had passed between the creation of the Vigilance organization and the final disposal of the case of Judge Terry; and the members of the executive board were now weary with their labors, and convinced that they had played the part for which they had come into existence. Hence the logical course was to disband. But they did not intend to cease their work without a flourish; with the good showmanship which they had manifested throughout their career, they determined to quit the scene as spectacularly as they had entered; they resolved to provide an exhibition which would not only attract by its picturesqueness but would impress by its demonstration of the size and power of the Vigilance forces.

It was on the eighteenth of August that the ceremony occurred. Then the watching thousands of citizens were treated to a parade of all Vigilantes—a parade which had many of the features of the triumphal procession of a conquering army. While strains of martial music filled the air, the members of the Committee advanced in long, imposing ranks, wearing civilian clothes, but marked by a certain uniformity thanks to their long frock coats buttoned up to the neck, their black pantaloons, their white gloves, their glazed or cloth caps, and their white satin badges shining from their left coat lapels. Most of the officers were mounted, and wore—of all incongruous combinations!—bouquets of flowers attached to their muskets! Through streets strung with flags, they slowly made their way; beneath long decorated streamers; along the curbs of sidewalks jammed with spectators; and past houses whose porches and

balconies were packed with the curious. With men marching
and counter-marching; with horses prancing and pawing; with
bayonets glittering in all directions; with the artillery solemnly
moving forward; with fifteen guns mounted as a manifestation of power, the scene could not fail to be stirring and impressive; nor could the display of the four infantry regiments,
the two squadrons of cavalry, the riflemen, the pistolmen, and
the police battalion, do otherwise than to carry conviction of
the great numbers and the resources of the Vigilantes.

Not least interesting among the day's exhibits was a miniature representation of Fort Gunnybags, which paraded the
streets on a dray, showing the sacks of sand, the cannon, and
the other features of the Vigilance stronghold. Apparently
the Committee was intent upon taking the most graphic means
of emphasizing its military character and strength.

*   *   *

Thus rang the farewell of Vigilance—yet in many ways it
was not farewell. The citizens realized that it would take more
than an arbitrary edict of adjournment to reduce Vigilance to a
ghost; that the basis of the organization remained, and that at
any time the pealing of the Monumental bell might summon
the thousands of members back to their companies. And this
thought was to exercise a sober and restraining influence upon
the community for years to come. As a matter of fact, the
nucleus of the organization was kept intact, despite the supposed
disbanding; the Committee retained its rooms, each company
was expected to continue its independent organization, and
meetings of the Executive Committee were still held, and business transacted. That the Vigilantes still were prepared to act
in case of need is demonstrated by the motion passed at the
meeting of January 23rd, 1857, to the effect that "the grand
marshal be requested to report . . . the number of men he

could collect within an hour's notice in case of emergency."

In the following chapter, we shall consider how Vigilance was to play its part in the subsequent life and politics of San Francisco. But first let us note a few incidental effects of the movement,—a few of its results to some of the chief actors in the drama. It was not to be supposed that Coleman and his associates could attack the criminal elements with absolute personal impunity; indeed, the surprising fact—the culminating proof of the awe in which the Committee was held—is that none of the leaders came to a violent end at the hands of the groups they assailed. This is not to suggest, however, that they were immune from molestation. By means of suits for damages, some of the heads of the Committee were persecuted unmercifully; by means of criminal charges, brought against them when they were out of the State and remote from help, they were subjected to all manner of annoyances and indignities. Thus Coleman, visiting New York in September, 1856, was arrested and held on $10,000 bail on the charge of J. R. Maloney, who had been banished by the Vigilantes; incidentally, he was subjected to numerous threats against his life, from the moment he boarded the steamer; and he had his footsteps dogged continually. Says Coleman, in a letter dated April 5, 1857, and addressed to members of the Committee:

"I dropped all other business and attended exclusively to the case for eight days—and nights too. Friend Truett was on hand, and with the many friends that rallied around, we had a pretty strong force, and actually outnumbered the 'roughs' in court, and carried the day by numbers as well as every other way. . . . The expense was large necessarily, but it wouldn't do to be at all parsimonious in a case like this; and as the opposition was moving heaven and earth as far as it could, it became us to be moving also—and we did."

Coleman goes on to mention that he had paid $2500 in counsel fees, and a great deal in smaller amounts; and he declares that, being out of funds, and having no chance of raising any in the East, he will find it necessary to draw upon the Committee. Sums of a thousand dollars had already been sent him on several occasions—for the Vigilance Committee could not allow its leader, stranded far from home, to succumb to the trap laid for him by the enemies of all he held dear.

M. F. Truett, the "friend" to whom Coleman refers in the above quotation, was another prominent Vigilante, who, arrested on charges brought by Maloney and Mulligan, had had to give bail for forty-five thousand dollars—an amount subsequently increased to two hundred and eighty thousand dollars, owing to two other suits. For months these cases were pending, until Maloney providentially died, and Truett was thereby released from the charges.

Another source of great anxiety to the Committee occurred in connection with the suits brought in California courts after the return of the banished men. It is an interesting commentary on human nature that criminals shipped away in the steerage never offered the Committee any further trouble, but that those deported as first-class passengers were, according to Coleman, "flattered and exalted . . . to the belief that they were important personages and had suffered great damages." Hence the numerous suits. In September, 1857, the Committee, deeming that "the necessity for maintaining the penalty no longer exists," rescinded its decree of exile against the expatriated men; with the result that numbers of them returned, and that some of them had the temerity to bring suits for damages against Vigilantes and steamship companies,—suits which succeeded only in one or two instances, but which invariably caused much annoyance and pecuniary loss to the targets of the attack. It is worth noting, incidentally, that a number of the cases were prosecuted by none other than attorney John Nugent, the one-time editor of the *Herald*, the paper that had ruined itself by its opposition to the Committee of 1856.

But despite the suits and other evidences of anti-Vigilance feeling, most of the returning "bad men" displayed a chastened and subdued mood, and never afterwards manifested their old potentialities for trouble-making. There were, unfortunately, several exceptions—one of which was provided by "Rube" Maloney, who was arrested at San Jose for taking undue liberties with other people's money, and subsequently broke jail in company with two other prisoners. And another exception occurred in the case of Billy Mulligan, who re-visited his old haunts in January, 1864, and remained until midsummer of the following year, when his career came to a sudden and spectacular end. It appears that "Billy," being too much a devotee of the whisky flask, was afflicted with delirium tremens; and during his attacks he was terrorized by hallucinations regarding the Vigilance Committee, which, he imagined, was coming to take him. Obsessed with these delusions, he finally barricaded himself in a room in the St. Francis Hotel, from which he poured bullets with indiscriminate recklessness. Never would he be taken alive by the Vigilance Committee! All attempts at conciliation failed; he shot and killed Jack McNabb, a former intimate, who sought to placate him; he shot and likewise killed John Hart, a fireman who chanced to be passing; and finally he in his turn, for the protection of the public, was brought to his death by the shell of a police officer.

Thus belatedly, indirectly, and in a grim and unexpected manner, did Vigilance claim its final toll.

CHAPTER XVII

THE RECKONING OF THE ACCOUNTS

Before attempting to compute the gains and losses of Vigilance, let us glance back briefly over the territory we have covered.

At the opening of our narrative, we traveled to an Arcadian California, where the inhabitants were few, the life simple, and the people honest and trustful. We saw how, upon this almost primeval society, there burst the frenzy of the Gold Rush; how the country suddenly swarmed with adventurous strangers, including not only sturdy pioneers but cutthroats, thieves and ruffians of a thousand varieties. We glanced at the State in a condition of anarchy, ruled by no responsible local authority, overlooked for political reasons by the Government at Washington, and delivered to the tender mercies of the predatory elements. We watched as crime lifted its blood-dripping head, as murder became an everyday affair, as the life of each man and the protection of his property came to depend on the strength of the arm and the quickness of the trigger.

Then, amid that chaos in which lawlessness was king, we saw how impromptu associations of citizens began to assert themselves, in order to overthrow villainy and establish some semblance of justice. We observed the uprising against The Hounds in 1849, and the dispersal of that gang of rogues by the citizens of San Francisco under Sam Brannan. We viewed the mass meeting and trial by which, early in 1851, the supposed robbers of Jansen's store were faced with one of the earliest popular tribunals; we witnessed the organization of the first Committee of Vigilance later that same year, and saw how four men were executed and many others deported or driven out of the State. But we noted how temporary, on the whole, were the results of the first Vigilance movement, and how quickly crime regained its lost stronghold, how speedily the assassins re-asserted themselves, how triumphantly the political rascals established their reign, to the accompaniment of stuffed ballot boxes, bought juries, venal courts, and a thousand other devices of fraud and corruption. Then, when the State had sunk to new depths of degradation, we beheld the rise of one whose voice was as a trumpet call; we saw how James King of William, the self-constituted leader of those thousands who until then had been leaderless, sprang up with an irresistible force and struck with sledgehammer blows at the very portals and pillars of established iniquity. And we noted how the death of this commanding figure—his assassination by one of the typical birds of prey that had been looting the city—was as the spark that precipitated an explosion, and produced that outburst of popular indignation which gave birth to the second Committee of Vigilance.

For the past few chapters, we have been following the activities of that second Committee, and have remarked how, like its precedessor of 1851, it hanged four men and exiled many more; how, also like the earlier Committee, it snatched two prisoners from the hands of the lawful authorities; how it brought a justice of the State Supreme Court to trial; how it developed a military strength without parallel in the history of popular tribunals, and at times was goaded until it might have been plunged through the terrors of civil war, to establish an independent and revolutionary government.

And now the question not unnaturally arises: what were the final results of the whole movement or series of movements, which began with the assertion of rights by a group of citizens in 1849, and culminated in the powerful organization of 1856? What was the net outcome of the popular revolt which, defying law for the sake of justice, and challenging the State for the sake of public security, was insurrectionary in its tendencies even if beneficent in its aims? Was California—and, for that matter, the entire United States—eventually the better or the worse for the rise of the Vigilantes?

Before turning to the larger phases of the question, let us consider some of the more immediate and more obvious results of the Committee of 1856. First of all, its effect in ridding the State of undesirables was by no means inconsiderable; for, in addition to the four men hanged, the twenty-five shipped away, and the five or more notified to leave, there were many who departed without waiting for the personal attentions of the Committee. In fact, it is estimated that as many as eight hundred thieves, corruptionists and desperadoes sought safety in flight, thereby removing the most foul element of society. It is true that these men left only in order to inflict their unwholesome presences upon other communities—which can hardly be considered a gain for the country as a whole; it is also true that there is no way of knowing how many of them subsequently returned to California; it may even be true that some innocent parties, coming under suspicion, were terrorized into fleeing; and yet, when all is said, it is hardly to be questioned that the tone of life in California was improved by the flight of so many vicious characters.

More important, and more fundamental, was the reform which the Vigilantes undertook by securing control of the political life of San Francisco at its very foundations. Profiting from the lesson of the earlier Committee, the organization of 1856 did not propose to let the affairs of the city slip back into the hands of the rowdies, the ballot-stuffers, and the professional job-hunters. Yet officially the Committee was nonpolitical; its leaders were sagacious enough not to gird themselves for formal entry into the political arena, and undertook to gain their ends by methods that were not too obvious.

On August eleventh a great mass meeting was held, not expressly sponsored by the Vigilance Committee, but espousing Vigilance principles, and manifestly brought into existence by the spirit of reform and social purification aroused by the Committee's actions and by the utterances of James King of William. It demanded the election of honest men to office, an unpolluted ballot-box and the thorough reformation of all departments of government; it called for an extension of education and the spirit of public service, and the elimination of waste and corruption. But it did not confine itself to formulating a program; it took practical measures to see that its objectives were attained. A committee of twenty-one, appointed to name candidates for the city and county offices, fulfilled its purpose by nominating men of a higher type than had ever before had a chance of obtaining public office in San Francisco; and, having nominated them, it did not permit them to be cheated of their just election by the old methods of rowdyism and manipulated ballots. On October 28th, a week before the election, one prominent man in each district was selected to stand guard over the election and each man received the following instructions (which, incidentally, show that the Vigilance Committee was still at the helm):

"Sir: You are hereby appointed by the Executive Committee of the Committee of Vigilance to take charge of the vigilance force which will be detailed to preserve the public peace and order in your district upon Tuesday, the 4th of November next. In assuming this responsible position, you are reminded that neither the Committee of Vigilance as a whole, nor its members in their official capacities, can assume any side in political controversies. . . . The duties confided to you are the preservation of the ballot-box from any attack, and the securing to every citizen, whether good or bad, the free exercise of his elective franchise."

But it was not to be the duty of the supervisors of elections to assert themselves merely by means of moral suasion; if necessity demanded, they might resort to more direct means. The instructions go on to say:

"Should it become necessary for the preservation of the public peace to make any arrests of drunken or disorderly persons, you may send them to the station-house, but should any person attempt to vote twice or put in two votes at once, or should there appear to be any organized attempt to destroy the ballot-box . . . you will at once dispatch a mounted messenger to the Executive Committee, and immediately arrest the perpetrators, and send them under a sufficient escort to the building in Sacramento Street lately occupied by the Committee of Vigilance. It is expected that by arranging reliefs you will obtain a sufficient force to protect from violence the officers and the ballots until the counting is finished."

In conclusion, an appeal is made to the pride of the Vigilante; to his satisfaction in the good work accomplished by his organization:

"You will remind every man that he is in some measure the representative of seven thousand freemen, and that new luster may be cast upon the good the Committee of Vigilance has already accomplished, by the energy, discretion and impartiality he may manifest upon election day, while the lack of any of these qualities may tarnish not only his own character, but the reputation of the body of which he is a member, and entail evil consequences upon the entire community."

Not in vain did the Committee send out these instructions! Not in vain did it see that the election booths were well policed, that the disorderly elements were checked and intimidated, and that all citizens were protected in the legitimate exercise of the ballot. The election of November 4th, which is regarded as probably the first honest election in the history of the city, resulted in an overwhelming victory for the People's Party— the party under the sponsorship of the Committee of Twenty-one. They elected their slate of local officers; and they took charge of the city finances in such a way that the municipality, on the verge of bankruptcy, was rescued from ruin, and enjoyed a reign of stringent efficiency and lowered taxes, and yet of improved public service. At the expiration of the first year, the officers had done so well, that the Committee of Twenty-one was asked to appoint its successor; and the new committee nominated a new group of officers, who likewise were triumphantly elected, and likewise acquitted themselves honorably and ably. And so things continued for about ten years, during which the People's Party remained unintermittently in power. No longer was it possible for a Casey to be elected to office without even running! No longer was it possible for a Sheriff Scannell to purchase his office for $100,000! No longer was it possible to pad the jurybox, and to secure witnesses to swear to anything for a price! No longer were murderers nestled to the gentle bosom of the law, and shielded while they shot honest citizens with impunity! No longer were the affairs of city and county managed as a lucrative racket, for the enrichment of rogues and the impoverishment and humiliation of decent men! No longer did vice triumphant snarl in the seats of the mighty, and exact its daily toll from the life-blood of the community!

All authorities agree as to the reign of good government that endured for at least a decade. "For ten years," declares Bancroft, "this new reform party did well, purging and purifying; during which time it was a common remark that no city in the world was better governed than San Francisco." . . . "Thenceforth, for years," concurs Josiah Royce, "San Francisco was one of the best governed municipalities in the United States." . . . It was ruled, remarks T. H. Hittell, "better than it has ever been governed at any time before or since." Only in the year 1865, when the heat of national politics was permitted to intrude, did the influence of the People's Party begin to wane; the nominating committee, by passing a resolution that barred the doors of office to all who had not voted for Lincoln and Johnson, split the party and dissipated forever its pristine strength and purity.

Even though much of the committee's accomplishment was to endure for years beyond 1865, one is forced to record that the passage of a second decade saw it almost completely obliterated. By the year 1877, political conditions in San Francisco, and in the State generally, had fallen far back toward what they had been during the reign of the Scannells, the Caseys, and the Mulligans. "Corruption," says Bancroft, "had crept into every department of government; nepotism had been reduced to a system, official peculation to a science. Almost any bill could be lobbied through the legislature with the aid of bribery; grants and subsidies could be purchased; and monopolies could obtain privileges at the public expense, while the masses were burdened with a tax that swallowed forty per cent of the income of a small property, and obliged the average citizen to work one-third of his time for a government which recklessly sank the money in useless salaries, subsidies, and peculations."

It was during the year 1877 that the Committee of Vigilance strangely came to life again, and offered the last manifestation of its power. At this time the country was suffering from a "depression," similar to that which has grown all too familiar to us of late, although less pronounced in type and extent; and the laborers of California, smarting under the ills of unemployment and low wages, staged an agitation which unfortunately followed channels of violence and race prejudice, and, in particular, sought to make a scapegoat of the Chinese. Nothing less than the expulsion of the Orientals, who were numerous in California and who worked for wages that outdistanced white competition, was demanded by the Workingman's Party; severe measures were advocated against employers of yellow-skinned help; and riotous attacks were made against Chinese laundrymen, and incendiary threats against the docks of Asiatic ships. In addition, there were threats of assassination of public officials, and of destruction of the city by fire—so that it is no exaggeration to state that once again a condition of public emergency had arisen.

Recognizing this to be the case, the citizens convened once more, and appealed to William T. Coleman to lead them as of old, and to organize a Committee of Safety. This he succeeded in doing, and within twenty-four hours the Vigilance Committee seemed to have been resurrected. More than five thousand men volunteered for service—but not, as formerly, to oppose the established authorities and take the law into their own hands. This time they enjoyed the aid of the State and the Federal governments; they were provided with arms and ammunition, and had the assistance of United States troops. Yet the weapons of the majority were nothing more lethal than pick handles, with which they patrolled the city, so becoming known as the Pick Handle Brigade. Thanks to their numbers and determination, they effectively overcame lawlessness; they put down riots, nipped incendiarism in the bud, and restored order to the city—after which they calmly vanished from the scene. But in them the old Vigilance movement had experienced a reincarnation which, though brief, was impressive and salutary; while their connection with the troublous early days is shown by their pass word: " '56 to '77."

*   *   *

Considering how soon the benefits of Vigilance were lost; considering that, in less than a quarter of a century, they had ceased to be visible, what was the net eventual gain from the entire movement?

It is, of course, not just to regard a reform as valueless simply because it is not permanent. All human efforts are merely temporal in their effects; all must disappear with time; and the difference between the most transitory change and the most lasting revolution is, in the last analysis, largely one of degree. To the citizens of San Francisco, in the years following 1856, the advantages of the renovated city government were real, even though they were not to bless succeeding generations; to the man whose life was protected from the assassin's gun, to the taxpayer who did not groan beneath onerous levies for the sake of preying politicians, to the voter who realized that his ballot was not being thrown into the waste-heap, the value of the improvement was sufficiently clear. And there can be no question that the energy expended, throughout the whole series of uprisings from 1849 to 1856, was more than justified by the disenthronement of the plunderers and the years of sound and efficient government that followed. It is regrettable, to be sure, that the gains were not more enduring; but, as a matter of fact, they actually lasted longer than might have been anticipated, considering that the innovations introduced by the Committee did not affect the basic political or social structure of the community, but were primarily changes in a state of mind, changes in the general attitude toward public morality, changes that could be expected to live only so long as memory of the rascalities of the Scannells and the Sullivans remained keen.

The entire record of the popular tribunals, from the affair of The Hounds to the adjournment of the Committee of 1856, is the story of the rise of public indignation, is the story of mass revolt against vice and iniquity, is the story of the gradual rousing of a frontier community to a sense of public welfare and security. That a variety of motives played their part cannot be denied—personal fear and the lust of revenge, the passions and audacity of the mob no less than the idealism of the reformer; yet the framework of Vigilance was in the spirit of righteous wrath against organized wrongdoing, and the movement flourished precisely in proportion to the strength of that spirit. Eruptions of this wholesome feeling occurred both in 1849 and 1851, but were not powerful enough to leave any prolonged effects; and, only after the appearance of James King of William and his blasting editorials, was the popular mind stirred to such impatience with corruption that eight or nine thousand men could combine spontaneously in a Vigilance Committee, giving freely of their time and energy in the effort to sweep the city clean. That the results of such a movement could endure for even ten years is extraordinary, for it owed its efficacy solely to the flame of public virtue engendered in the minds of the citizens; and in a growing and changing community, with new members constantly being admitted from without, with a new generation growing up, and with no new measures in vogue for training the citizens in political morality, it was to be expected that the old spirit of corruption would gradually creep in again and the gains be eventually dissipated and lost.

One of the objections most frequently leveled against the San Francisco Committees of Vigilance is that they were lawless organizations, founded without any shadow of legal right, and operating in opposition to the duly established authorities. This argument, it appears to me, would have much more weight if there had been any "duly established authorities"; but in a community where most if not all the public officers owed their power to purchase, fraud or other means of usurpation, it would be difficult to stimulate any great amount of virtuous enthusiasm for the representatives of legality. Certainly Sheriff Scannell, paying for his election with a huge gift to the Democratic nominating committee and reimbursing himself while in office, was not in a moral position superior to that of the Vigilantes, even though the latter did not act under tne hypocritical color of law; certainly, he was less the representative of the law's *intention* when he shielded criminals such as Cora and Casey, than were the Committee members when they marched against the jail and illegally removed the prisoners. So far as San Francisco itself is concerned, it is unquestionable that the Vigilantes, acting without any shadow of constitutional right, came nearer to fulfilling the aims of justice and maintaining a rule of order, than did the set of office-holders they so vigorously opposed. Grim, sinister, and dictatorial as they were, and self-invested with martial authority, they yet accomplished the purpose for which they had organized; and the token of their sincerity is to be seen in the rapidity with which they disbanded once they had achieved the avowed ends for which they had worked.

There is, however, a larger phase of the question which must be considered—and one that reaches beyond the boundaries of any single city or state. Even though the Vigilance Committee proved salutary for San Francisco, does that mean that it was beneficent in its wider influence, that it set a happy precedent for the country as a whole, and moved by the power of a blessed example? Here, unfortunately, our answer must be less favorable. It is manifest that the effects of the Vigilance movement were far-reaching; but it is equally manifest that they were not unmixed. In widely scattered sections of the country, but particularly in the West—in Idaho, in Montana, in Nevada, and other states—Vigilance organizations sprang into being; organizations which did not always follow the scrupulous methods of their San Francisco predecessor; which did not always keep written records, conduct cautious trials, or decide with discre-

tion or impartiality. Sometimes, indeed, they capably filled a
hiatus in the law, and rid the country of predatory gangs of
ruffians; but at other times they succumbed to prejudices, sec-
tional or racial animosities, and the brutal impulses of the mob.
Thus the Vigilantes of Montana, though one of the best of the
organizations, maintained strict secrecy of membership, and
had a habit of trying and passing judgment on suspected criminals even *before* they were caught; thus, the committees in
Oregon, Idaho and elsewhere tended to degrade themselves
into the tools of ambitious or passionate individuals, and sometimes deservedly ended as objects of public denunciation; thus,
in Texas, an abolitionist was as likely to fall victim to the committees as was a criminal, and in innumerable cases the prey of
mob wrath was executed without more than the travesty of a
trial. Worst still were the horrors perpetrated by the so-called
Vigilantes of the night-riding variety: the Knights of the White
Camelia, the Ghouls of the Ku Klux Klan, and the agents of
other secret societies, who presented the spectacle of lynch law
in some of its most shocking and outrageous forms.

Today, the term Vigilante is used to denote almost everything that the original Vigilantes were not. Today, the perpetrators of a thousand and one diverse atrocities, while knowing nothing of the original Vigilance movement, use the name
of Vigilance to justify them in their villainies. Ironically, it
may be pointed out that the targets of the first pre-Vigilance
organization—the rascally society of Hounds—would, in
present-day parlance, be known as Vigilantes when staging
their dastardly attack upon the Chilean quarters.

Thus it will appear that, beneficent as the San Francisco Committees may have been in the immediate results they attained,
they have possibly done more damage than good in the long
run. In common with many other groups of rebels and re-
formers, they have lent themselves to imitation in their worst

features; or, rather, their worst tendencies have been exaggerated and perpetuated, while their better characteristics have been overlooked or forgotten. They were, unquestionably, composed in the main of sturdy and conscientious men, indignant at the spectacle of crime unleashed, and honestly trying to find a remedy for a flaw in the social structure; yet their successors, in too many cases, were neither sturdy nor conscientious, were dominated by personal bias or passion, and committed crimes that made the name Vigilante a reproach and a warning.

It will, accordingly, perhaps be forever impossible to determine whether the Vigilance movement was a success or a failure; whether its immediate benefits were sufficient to counteract its long-range disadvantages; whether the cleansing of a single city or state for the period of a few years was compensation enough for the establishment of a precedent that too often has been viciously interpreted.

In any event, there was a rousing strength and courage about the men of the original Vigilance Committees; and this must always awaken admiration in a world where weakness and pusillanimity are so common. And, no matter whether we be driven to condone or to condemn the Vigilantes of San Francisco, it is well that we know the facts, so that we may realize that they were far different than is often imagined, and that, whether justified or not in the course they took, they were sincere, struggling humans seriously trying to cope with a social emergency. The conditions that produced Vigilance, as we have seen, were unique in history—as unique as the causes of the Crusades, or the Inquisition, or the settlement of New England; hence it may safely be asserted that never again will the world witness such a sudden mass surging of a riotous, adventurous population to a land on the outskirts of civilization. But precisely because it will not recur; precisely because it was novel and unprecedented, the situation that gave rise to Vigilance will perennially reward our attention. We may offer up secret prayers of thanksgiving that the need for a similar movement does not exist today; we may fervently hope never to observe such civic strife as convulsed San Francisco in the years between '49 and '56; but we must admit that life in those days had a zest, and that we would have felt fully alive had it been given us to range the streets of that reckless city, to mingle with its vari-colored crowds, to hear the clattering of its carts and the clangor and blasphemy of its gambling halls, to participate in the energy and bustle of its shops and ships, to grow red with indignation as we snatched up the latest paper and read the scathing editorials of James King of William, to press in shouting rage about the jail that guarded the assassins Casey and Cora, and to enroll in the great association whose avowed object it was to uproot villainy.

Yes! life in those days, though often ended abruptly, must have been worth living; and the picturesqueness, the color, the glamour of that long-vanished epoch, the fiery daring of James King of William and the vigor and stern resolution of Coleman and his followers, will retain their breathing reality long after the question of the justification or non-justification of the Vigilance movement possesses no more than an academic interest.

PRINCIPAL AUTHORITIES CONSULTED

BOOKS AND PAMPHLETS

Bancroft, Hubert Howe, *California Inter Pocula*. San Francisco, 1888.

Bancroft, Hubert Howe, *California Pastoral*. San Francisco, 1888.

Bancroft, Hubert Howe, *The History of California*. (Seven volumes). San Francisco, 1884-90.

Bancroft, Hubert Howe, *Popular Tribunals*. (Two volumes). San Francisco, 1887.

Bari, Valeska, *The Course of Empire*. New York, 1930.

Barry, T. A., and Patten, B. A., *Men and Memories of San Francisco*. San Francisco, 1873.

Burnett, Peter H., *Recollections and Opinions of an Old Pioneer*. New York, 1880.

Christman, Enos, *The Letters and Journal of a Forty-Niner*. New York, 1930.

Cleland, Robert Glass. *A History of California. The American Period*. New York, 1922.

Eldredge, Zoeth S. *Beginnings of San Francisco*. San Francisco, 1912.

Fargo, Frank F. *A True and Minute History of the Murder of James King of William*. San Francisco, 1856.

Frear, Rev. Walter, *Sermon on the Death of James King of William*. Iowa Hill, 1856.

Hittell, John S. *A History of the City of San Francisco*. San Francisco, 1878.

Hittell, Theodore H., *History of California*. (Four volumes). San Francisco, 1885-97.

Letts, John M., *California Illustrated*. New York, 1852.

O'Meara, James, *The Vigilance Committee of 1856*. San Francisco, 1887.

Rivors, *A Full and Authentic Account of the Murder of James King of William*. Rochester, 1857.

Royce, Josiah, *California, from the Conquest in 1846 to the Second Vigilance Committee in San Francisco*. Boston, 1886.

Scherer, James, *The First Forty-Niner*. New York, 1925.

Sherman, General William T., *Memoirs*. (Two volumes). New York, 1875.

Shuck, Oscar Tully, *Representative and Leading Men of the Pacific Coast*. San Francisco, 1870.

Shinn, C. H., *Mining Camps. A Study in American Frontier Government*. New York, 1885.

Soulé, Frank, Gihon, John H., and Nisbet, James, *The Annals of San Francisco*. New York, 1855.

Smith, Frank Meriwether, *San Francisco Vigilance Committee of '56*. San Francisco, 1883.

Taylor, Bayard, *Eldorado*. New York, 1856.

Taylor, Rev. William, *Seven Years' Street Preaching in San Francisco, California*. New York, 1857.

Williams, Mary Floyd. *History of the San Francisco Committee of Vigilance of 1851*. Berkeley, 1921.

Williams, Mary Floyd, *Papers of the San Francisco Committee of Vigilance of 1851*. Berkeley, 1919.

Woods, Daniel B., *Sixteen Months in the Gold Diggings*. New York, 1851.

PERIODICALS AND MISCELLANEOUS ARTICLES

Alta California, San Francisco, 1849-56.

Ayres, W. O., *Personal Recollections of the Vigilance Committee*, OVERLAND MONTHLY, August, 1886.

Coleman, William Tell, *San Francisco Vigilance Committee*. CENTURY MAGAZINE, November, 1891.

Daily Herald, San Francisco, 1850-56.

Evening Bulletin, San Francisco, 1855-56.

Evening Picayune, San Francisco, 1850-52.

King, Charles J., *Reminiscences of Early Days in San Francisco*, OVERLAND MONTHLY, March, 1888.

King, Joseph L., *The Vigilance Committee of '56*. OVERLAND MONTHLY, December, 1916.

Lyman, George D., *The Sponge, its Effect on the Martyrdom of James King of William and the San Francisco Vigilance Commitee of 1856*. In *Annals of Medical History*, New York, 1928.

Richardson, D. S., *Duels to the Death*. OVERLAND MONTHLY, August, 1888.

Woolley, Lell Hawley, *Recollections of Pioneer Experiences in California*. OVERLAND MONTHLY, January, 1917.

INDEX